Scripted drama

Scripted drama

A practical guide to teaching techniques

ALAN ENGLAND
Lecturer in Drama, Division of Education
University of Sheffield

CAMBRIDGE UNIVERSITY PRESS

Cambridge
London   New York   New Rochelle
Melbourne   Sydney

Published by the Press Syndicate of the University of Cambridge
The Pitt Building, Trumpington Street, Cambridge CB2 1RP
32 East 57th Street, New York, NY 10022, USA
296 Beaconsfield Parade, Middle Park, Melbourne 3206, Australia

First published 1981

Typeset by Ward Partnership, Widdington, Essex
Printed in Great Britain at the University Press, Cambridge

British Library Cataloguing in Publication Data
England, Alan
Scripted drama.
1. Drama — Study and teaching (Secondary)
I. Title
792'.07'12   PN1701   80-41013
ISBN 0 521 23235 X hard covers
ISBN 0 521 28179 2 paperback

to Mary

Contents

CONTENTS

Acknowledgements

I should like to thank

David Bradley, Head of Drama at Norfolk Comprehensive School, Sheffield, for putting my ideas to the acid test, allowing me to experiment with his classes and nailing my feet to the ground.

Dr Stanley Collier of the Dept of French in the University of Sheffield for translating the extracts from *Tartuffe*.

Eyre Methuen Ltd. for permission to print extracts from *Theatre Games* by Clive Barker.

David Gregg, a former student of mine, for a transcript of the discussion in the *Merchant of Venice* workshop.

Mrs Velda Harris of Sheffield Polytechnic for the description of her movement work on *Antony and Cleopatra* and for making available the fruits of her experience as a drama teacher.

Dr Bernard Harrison of the Division of Education at the University of Sheffield for the account of his collage of *Much Ado about Nothing*.

Heinemann Educational Books Ltd. and H.E.B. (inc) New Hampshire for permission to print extracts from *The Travails of Sancho Panza* by J.M. Saunders.

David Hirst of the Drama Dept in the University of Birmingham for alerting me to the usefulness of the ideas and practices of Rudolf Laban.

Christopher Parry for permission to quote freely from articles in *The Use of English*.

Geoff Readman, formerly Head of Drama at the Portland Comprehensive School, Worksop, for letting me share the teaching of his drama classes.

Professor Peter Thomson of the sub-Department of Drama in the University of Exeter for permission to print extracts from letters to me.

The Pocket Theatre Company for the extract from their version of *Othello*.

ACKNOWLEDGEMENTS

Sheffield University Research Fund for a helpful grant.
My wife, Mary, for her endurance and her uncompromising and helpful criticisms.

Introduction

By contrast with the avalanche of books on the teaching of improvised drama, the output of books on the teaching of scripted drama has been small. There could be a number of reasons for this. Perhaps it is felt that scripted drama is of less educational importance; it could simply be that unscripted drama requires an endless supply of ideas and material; possibly procedures for dealing with scripts seem self-evident. However, the actual use of scripted drama in schools is widespread. Stage, radio and television scripts find a ready market. A play still qualifies as literature in the eyes of English departments and examining boards and the impossibility of examining the unexaminable forces even unwilling drama specialists to make room in their syllabuses for texts on the grounds that they are something about which answerable questions can be asked.

Relevant teaching approaches are not nearly as ubiquitous as the material, approaches, that is to say, based upon an appreciation of the true nature of the artefact and the kind of experience it makes possible. Spoilt by the excitement and quicker returns of developmental drama, some practitioners find the transition to the text a hard feat. Caldwell Cook cried in the wilderness but Frank Whitehead, in the very first issue of *The Use of English* in 1949, was confident that there was at least one assumption he could make: 'I assume a measure of agreement that drama lessons will necessarily take the form of acting by the children', and drama lessons in this context meant working with scripts. But in 1954, A.K. Hudson, in *Shakespeare and the Classroom*, still felt the need to inveigh against 'the construe method' and my experience and observation lead me to believe that the battle remains to be won. Yet work on the script is uniquely placed to satisfy the demands both for freedom and for discipline and to fulfil an impressive range of educational aims.

As a 'new' activity, developmental drama adopted the educational objectives which were fashionable in its infancy. The emphasis is on personal development, defined as the progressive achievement of selfhood, of self-discovery and self-definition, of 'uniqueness'. Education, as Brian Way declares in *Development Through Drama*, had hitherto concerned itself too exclusively with 'sameness'. Drama should develop the whole person and redress the neglect of the emotions. Reality should be explored not merely through words but through bodily sensations and movement. Spontaneous discoveries are genuine ones. Involvement is more important than communication, the process than the product. The audience is unnecessary, criticism anathema.

This upgrading of the learner is welcome and much else in Way is worth saying. Unfortunately, scripted drama work has tended to be dismissed as 're-creative', a reliance on other people's achieved insights. Privileged access to these could give a teacher the excuse to adopt an authoritarian role. When bracketed with 'theatre', scripted drama reveals its dependence on presentation to an audience. Practitioners need acquaintance with skills, techniques and conventions. Bracketed with literature, it exercises a narrower range of personal attributes and is available mainly to those who can read.

While acknowledging that there are certain vital differences between the two areas, it seems to me that some of the objectives pursued by those working without a script can be encompassed also by those working with or from one. The very nature of the play text makes this possible. The text of a play differs from the novel or poem insofar as the words do not in themselves contain the complete experience. The writer of a play does not intend it simply to be read.

The dramatist does not simply write down sentences as he hears them half-spoken in the silence of his own mind; he invents them to be coloured by the spoken voice. And more than this, he knows that they will be part of the total performance of the actor who speaks them; physical bearing, gesture, appearance, state of mind, sexuality, position on the stage, will all affect the precise impression made by the words the dramatist writes down: and the tempo and rhythm with which the actor acts and speaks at the moment of utterance. And they will also be affected by the spectacle, music, sound, setting, by the actors and by the audience – by everything that happens on stage *as* it happens.

(*Effective Theatre* by J.R. Brown, p. 11)

Even a radio playwright must take into account the quality and behaviour of voices and the orientation of the speakers. Playscripts, then, must of *necessity* be bracketed with theatre. The basic medium of theatre is the actor, the human individual, and however hard he and the director may strive to realise a given experience, neither of them is an automaton. The successful actor will to some extent have based his creation upon his own experience and observation of life, understanding the unknown with the help of the known. He will have used his own imagination; the images he receives from the play will have been modified and put to work for him. In Michael Chekhov's words, in *To the Actor*, he will have engaged with them in an act of 'creative collaboration'. Whatever functions his character may have been assigned in the play, the actor will have to appear, inescapably himself, when the character 'enters'. Some sort of logical consistency, some personal 'knowledge' of the character and its life outside what is given in the play, may improve his exercise of his craft and help his morale. Even if a dramatist is concerned with distancing the actor from his part (e.g. a Brecht or a writer of satirical comedy), the actor must be convinced that it is possible human experience he is dealing in. The words he says must eventually seem, given the premises of the play, as inevitable to him as his own.

What happens to a developmental drama class and what happens to the cast of a play are in some ways similar. At the preparatory stage at least, the actor is involved in the process of defining himself with relation to his role and of discovering which aspects of his personality are relevant to the task of portraying it. As Charles Marowitz observes: 'The actor has only himself at his disposal. He can work only with *his* emotions, *his* temperament, *his* store of memories. Should he fail to work with himself, he is in danger of imitating or faking so, of course, he must return constantly to his own wellsprings.' (*The Act of Being*, p. 14.) Ultimately an actor will probably be forced to 'fix' his performance — or at least devise some mechanism for recalling emotions at will. Skill and technique, it has to be admitted, are part and parcel of the stage actor's equipment. But both he and a good director will nevertheless be concerned to preserve the spontaneity of his performance lest it lapse into habit and lose conviction. The general direction for such a person may be known in a way that it is not known for the improviser but the route can and should vary with every fresh assay. He will need to be alert to build upon the element of unpredictability, which is inevitable in any case in an enterprise consisting largely of the interaction of human beings.

The actor in a theatre and the acter-out in a classroom both use facets of their personality. The activities of both require the use of intelligence but are ruined by the intellect that meddles, by preconception and a striving too assiduously for 'results'. Both need to

3

think with mind and body, both to understand through feeling and intuition, to understand the significance of space and spatial relationships. In both, the imagination, the symbolising power, is of prime importance. Both explore the possibilities not merely of verbal but of non-verbal expression.

Insofar, then, as a student working upon a script proceeds in the manner of an actor, he may achieve the kinds of enlightenment available to the free improviser. There are other respectable educational aims, however, which in practice guide the teacher of developmental drama and for which the dramatic script can be an invaluable resource. Personal development itself, looked at from a broader angle, requires the aid of other people. As Lawrence puts it: 'Though man is first and foremost an individual being, yet the very accomplishing of his individuality rests upon his fulfilment in social life.' (*Education of the People* in *Lawrence on Education*, edited by Joy and Raymond Williams, p. 145.) Growing may involve discovering differences but the 'sameness' that Way rejects is not altogether irrelevant. The fact that an insight is shared does not mean that it is not personal. The individual needs some reassurance that his discoveries and conclusions are validated and confirmed by someone else. Even developmental drama works eventually in terms of groups. It is true that some groups can be frustrating for their members. Where the origination and processing of ideas is officially the duty of the group itself, certain dominant members can swing things to their own advantage, consigning less assertive members to minor roles each time. A good drama teacher will make socialisation a high priority.

Unless you are doing *Krapp's Last Tape*, a scripted play inevitably involves the participants in interaction with and adjustment to other actors, both in their roles and as themselves. An actor will react to the way the other person is playing his part and will need to accommodate this in his own scheme of things. Clive Barker describes the benefits to University students and trainee actors of the theatre work he did: 'Since the processes of acting are so inextricably linked to the processes of personal and social behaviour, the work became a framework within which the student could come to terms with his own personality and that of others.' (*Theatre Games*, p. 217.)

Another person even the player of Krapp will encounter is the playwright. The playwright may have mapped the territory but he can also negotiate the hazards. He can make possible the exploration of embarrassing or frightening experience from which the improviser

4

might shy away. He can supply a wide range of characters and situations. He can encourage an awareness of verbal registers and of the appropriateness of language to context, but he can also present such registers for ironic criticism. He can exercise the pupils in a considerable range of linguistic functions, as stage dialogue conveys information, reveals personality, provokes activity, persuades and influences, summarises and glosses. He can make available varied modes of expression, liberating the actor or student from the temptations of easy naturalism.

The precise status of a text is not easy to establish. Although the words are only part of the play, and although we may agree with Christopher Parry that a play is 'not a textbook' but 'a happening concerning people' (*English in Education*, Vol. 1, No. 2, p. 31), it is to the words that we refer when trying to justify our interpretations. Unless the actor/student at any level engages in some way and at some stage with these, he is not 'doing the play', even though what he is doing may be valuable on other grounds. A good play is a work of art, offering aesthetic satisfaction. The exhilaration of discovery open to the student is dependent on enjoyment of its artistic qualities. What the actor does with the text is also subject to the interpretation that can be agreed by the group or with the director on behalf of the group. If he cannot adapt, the director would be within his rights to ask him to leave the company. The teacher in the classroom is not under threat from the paying public and the baying critics and it would be totally improper for him to inflict such drastic ostracism. Nevertheless a pupil who is acting will at least have to argue the case for his idiosyncrasies. A good text will inhibit the self-indulgence and the worst excesses of raw emotions that the improvised situation is sometimes heir to. However lovable the pupil finds Falstaff, sooner or later he will need to test for himself the validity of the dramatic logic which argues that the Prince should reject him. A good director will take it upon himself to remind his actors how their roles fit into the whole construct and establish with them the appropriate style of presentation. Insofar as the teacher also accepts this function he helps the students find form for their expression and to discover meanings and ironies. Both director and teacher will encourage their charges to be mindful of the spectator-viewpoint; both will be concerned to keep things in perspective.

Good scripted drama is 'artificial' in a good sense, but it can be argued that an element of artifice gives meaning and viability to

5

developmental drama also. Although Brian Way denies it, developmental drama has its conventions. It has to start somewhere and the previous life-history of its characters is 'assumed', or established by artificial means. I saw a girl improvising the part of a lonely old woman in a high rise flat, going about her daily routine. Some 'kids' were playing outside and would soon start to annoy her. She talked to herself about her predicament, as such a person would, but when we watched her, her speech spontaneously took on more and more the expository function of a soliloquy. Developmental drama also makes assumptions about time and place. It, too, can issue in a 'statement'.

Neither the actor nor the member of a developmental drama class is 'doing' life itself. The argument about whether an actor at any point actually 'feels' the emotions of his character has raged since Diderot. Bertram Joseph maintains that he does. Brian Stone, in Unit One of the Open University Modern Drama course (p. 10), maintains that he doesn't.

Acting is a style of imitation to which both cognitive and affective processes contribute, both in the preparation and in the performance . . . For example, in *The Bacchae* the actress playing Agave does not, at the moment when Agave recognises the head that she is carrying, feel the horror and despair that Agave feels and expresses. In her art as an actress, she knows what that horror and despair are (cognitive) and, responding to knowledge of and empathy with those emotions (affective), is able to project a living representation of Agave.

Certainly, as Stanislavsky recognised, many of the actor's feelings are feelings he has recalled and pressed into service, but this does not make them any less real. There is some truth in both opposing positions. Ron Hayman, in his book *Techniques of Acting*, quotes the actress Geraldine Page:

When you take the character over and use the character, you wreck the fabric of the play, but you can be in control of the character without taking the character over. When the character uses you, that's when you're really cooking. You know you're in complete control, yet you get the feeling that you didn't do it. You have this beautiful feeling that you can't ruin it.

(Pp. 46–7)

Like the actor, the student both of developmental drama and scripted drama is called upon to use himself rather than to be himself, to use emotion without becoming a prey to it.

If emotion is vital to learning, certainly in learning about people, reflection is vital to realising what one has learned. Here the interests of the stage or studio artist and the drama student may be different. Critical enlightenment may be a spin-off for the artist but it is a most

6

important long-term goal for the student. If a part in a play is badly written, an actor may 'make something of it' by the sheer force of his presence or by technique. The main benefit for the student may be an awareness of its inadequacies and of the reasons for these. In a society where some form of drama is a daily experience for many people, there is a special need for a discriminating public and in the individual there is a need to recognise the truly rewarding dramatic experience.

The pursuit of contemplation may lead to the use of discussion. Some teachers of developmental drama are suspicious of discussion on the grounds that it is at best superfluous and at worst harmful. But evaluative talk if carefully handled can improve the quality of an experience, especially if it involves the talkers not merely in reinforcing what can be endorsed but in reconstructing the experience where necessary along more personally meaningful lines. Developmental drama itself involves discussion among participants aimed at clarifying situations and making collaboration possible, but similar activities are open to pupils working on a script.

If evaluative discussion can raise rashes, the notion of an audience can raise bigger ones. The fear with the audience is that exposure to it introduces an element of exhibitionism and an anxiety to 'arrive'; this fear has often been justified. The very form of scripted drama creates an audience-consciousness and teaching method will have to take this into account. But an audience trained to offer the right kind of sympathy and to encourage the right kind of priorities can only improve the educational process. A play is a collaborative venture to produce an event.

Ideally a class in scripted drama will be reflecting not simply on the literary qualities of a script but on what it makes possible in terms of performance, what it can do to actors, director, designer, audience. What is the likely educational effect of all this? In any individual case the results may be literally incalculable. Definite changes in personality as a result of any kind of drama work may be suspected but cannot be proved. Talking of the process of exploring a Shakespeare play, L.C. Knights has this to say: 'How that process develops, in each different individual, must remain something of a mystery, and although the teacher can help, he must always remain aware of the limits of what he can do: he must always leave an area of privacy in which growth can take place.' (*Teaching Shakespeare* in *The Use of English*, Vol. 1, No. 19.) The aim of our teaching, he goes on to add, is 'to foster ... the sense of personal creative discovery ... however far it may sometimes seem from the actuality of the classroom and the more obvious demands of the educational system.' Perhaps the only verifiable gain is insight, understanding acquired principally through the use of the imagination, but, if this is so, it seems to me a not unworthy one.

1
Activities

The procedures a teacher adopts ought to be the result of his assessment of the needs of individual pupils in particular contexts. However, if pupils can learn from one another, so can teachers. A colleague's idea or teaching method may not work for us in quite the same way it worked for him but with a little modification it may be just the answer for a problem of our own. The first test is always whether it squares with our educational principles.

My own preference is for practical activities, or at least for activities which awaken in the mind an awareness of the play as a theatrical event. A number of activities undertaken by stage artists or other members of a production team and the functions of the critic and audience represent helpful approaches for the student also and can be carried out naturally and painlessly by a desk-bound class. The most important operations, though, are those involving the interaction of actors with each other, with the director and with the audience. It follows that it is educationally desirable that the teacher should need a good excuse before he refrains from bringing his students into both physical and vocal confrontation and from affording them the experience of relating in space. (Even the excuse that students are preparing for a written examination and that all this prancing around is a waste of time is not really valid. Practical work provides a marvellous incentive to scrutinise the text very closely and in any case exam boards even in English are now recognising the theatrical nature of the play text by angling questions towards this.)

With all work on scripted drama the main problem is to liberate the imagination from the hypnosis of print without actually liberating it from the play altogether. A book in hand may be especially galling to the actor trying to look another in the face or to the director trying to keep an eye on what A is doing while B is speaking; but the practical exigencies of the job do eventually take them along the road to this freedom. Acting out becomes not merely an extension to a reading but a (or perhaps we should say the) way of reading a play; acting out and reading should, in fact, be parts of an integrated process. An actor is faced with the problem of how to behave; unless he understands what he is saying and other people are saying he will not know what to do and the director will need to share that problem if he is to help him.

In educational terms, what we will be doing is looking at the ways in which acting and directing the script and watching actions and hearing the words performed can be used as methods of investigating and establishing meaning. The teacher's aim is not primarily to teach theatrical skills so much as to use the activities to illuminate an experience. It is also true, however, that the more expressively the student learns to move, gesture or deliver lines, the greater will be the personal satisfaction to be derived from the encounter with the script. The question then arises for the teacher how far he should encourage his actors to go along the road to performance. A play exists in time, its meanings partly determined by the rate at which the action unfolds. It seems logical, then, that the students should be given the opportunity to experience tempo. Enough 'polish' to read the play or part of it at an expressive pace would seem to be the minimum requirement. With lines actually learned, of course, the actor's range is enormously increased, but there may be too little time to spend on this. The test, it seems to me, is to decide whether the repetition is becoming tedious and killing the creative involvement of the students. In a classroom context it may be that there will be time for the learning of only a very small section, but I believe that we should be thankful for mercies of any size and that first hand knowledge of what dramatic experience is really all about is worth an age of talking about it. Actually, once the importance of movement, facial expression and gesture have been appreciated, the lines tend to fall into place as one element in a grand design and pupils glance up from the book with phrases learned unconsciously and called forth by association.

How far should the teacher encourage the use of properties, costumes and lighting? With scripts in hand, of course, properties are often hard to wield and with fancy lighting changes, reading becomes impossible. There is a lot to be said for firmly establishing the 'poor theatre' convention early and forcing the imagination to do the work. With lines learned, however, many things are made possible and the teacher may find that theatrical paraphernalia do give the lazy imagination a useful fillip. Stanislavsky was in no doubt about this. Even the most elementary item of costume can help an actor embody his conception and create his 'image'. As Tortsov says in *An Actor Prepares*: 'Without an external form, neither your inner character nor the spirit of your image will reach the public. The external characterisation explains, illustrates and thereby conveys to your spectators the inner pattern of your part.' For the teacher the issue is whether the aids remain springboards or become substitutes for creative energy.

When the pupils are functioning as audience in a classroom, what should they expect of a performance? Their appreciation is something a teacher should gently train, not in the sense of surreptitiously determining the way they react but establishing priorities. He should help them to understand their own responsibility in the creative act. A performance is not a one-way communication from one group to another but an occasion for what Peter Brook has called 'a change of perception' on everybody's part. The audience should be encouraged to make some allowance for good intentions as well as actual achievement. What is important is the meanings that are possible.

In órganising his classroom, the teacher should set himself the ideal of involving each child in as many aspects of the work as possible, or, bluntly, trying to ensure that everybody has a go at everything. His chances of achieving this may be generally remote, but nobody wants to be a permanent member of a crowd, either onstage or off. Teachers who divide their children into Acting Companies and give them specialist jobs run the risk of allowing individuals to exercise only a limited range of expression. This is not to deny that some students are able, say, to read, mimic or design more confidently than others, and whether you believe that this is 'talent' or merely 'a greater individual capacity for experiencing' (Spolin, p. 3), I would agree that they have the right to operate at their level also. Indeed, their special capabilities (and the teacher's!) may legitimately on occasions be mobilised in the interests of the corporate enterprise. But what I am saying is that they will not be the only ones with the desire to attempt Mark Antony or Beatie Bryant and if the time is available some compensatory satisfaction for the others would seem only fair and just.

Flexibility of function needs to be matched with flexibility of grouping, with groups descending in size from the whole class to the pair. Sometimes, the groups within a class will be doing the same kind of work, but in a class with a wide spread of ability or sophistication some groups may be working directly on the text while others approach it more obliquely. According to my conception, all work on scripted drama will at some point engage with the words and it is true that children — and grown-ups — are not equally happy handling them. However, the fact that drama does permit of such a wide variety of responses means that there will be ways in which even the less literate can shine, and this should encourage the teacher to be bold in his mix. The more autonomously the students are able to operate the better. The teacher will have to ensure that active groups are not under the heel of a dictatorial 'director' living up to an image he has acquired from the media. A leader will need to be reminded of his responsibility to the others and if necessary his role could be restricted to the recording of group decisions and reminding the group of the audience viewpoint.

What even the most adaptable of teachers can attempt is affected by size and composition of class. He will need a certain amount of luck, also, with the room and facilities he has available to him. Some drama teachers have a studio with space that can be modified at will, chairs that can be arranged to create a variety of relationships, rostra and tables to vary physical orientation, blackout curtains and lights to assist with atmosphere and focus, electric sockets, record player and tape recorder, a cupboard with material for costuming, display boards on the walls and a supply of make-up and mirrors. An English colleague may have a room that is so full of desks and bodies that he is gasping for air, it may be separated by paper-thin walls from an irascible mathematics teacher, and it may have none of the theatrical luxuries.

All the approaches I shall discuss are aimed at finding acceptable contexts, vocal, physical and personal, for the words of the play and the actions specified or implied by the text. But some of these approaches are more direct than others, insofar as they involve the pupils immediately in wielding the words and actions as given. Others allow the pupils to be more inventive and the relationship of what they do to the text is in the first instance more oblique. I was tempted to distinguish these indirect approaches as 'improvisatory' since the most ready definition of improvisation that people would offer would be something on the lines of 'making it up as you go along'. But I hesitated, as the word can in fact be taken in different ways. As David Male succinctly puts it:

There is a great diversity in the meaning of the word 'improvisation'. It may involve invention, exploration, elucidation, observation. All these activities lead to a spontaneous and imaginative response in words and actions that can be free and open-ended or shaped into a dramatic structure. With all these alternatives, it is worth while knowing which of them you are engaged in at any one time.

(Approaches to Drama, p. 32)

Accordingly, direct work on the text as written, if it is exploratory and experimental, if it allows the pupil to try out different versions of a dramatic experience with the aim of seeing which merit his personal endorsement, can also legitimately be categorised as improvisation.

2
Acting the text

Distinguishing between methods at all may seem a somewhat academic exercise but I have found it convenient when it comes to discussing their particular merits. Given this, a logical procedure is to list a variety of activities and illustrate each one by reference to a number of plays. This is, in fact, what I have done when discussing reading, planning a production and the less direct approaches to a text. With practical work on acting, however, described in this chapter, and with that part of a director's work which involves the handling of actors (in *Exploring Further*), I have decided rather to make do with a limited number of examples and to choose those which permit me to show the operation of a wide range of activities. I worked on the principle that, in the first place, the reader would find it less onerous to have to refresh his memory of a few rather than of many texts and that, in the second place, I would be able to refer back to these examples when discussing further approaches. Sometimes I have referred to one play, sometimes picked material from different plays by the same playwright. Where I have homed in on a particular scene, I should like to stress that the selection of activities described is not intended to represent a strategy for that scene as a whole. The chapter entitled *Strategies*, in fact, is devoted to procedures both for conducting individual sessions and for dealing with plays as a whole. There I have tried to show how kinds of activity can and should be mixed together according to the nature of the material and the needs of the class. Where here we are concerned with creating contexts for valuable educational experiences, there we shall be examining the extent to which these experiences can be or have been arranged in a profitable sequence.

Activities vary in appropriateness according to the style of the play being worked upon. Consequently I have chosen examples which represent a variety of dramatic modes. A case could be made for saying that there as many modes as there are plays, but groups of plays do share particular features and one play may provisionally do duty for many. However, I have not even tried to make an exhaustive summary of possible categories of play. What I have really hoped to do is to establish the principle that what is being explored is the distinctive nature of the piece and that this is an important factor in determining the effectiveness of what pupils actually do.

From time to time, I have found it profitable to borrow and develop ideas from pundits writing on the art of acting. Some of their suggestions seem to have particular relevance to particular styles of drama, although in certain cases they have wider application than people give them credit for. My own position as a teacher of drama would be that one shouldn't be prejudiced by theory, but should be prepared to try anything. One cannot be certain how useful an activity is until one has tried it. From a teaching point of view, even the discovery that an approach doesn't work can be edifying. I should like briefly to clarify those ideas and terms to which I shall later refer.

Activities recommended by Stanislavsky are often thought to be specially useful in tackling the acting of plays with psychological depth and elaboration, and his 'system' is often identified with a naturalistic theatre where Chekhov and Ibsen flourish. *An Actor Prepares* describes his psycho-technique, but the teacher also needs his later book, *Building a Character*, where physical skills and observable effects are given their due of attention. His belief in the interconnection of mind and body and his suggestion that the discovery of an appropriate action can trigger off an appropriate psychological state are particularly useful. The 'magic if', where the actor asks himself what he would do if he were in the situation of the play, is a device for identifying with the character. Stanislavsky recommends the actor to research into his character and discover the 'given circumstances'. He defines this expression as follows:

It means the story of the play, its facts, events, epoch, time and place of action, conditions of life, the actors' and régisseur's interpretation, the mise-en-scène, the productions, the sets, the costumes, properties, lighting and sound effects, — all the circumstances that are given to an actor to take into account as he creates his role.

(*An Actor Prepares*, p. 51)

He further recommends the actor to seek for the character's basic drives and 'objectives' which may persist through a 'unit' of action and may be linked with a 'super-objective' running through the whole of the play. Another concept I have found valuable is that of the 'subtext', which he defines as:

the manifest, the inwardly felt expression of a human being in a part, which flows uninterruptedly beneath the words of the text, giving them life and a basis for existing. The subtext is a web of innumerable, varied inner patterns inside a play and a part, woven from 'magic ifs', inner movements, objects of attention, smaller and greater truths and a belief in them, adaptations, adjustments and other similar elements. It is the subtext that makes us say the words we do in a play.

(*Building a Character*, p. 113)

This again has an obvious application to a naturalistic play where the words hide more than they reveal. The best known of Stanislavsky's ideas is the 'emotion-memory', in which he invites the actor to utilise features of his own past experience to release (in Pavlov fashion) an emotional charge which will help him express an emotion the text requires.

It is true that many of Stanislavsky's activities will be less helpful when it comes to tackling plays where character functions in a non-naturalistic way. Sometimes they will suit Shakespeare, sometimes not. Dr Stockmann in *An Enemy of the People* by Ibsen may have a 'super-objective' but has Hamlet? In a political production such as *John Ford's Cuban Missile Crisis* the actor may have to adapt to widely varying functions. Sometimes a subtext will be 'declared' in a soliloquy. Stanislavsky himself, though, did not want his system to be seen as creating a style of acting, but rather to be a technique. Actors in Molière, for instance, are recommended to seek for a super-objective.

Acting in some plays may require especial attention to the express-ive powers of the body in relation to space and to other actors. Instead of focusing on inner psychological truth, it may pay the actor to concentrate on the accuracy of the image he creates and of the stage picture. He may need to be reminded that words are not automatically the dominating element and the ideas of Artaud (*Theatre and its Double*) may be more relevant than those of Stanis-lavsky. Activities suggested by Rudolf Laban may help him compose a picture of the play in terms of movement and time. They may also give him a means of access to the sorts of extreme states of mind that fascinated Artaud. If a play depends on keeping an audience alert to the political issues it raises and wishes to remain as 'open' as possible, leaving the audience free of emotional pressure so that it can make up its own mind, it may be that the actor will have more to learn from Brecht. He may find his portrayal is required to be emblematic, stylised, clear and direct.

16

When confronted with a part in a play, the actor has to ask in Styan's words, 'If I were playing this part, how much reality would be expected of me to make the play work?' The answer to this, he goes on, 'depends upon the convention of the play, the tacit agreement with the audience about how much make-believe is allowable' (*The Dramatic Experience*, pp. 54—5). A director will also have to decide in what terms the play presents its vision of the truth and he may help the actor by devising appropriate rehearsal activities for him. The actor, like the pupil, though, is an idiosyncratic human being and individuals require different stimuli to help them experience relevant sensations. I can but show how I think material can affect the choice of activity in the classroom, but I would not presume to be prescriptive, as final decisions about the material are in the hands of the teacher and the pupils and will depend on experiment.

I have tried from time to time to indicate possible ways of deploying pupils when a particular activity is being examined. The scope is considerable. Sometimes students function as individuals, giving them the chance, for instance, all to be the same character for a spell. Sometimes they are envisaged as working in pairs — say to practise a duologue or for one student to hear and see the other perform — exposure to an audience on a less daunting scale. They may function in class as a chorus or the teacher may, in a major role, address them as a crowd.

A popular old-fashioned approach was for a group of talented actors or good readers to perform before the rest. This is certainly better than no active work at all and can, in a modified form, be made to satisfy the educational principles I have outlined. The group has to be thought of as exploring the play on behalf of the spectators rather than presenting something to them. In fact, the 'spectators' also function as co-directors with the teacher, encouraging, inspiring and advising the cast. The teacher should take every opportunity for the exchange of roles between and among his pupils and be prepared to invite one of his co-directors to demonstrate his point in role as actor rather than state it in words; or he may stop the rehearsal and indulge in a class exercise in which everybody can actively engage in finding solutions to a particular problem for themselves. But he will need to beware of chopping and changing too frequently and should try to give everybody a reasonable slab to get his teeth into before he is translated to the 'audience'. A re-run with

17

a selected cast will help restore the sense of continuity at the end.

One advantage of what one might call 'production by committee', that is to say where the rest of the class share the acting problems of a selected cast, is that the teacher is able to clarify the nature of these problems as they arise and alert the students to the implications they may make. It is useful for youngsters who have no theatrical background to call upon or none of the benefits of previous work in developmental drama or are poor at reading. I have also found this method useful with adults with similar deprivations. As far as classroom management is concerned, an advantage of this method is that once the 'audience' realise the rehearsal is in their hands, threats to good order tend to be minimised. Another advantage of this method of organisation is that it allows the teacher more easily to draw attention to those aspects of the director's function that depend on his being able to stand back and identify with the potential audience, to his responsibility for focus, composition, tempo, pace and rhythm.

The class will first have to agree on the shape of the acting area and the presence and the provisional placing of rostra or furniture. The cast can be chosen by testing the preferences of the class or the teacher can ensure, for this particular exercise, that his performers have the minimum reading ability in the sense that they can decipher the signs without too much sweat. How the teacher casts depends on how he intends to follow up the work. If he intends to have the whole class exploring the same scene or episode in groups afterwards, then a capable cast can speed up what is a slow process of preparation. With the groups established, the teacher can either circulate and comment or he can be an audience of one. If the actors are shy, the group can report its findings at the end, but if they are prepared to show their work this is easier than to describe it. One hopes that the teacher will have encouraged in them an awareness of the need both to build on their encounter with the text and to allow for the interpretations of others; to realise, that is, their responsibility towards their fellow players. 'Characters' are affected by what the individual can make of them: if, in *The Merchant of Venice*, the actor can only play the suffering side of Shylock with any degree of conviction, Portia will have to try to compensate as best she can; otherwise she will come out of the trial scene as a heartless prig.

The danger, of course, with what we have called 'production by

18

committee' is that the teacher is easily able to dominate the process and he may do it unwittingly. Although it might be helpful to some groups to see issues raised and solutions tried, official prestige can be given to those ways of doing things that the representative cast settle upon. The teacher might draw some consolation from the fact that, even though all the groups may be working in the same-shaped space, and even though the less inventive do rely on the agreed decisions, the very fact of the actors being individuals will ensure a difference of emphasis and flavour and therefore of meaning; but he will have to be perceptive and quick off the mark to bring this out.

The teacher who spurns such consolations may prefer to divide his class into groups from the beginning and either set up an experiment or leave them to discover the problems for themselves. I must confess I have been surprised how much ingenuity even unsophisticated children can display when confronted with an open-ended challenge like this; but in general, as I say, I have found that one needs to be sure that the groups have a degree of experience either in improvisation or in theatrical realisation, before one can turn them loose with any degree of confidence.

The rest of this chapter, then, discusses approaches to the work of particular playwrights and particular kinds or styles of drama. The activities concentrate on working on the text as written and face the pupil, at this stage, with the challenges and decisions of the actor.

Macbeth

The Shakespearean actor may be required to cope with a variety of functions, constantly adapting his activity to the style of a scene or episode. He is not required completely to immerse himself in a role and conventions such as the soliloquy discourage attempts at creating illusion. In a play such as *Macbeth*, though, (a favourite with the fourth year and upwards) the acting at times needs to be psychologically expressive and the actor will be concerned to discover subtle individual motivation, sometimes declared and sometimes undeclared. For the young performer, the sheer scale of the passions in this play can make it difficult for him to take full possession. Then there is the language, which must make sense to him before he can speak it but which must do so much more than any language he has ever used.

Even if the teacher confines himself to direct work on the text itself, a workshop on a scene such as Act II, Scene iii can involve a fair variety of activities. This is the scene where the news of Duncan's murder breaks. Macduff has arrived, is requested to give the king an early call and has gone to the royal bedchamber. Onstage are Macbeth and Lennox. Lennox chats; Macbeth, who has done the murder, has his mind on the return of Macduff. The setting is susceptible to experiment and to try any play in a locality other than the one intended by the playwright can open up new styles of playing and hence new meanings. For the moment, though, we will stay where Shakespeare puts us. We are in a courtyard and no furniture is required. Characters come on from different parts of the castle. When pupils are functioning entirely as actors, new arrivals could enter the acting space from any direction. If an audience viewpoint is important, an arena or thrust stage would still allow entry from four corners. A simulated Elizabethan stage, however, would require the scrapping of two of the corner entrances (the downstage ones). In this case, the actors could be encouraged to spread the action as wide as possible, since their Elizabethan counterparts had about forty feet of width to play with.

For small-scale work, the scene divides itself conveniently into sections, often marked by an exit or an entrance. The order in which the teacher might tackle such sections and the weight he gives to them is, of course, his decision; and that particular problem is one of strategy. Let us, for the sake of the present exercise, which is to examine approaches, look first at the duologue between Macbeth and Lennox, leading up to the arrival of Macduff. All my quotations are from the Penguin edition.

Lennox: Goes the King hence today?
Macbeth: He does; he did appoint so.
Lennox: The night has been unruly. Where we lay
      Our chimneys were blown down, and, as they say,
      Lamentings heard i'the air, strange screams of death,
      And prophesying, with accents terrible,
      Of dire combustion and confused events
      New-hatched to the woeful time. The obscure bird
      Clamoured the live-long night. Some say the earth
      Was feverous and did shake.
Macbeth: 'Twas a rough night.
Lennox: My young remembrance cannot parallel
      A fellow to it.

Some teachers might consider that such a passage, in the context of the whole, does not merit a great expenditure of time. But one can always argue for practical work that it encourages habits of thought that can have a useful spin-off. Lively class-work can be done on the speech by Lennox. This turns out to be no mere fill-in, and it gives the students a foretaste of the confusion and disorder which the unnatural deed is about to unleash. The night has been unruly and there are five examples of its unruliness. If each item is taken in turn and members of the class at random are asked to read them aloud, the words soon acquire a familiar ring. Items can then be distributed so that every member of the class has one. The teacher says: 'What happened last night?' and points at a pupil. By his tone of voice and demeanour, by his eagerness to know, the teacher aims at encouraging the pupil to deliver his piece of news as vividly and expressively as possible. With a cooperative class the items could be enacted by groups in terms of movement and sounds, building up the sequence. Volunteers who now read the whole speech should be less inclined to gabble the lines, more aware that they are actually saying something and that they are keen to say it. No subtle insight into character has been attempted and the outrageousness of the events seems justification in itself for describing them. The thematic function of the speech has been paramount.

Next, the class can be asked to concentrate on Macbeth's thoughts during this section. Perhaps he would be imagining what Macduff was doing at that very moment; perhaps he would be imagining how he ought to behave when Macduff returned. Pupils can be asked to speak these thoughts aloud. After this, the class can be divided into pairs as Macbeth and Lennox are invited to produce their own versions of the sequence. The work on Macbeth should give the actor a better chance of revealing through his (distracted?) behaviour an appropriate subtext.

Our second section is defined by the entrance of Macduff and the exit of Macbeth and Lennox to 'confirm' the reported murder.

> (*Enter Macduff*)
> *Macduff*: O horror, horror, horror!
> Tongue nor heart cannot conceive nor name thee!
> *Macbeth and Lennox*: What's the matter?
> *Macduff*: Confusion now hath made his masterpiece;
> Most sacrilegious murder hath broke ope
> The Lord's anointed temple and stole thence
> The life o'the building.
> *Macbeth*: What is't you say? The life?
> *Lennox*: Mean you his majesty?
> *Macduff*: Approach the chamber and destroy your sight

With a new Gorgon. Do not bid me speak.
See, and then speak yourself.
(*Exeunt Macbeth and Lennox*)

Lines like "O horror, horror, horror!", ("Oh, by whom?" coming later in the scene is such another) can, if they fall flat in reading or performance, be hilariously funny. Macduff's whole message might seem as unnatural to the pupils as it seemed to James Thurber's American lady, who thought that any normal, innocent person would have said: "My God! There's a body in there!" It is, of course, arguable that the imagery used invokes a necessary awareness in the audience of the enormity of what Macbeth has done or even of a scheme of values against which he has offended, but this time there is psychological motivation behind the apparent circumlocution and youngsters (as might actors) will find it more helpful to focus initially on this. Something literally unspeakable has occurred. Macduff cannot bring himself to describe it and this, in itself, adds power to the impact. The speech might also be designed to bring home to Macbeth the enormity of what he has done, giving the actor playing the part something to react to, and finally, it could be designed to strike awe into the audience. From the pupil whose mind is concentrated on the jobs the lines are required to do, a heightened delivery is more likely to be drawn forth quite naturally. For the teacher trying to help his pupils understand Macduff's frame of mind and deliver his lines convincingly, there are various possible experiments. They might act out the entry to the bedchamber and the registering of its contents. The teacher might try to arouse sympathy by inviting them to imagine cases nearer home where the delivery of bad news would be so painful as to be almost impossible. He may decide to experiment with the lines themselves. Suppose that the exchange were pared down, cutting out the 'evasions':

Macduff: O horror, horror, horror!
Macbeth and Lennox: What's the matter?
Macduff: Most sacrilegious murder . . .
Macbeth: What is't you say?
Lennox: Mean you his majesty?
Macduff: See, and then speak yourselves.

This simplified version can be tried in pairs to see what effect it creates and then the true version, either by the same pairs or by volunteers. By this means the squeamishness of Macduff may be thrown into relief. If this exercise does not make the "horror" line much easier to say, students can experiment with pace, posture and

22

position. Try out the line with pauses, releasing the next word only when it can be done with conviction. Pupils can investigate whether the line seems more appropriately said to Macbeth and Lennox or by the speaker to himself. They can experiment with the physical circumstances. One pupil, for instance, might find it easier to deliver the line if he is leaning against a doorpost, eyes hidden against his forearm. Finally, in this particular extract, a thorough treatment would once again require attention to the subtextual meanings expressed by Macbeth's silent reactions and work in threes brings the whole thing within everybody's field of responsibility.

Alone on the stage, Macduff sounds the alarm. An opportunity occurs here to involve the whole class in collaborative experience. This can be done with one actor as Macduff and the rest of the class as inhabitants of the castle. The sense of filling a stage gives all a first hand impression of public reverberations. As they respond to the alarm, making up conversations, they rehearse the initial bewilderment that major characters are to feel. Macduff has now to speak to individual arrivals. Two pupils can be invited to play Lady Macbeth and Banquo. Lady Macbeth will actually have a public before whom to put a public face. Two other notorious and potentially hilarious lines: "Woe, alas!/What, in our house?", can, by virtue of being easy to memorise, be here delivered directly to faces and not to the page of a book — or, if the actress prefers, delivered merely with a consciousness of the eyes that are watching. The eyes will also be on Banquo and this actor, too, will have to decide, on the basis of his function in the play up to this point, what silent reactions might be likely for him. Other actors can take their turn at being both Lady Macbeth and Banquo.

I have suggested that it is possible to act out descriptions of events chronicled in Lennox's speech and some teachers see the same approach as a way of giving force to metaphors. Here I think one has to be more careful, as, if it gives rise to silliness, it can have the opposite effect. Macduff's speech as he rouses the sleepers includes an image of the Last Judgement:

> As from your graves rise up and walk like sprites
> To countenance this horror.

Such an image would be part of the mental equipment of the contemporary audience and it recalls a closing scene in the Mystery Cycles. If the class lie on the floor and rise slowly to their feet to the accompaniment of chilling music such as Penderecki's *Threnody to the Victims of Hiroshima*, it can provide a vivid impression of the imaginative impact the filling of the stage might achieve and give a clue to the actors as to a possible style of performing and presenting it.

Macbeth's first speech on re-entry faces the actor with a crucial choice of interpretation:

> Had I but died an hour before this chance
> I had lived a blessed time; for from this instant
> There's nothing serious in mortality
> All is but toys, renown and grace is dead,
> The wine of life is drawn, and the mere lees
> Is left this vault to brag of.

Is the character genuinely appalled by what he has done or is he putting on an act? Should he try to convey one impression to the people onstage and another to a theatre audience? To give the actor the opportunity to experiment, the hearers in the classroom will need to be flexible in the role they adopt at any given time. The teacher may need to encourage them to be both a sounding board by their presence and an audience by their critical function. Once again, various volunteers can try the entrance and the speech, and the validity of each version can be discussed. As with Macduff, it will help if the actor is made aware of all the circumstances surrounding the character's entrance. He will need to realise that Macbeth has just come from killing the grooms and that the people onstage will by now have learned about the murder of Duncan. He could try the speech addressed largely to Lady Macbeth. He could see what effect it has if spoken largely to Banquo.

Malcolm and Donalbain arrive to receive the news and Macbeth is forced once again into the public spotlight by his actual confession that he killed the grooms. The structure of this speech can be approached and apprehended simultaneously by the class as a whole. The speech is chanted and the class faces in a different direction as the sense dictates. The first part directly apostrophises a listener (or listeners):

> Who can be wise, amazed, temperate and furious,
> Loyal and neutral, in a moment? No man.
> The expedition of my violent love
> Outran the pauser reason.

Next the actors incline (say) to the right:

> Here lay Duncan,
> His silver skin laced with his golden blood,
> And his gashed stabs looked like a breach in nature
> For ruin's wasteful entrance;

24

Then to the other side:

> there the murderers
> Steeped in the colours of their trade, their daggers
> Unmannerly breeched in gore.

Face front again for the final rhetorical question:

> Who could refrain,
> That had a heart to love, and in that heart
> Courage to make's love known?

The different orientations are not intended to indicate, literally, a way of performing the speech onstage. It is hoped that if the physical movement becomes internalised, it will help the delivery of the lines. How the individual pupil performs the movements is up to him. Does he feel that Macbeth is trying to present his actions as inescapably clear-cut and logical? Is the effect more clumsy than Macbeth thinks? In looking at the structure in this way we are trying to acquire an inkling of the possible intentions behind it. Physical movement used in this way can also be applied to speeches where the change of direction is purely emotional and in no way literal.

Apprehension of an overall intention or of an emotional framework can help the pupil not to ignore but to cope with detail. With the speech under discussion the general 'sense' might be summed up by discovering the signposts and focusing on them:

> Who can be wise, amazed, temperate and furious,
> Loyal and neutral, in a moment? No man.
> Here lay Duncan . . .
>   there the murderers,
> Who could refrain?

The pupils say just this but attempt to make what lines they have got as expressive as possible; to try to conjure up, say, outrage and sorrow with "Here lay Duncan" and scorn and disgust with "there the murderers". What they should discover in returning to the speech as written is the purpose behind the detail and just how helpful the detail is to the actor.

Until he has grasped the sense of what is being said, the young actor cannot be in complete control whatever the play he is performing. I have suggested a mental (it could be physical) underlining of key phrases or signposts: key words for emphasis or 'pointing' can also be useful to isolate. Clive Barker (*Theatre Games*) recommends the underlining of verbs in particular and Charles Marowitz (*The Act of Being*) finds that the syntactical shape of a speech can be high-

25

lighted by having the actor playing the role, or the rest of the class who are listening, speak out the punctuation.

Sense is important, then, and so is intention; that is to say, what the pupil as character, chorus or whatever, is trying to achieve. With verse drama, the actor may be the originator of reverberations of a more formal kind. Cecily Berry describes the state of mind of an actor tackling *The Duchess of Malfi* by Webster:

In coping with a text like this you have to find the reason of the speech — that is you have to make the top logical sense clear and pursue the thought. You must weave your way through the extravagance of its utterance, which involves experiencing the weight and form of those particular images so that the audience can realise them fully. You also have to root all this down to the particular emotional need of the character which is contained in those precise words, their sound containing some of their meaning.

(*Voice and the Actor*, p. 135)

In the speech of Macbeth that we have been discussing, "Who can be wise . . . ", the audience might be busy linking up images with other images, thematic references to 'nature' and 'courage' to other examples of it, and the teacher is, of course, at liberty to point this out. But he might be well advised to direct his young actors in the first place to what the character intends. Could it be that 'courage' and 'love' are being used in this context as rhetorical weapons?

The danger for any actor with verse drama, or even with highly formalised prose such as Shaw's, is that they feel bound to adopt an incantatory delivery. So hard do they concentrate on *how* the lines are to be said that a mental tune is set up which may have little to do with *what* is being said. In a production I did of *The Merchant of Venice* a young actor got hypnotised by his impression of the rhythm of a speech by Shylock, one of his speeches in the trial scene.

> You have among you many a purchased slave
> Which like your asses, and your dogs and mules,
> You use in abject and in slavish parts,
> Because you bought them, shall I say to you,
> Let them be free, marry them to your heirs?

He emphasised the 'many', but since slaves had not hitherto been mentioned it made no sense at all to do this. I made him convey to me the gist and intention of his own words and the long hard road to emphasising 'slave' began.

B.L. Joseph thinks an actor might benefit from an awareness of rhetorical and metrical structure, particularly of verse drama, but he is at pains to stress that the actor's attention should not be for long diverted from the real problems of playing a character in a situation.

Imagery and figurative language, so he says, should be tackled initially by asking why the character needs to use it or what function it fulfils by being introduced into the performance at that particular moment. What matters for the actor is what lines, whether containing imagery or not, can make him do, think or feel in a given theatrical context. Joseph strives hard to eschew an incantatory approach, but his own, if carelessly embarked upon, may have that very effect. It takes the actor through the stage of self-consciousness where many shipwreck and no further get, the 'how' coming before the 'what'.

The 'reasons' for Lady Macbeth's fainting have been long debated. It may be that she is more sensitive than she has seemed; it may be that demons which possess her choose this moment to leave her. But it is also true that she faints immediately after the speech of Macbeth's that we have been discussing and that, in performance, a distraction of the suspicious attention that her husband has drawn gives the actress a convincing dramatic motive. Attention to questions of theatrical expediency can have the effect of curbing the more ingenious flights of critical fancy. The unspoken reactions of Lady Macbeth since she first received the 'news' need discussing with the class. Her fainting can then be explored in the context of group performances of this sequence. Not simply the intuitions of the actress but the effects of her action on the audience can then be considered.

One thing her fainting does is to change the focus, as then Shakespeare narrows the audience's field of concentration to take in only Malcolm and Donalbain:

Malcolm (*to Donalbain*): Why do we hold our tongues,
    That most may claim this argument for ours?
Donalbain (*to Malcolm*): What should be spoken here where our fate,
    Hid in an auger-hole, may rush and seize us?
    Let's away. Our tears are not yet brewed.
Malcolm (*to Donalbain*): Nor our strong sorrow upon the foot of motion.
Banquo: Look to the lady!
        (*Lady Macbeth is taken out*)
    And when we have our naked frailties hid
    That suffer in exposure, let us meet
    And question this most bloody piece of work
    To know it further. Fears and scruples shake us.
    In the great hand of God I stand, and thence
    Against the undivulged pretence I fight
    Of treasonous malice.
Macduff: And so do I.

27

All: So all.
Macbeth: Let's briefly put on manly readiness,
          And meet i'the hall together.
All: Well contented.

A section such as this will be best done as class or group production. The onstage 'crowd' is now not officially aware of what is going on and the audience viewpoint is necessary if the whole experience is to be taken in. We need to register the physical isolation of Malcolm and Donalbain, to experiment with the kind of focus necessary while Banquo is delivering his declaration. Does he take in everybody or does he batten especially on Macbeth? Does Macbeth join in when All say "So all"? Is there a rapport between Macduff and Banquo or do you keep them suspiciously apart? Certainly Malcolm and Donalbain stay apart from the rest when the world, which they feel is against them, leaves the stage.

The overall shape and rhythm of the scene are obviously also important to the meaning. A simple walk-through in terms of entrances, exits and actions in itself shows the gradual filling of the stage, and then the gradual emptying, the widening and narrowing of focus. But I have been discussing the kinds of practical activity one might engage in rather than recommending an actual strategy for the whole scene. How many or how few of my experiments one did would be at the entire discretion of the teacher.

Oedipus Rex

The young actor tackling *Macbeth* had to cope with poetry and rehtoric on the one hand and subtle, individualised psychology in or beneath the text on the other. In Greek tragedy he meets characters who are simplified and enlarged, a manner which approaches the operatic and a structure which builds powerfully towards a crisis. Sophocles, for instance, may not be interested in mannerisms or in finding psychological motivations for acts of his characters. This is not to say that what we are shown is not true to life or that observation of people is not important for the actor as it is in more naturalistic plays. Nor is it to say that we may not find some psychology, too, if we keep an open mind and put the play to the test. The actor has to reconcile himself to a comparative lack of physical interaction with other performers and of furniture and objects with which to relate. He is thrown back on the resources of his voice and on his power to make gestures which are clear and stark.

One problem for the teacher is devising methods which will make strange conventions accessible to a set of unsophisticated youngsters. It is a problem David Raeburn faced in producing such plays: 'We may say, then, that the Chorus, the Messenger and powerful conflicts between two personalities or points of view are the very stuff out of which Greek Tragedy is made and that a production which fails to high-light these features as such is in danger of going astray.' (*Didaskalos*, Vol. I, No. 1, 1963, p. 124.) Another problem is to make understandable attitudes and assumptions — particularly attitudes to the gods and to fate — which it is difficult for any modern person brought up in a Christian tradition to accept. Direct work on the text of a tragedy such as *Oedipus Rex* is not possible for most of us and the teacher will have to rely on translations. These may range from the stilted to the chatty and the teacher not knowing Greek will need to make a judgement as to which is the most appropriate from the actions and conventions of the play. Lines which the actor will find impossible in the context to say are bad lines whoever wrote them and feasibility is at least one useful criterion. MacLeish's translation for schools of *Oedipus Rex* seems helpful and clear and it is from this I shall quote in my discussion.

In structure, the plays divide into movements, separated (or linked) by choral odes. MacLeish calls them 'scenes'. For convenience let us focus on one of these which presents many of the challenges the actor is likely to meet, namely the one that MacLeish calls Scene Four, the anagnorisis, starting, say, at the point where Oedipus comes to be told by Jocasta that a Messenger has brought news of the death of Polybus. In this scene, the student must accommodate the phenomenon of an 'oracle' being fulfilled to the letter. He must also swallow or roll round his mouth the fact that the Messenger just happens to be the man who received the baby Oedipus and that the shepherd who found the child just happens to be the one already sent for on another matter. He can be encouraged to seek what drives (if any) there might be at this juncture for the actor to work upon and what effect he can or should produce on his audience. Hopefully, this may mean that he is distracted from being enticed by the traditional red herring, the dilemma of whether Oedipus could have avoided his fate or not.

Group work can be done on the action as far as the exit 'in great distress' of Jocasta after it has become plain to her that Oedipus is, after all, her son. Each group can contain an Oedipus, a Jocasta, a

Messenger and — at this stage — a single spokesman (A townsman or woman) representing the Chorus. The pupils will have acquaintance with Oedipus as a forceful, possibly noble, possibly arrogant, possibly headstrong person and Jocasta as a person who would prefer not to know the unpleasant truth. If the teacher familiarises his class with the whole story in advance, he will be according them no privileges that the ancient Greeks did not share. No orientation to an imaginary audience need be made and Oedipus and Jocasta need only come from and go to the same 'place'.

In the groups, the pupils will be making discoveries about the style and nature of this section of the play and testing their reactions to it as an interpretation of human experience. The teacher, as monitor, might wish to provoke their thinking on a number of issues. Which lines mark a change or a new development in the action? Did Jocasta react? Should she have reacted? How? How did the actress playing Jocasta feel she ought to behave while Oedipus grilled the Messenger? Did the actor playing the Chorus feel silly announcing to Oedipus that the second shepherd is the very one Oedipus has sent for? Is there any room for a 'realistic' reaction from Oedipus to this improbability? Would it be in key with this scene? Did the Messenger feel able to make anything of his part? (He does say he hopes there might be something in it for him, delivering good news.) Did Oedipus feel like a character with an understandable desire to know or did you, in playing him, feel he was single-minded and callous? How did the reactions of the girl playing Jocasta affect your answer to this question? Having worked on this section, the actors might be asked to see if they can discover or define desires or 'objectives' for the characters that might help them in a future rehearsal.

So far, the actors, in exploring the nature and limits of 'characterisation', have concentrated on their own interrelationship. As actors, though, they also need to have some idea of the demands made on them in a theatrical setting. Is it best to simulate an ancient Greek auditorium or acknowledge the fact that the audience would actually be in a classroom and adapt the play to the given space? Will it help with the understanding of style and conventions of the play; will it facilitate an adequate grasp of meaning if the students can be alerted to the nature of the original conditions? Only experiment can settle the matter.

One ancient convention likely to cause headaches is the Chorus. In making the Chorus into a solitary 'Townsman', we have so far ducked the question of his representative quality. If we have a large enough class, we can now pick a cast to play the individual parts and let the Chorus consist of the rest of the pupils. We can place the Chorus in front of the 'platform' (real or imagined) in rows in the position of the ancient Greek 'orchestra'. As the Chorus in the extract so far has only a couple of short speeches (giving information and making explicit Oedipus's own anxieties), pupils can watch all the main action, feel part of it and at the same time be a critical audience. The short choral bits, when they come, can still, if preferred, be left to a chosen representative, since a number of pupils will have had experience in the previous exercise of handling the lines, or all can chant them together to emphasise the communal nature of the viewpoint.

The platform can be accessible from both sides as in the Greek theatre and upstage can be a 'door to the palace'. Downstage, central, a table could stand for the altar to Apollo. We have been concerned to give priority to the experience of acting the Chorus, but the teacher may find that to give part of the class at a time the chance to watch a Chorus at work not only gives them an idea of the function of the Chorus in the action but gives any subsequent playing itself more sense of purpose. He might experiment with disposing the Chorus around the platform itself if the room is too small to accommodate an 'orchestra'. Any splitting of the group will make concerted action more difficult and the effects of this on meaning can be highlighted.

When Jocasta has gone into the palace, the Chorus sings a brief ode, keeping alive both the confidence of Oedipus that a satisfactory outcome is toward and his uncertainty about his identity:

> Cithaeron, tomorrow you shall fill our song:
> Tomorrow Thebes will be dancing in your honour!
> For Oedipus is no one's son but yours:
> You are his father, his mother, and his nurse —
> On your fair slopes the King of Thebes was born!
>
> Who was your mother, Oedipus? A mountain-nymph,
> Immortal bride of Pan who walks the hills?
> Apollo loves our rolling meadowland — was he
> Your father? Or was it Bacchus, who prefers to roam
> The grassy haunts of the Muses, far-famed Helicon?

The lines were probably intended to be chanted in concert while the chanters performed rhythmical dance movements. To achieve this precise effect in a classroom would require a degree of drilling and technical accomplishment that would be impossible in the available

31

time and space. Another difficulty for modern actors is the fact that the Chorus represents a complete harmony of viewpoint and there may be little in our social life with which to draw analogies. The pupils will have chanted prayers together in Assembly but not necessarily with equal fervour. They may, of course, have chanted their more concerted support for a football team.

The teacher might experiment with the distribution of voices as he does in his 'choral speech' lessons. Suggestions from the pupils can be elicited as to when single voices, when duets, when the whole choir might be tried. They can also experiment with the placing of stresses, the underlining of words, the standardising of a tune. The strophe/antistrophe effect of the two verses might be simulated not so much by having a similar pattern of movement repeated in a contrary direction, but by dividing the chanters into contrasting halves. Psychologically, the most fruitful approach to the acting could be to explore the function of the Chorus less as the expression of a long-lost and putative organic community than in terms of its effect on a likely audience at a particular performance and on other actors on the stage. How do you want your audience to react to your expression of encouragement to Oedipus? Are you giving voice to hopes the audience would like to feel but know they can't? Try the lines on that assumption. When you chant the choral section at the end of the scene, beginning: "Can any man claim true happiness as his?" to what extent do you want the audience to share these sentiments? What tone of voice seems appropriate?

For the actors playing Oedipus and the Messenger as they wait for the Old Shepherd to arrive, the problem is whether or not to react to the earlier chant. Miss out this ode altogether and then reinstate it. Does it make any difference to Oedipus's behaviour? Compare the effects on the main action of having them express their grief, triumph or anxiety before a set of townspeople with the effect of the presence of only a single representative in the previous exercise. Pupils may clarify their answers to questions such as whether Oedipus's quest is purely and simply personal or whether the omnipresent townspeople serve to remind him that he has a promise to live up to. When pupils play Jocasta they will have to decide whether she should show to the townspeople all that she shows to the theatre audience.

Scene Four also contains examples of stichomythia, the quick-fire interchange as Oedipus grills the Old Shepherd. Both characters have clear objectives and a reminder of the need to focus on these might help pairs of actors to avoid the danger David Raeburn warns against, that of the interchange becoming 'a flat series of questions and answers' (p. 128). He recommends that 'voice inflexion must be suitably varied to convey the nuances of meaning, and skilful timing is essential. Young actors need to hold a pause, a particularly valuable point of technique in acting Greek Tragedy.' (p. 128). Mr Raeburn is concerned with the director's task of preparing the play for the stage. The classroom actor is concerned to discover when his 'character' deems it profitable to 'push' and in what ways it is acceptable to resist or evade the pressure.

Despite the setting, some actors may have felt the desire to move freely around the stage and this may seem more appropriate in this particular classroom atmosphere than it would be in a Greek amphitheatre. In view of the fact, though, that Sophocles would have envisaged a more static and formal presentation, it might be fair to give the pupils a chance to experience this formality, at least so as to open this choice up to them. Masks as simple as those worn by the Lone Ranger or a Western bandit can be easily made from cereal packets, and a run-through of the same scene carried out with a different cast. This kind of mask allows for mobility in the bottom half of the face. Denied some facial expression, the pupils should at least realise how important the voice is likely to be. The teacher may decide to involve the whole class again by masking them all and putting them into groups of four or he may experiment, for instance, with Jocasta's silent reaction, denied even the voice. The teacher, if he is adept, can read both Oedipus and Messenger, hamming up those lines which would provoke a strong reaction from Jocasta. For example:

Oedipus: My ankles! They've always been weak —
    but how did *you* know about them?
Messenger: They were pinned together when you came to me,
    and I released them!

Jocasta knows all about the pin and what it tells her about Oedipus, and the whole class, working as individuals, acts out its version of Jocasta's pain and separation. In masks, even boys in a mixed class can play Jocasta without embarrassment. At the point where Jocasta is asked to confirm the identity of the coming shepherd, the class pairs off and enacts the duologue between herself and her husband. Masks can give a different feel to the way you act and students can be led to consider the merits of that kind of acting as against the

33

more naturalistic type of acting that will probably have been encouraged by the first work in groups. They will need to ask which style seems appropriate to the play as written (and translated) and to the classroom setting in which it is made to happen.

It will be difficult for youngsters to accept that Sophocles has succeeded in justifying the ways of these particular gods to men. But the struggle of Oedipus to know and of Jocasta to evade the truth, and their ultimate acknowledgement of their presumption, may be something with which pupils can be helped to identify. The archetypal Freudian situation may trigger off vibrations of its own but there may be experiences of a less disturbing kind that the teacher can invite his actors to capitalise upon. They may remember occasions when they desperately wanted to know something about themselves that other people knew and wouldn't reveal, and aspiring Jocastas may find an impetus in a memory of an occasion when they wanted something embarrassing hushed up while an infuriating relative insisted, for reasons of his own, in talking about it. One is not saying that the analogies are in all respects similar but that they may contain enough similarity of feeling to provide a starting point.

Molière

In acting Molière, the pupil is working within a set of conventions which expects characters to be simple, unified and exaggerated. They are nearer to being embodiments of social attitudes than to having a private life. The actor is sometimes engaged both in playing the character and holding him up for audience criticism and ridicule. As the character, he must take himself seriously, but, as an actor, he must be aware of the character's absurdity. The ability to maintain a poker face is very important. Sometimes a character has an obsession, but although he may achieve enlightenment in the end, personality remains fundamentally consistent. Many of the situations and devices, even in Molière's mature dramas, draw on the popular Commedia dell'arte tradition and, to appreciate the style and consequently the meaning, actors need to be given the opportunity to explore the visual dimension of the comedy: the gesture, the facial expressions, the timed movement, the violence which veers towards farce.

A Doctor in Spite of Himself is very accessible to third and fourth year pupils. Sganarelle and his wife Martine quarrel, Sganarelle beats her and she vows revenge. Old Geronte has a daughter who has lost her voice and he sends out two servants to find a doctor capable of curing her. Martine tells them her husband is a doctor but will not admit it until he is beaten, Sganarelle gets his beating but has to carry through the medical charade, an impersonation Molière carefully equips him to do by giving him a smattering of pretentious learning. The play is both farcical and satirical and there is a danger with youngsters that the satire will be lost in favour of the knockabout. However, much more damage would be done to Molière's greater plays by this distortion and the enjoyment generated by the farce is attractive to pupils fairly new to scripted work.

The characters are traditional and any preliminary work on Punch and Judy, for instance, can suggest a style for the quarrelling husband and wife. What caused the particular quarrel in Act One is not specified but there are precise accusations: that Sganarelle, for example, is a glutton, a debauchee and a waster. They may slightly sway an audience in favour of Martine but mainly so that, when Mr Robert, a neighbour, comes in and interferes, her rounding on him has more comic effect. The nature of the grudges needs to be clarified, so that the attack can be better directed. The characters are resilient, though, and the violence is a feature of the style rather than a real experience. This can be tested by allowing the actors to introduce comic violence at points where it is not specified as well as where it is. If Sganarelle has a rolled up newspaper and is invited to use it whenever it helps him to make a point, he will find it a most effective way to discover and punch home the key words in the following exchange. The translation is by John Wood.

Mr Robert: I beg your pardon friend, most sincerely. Carry on, beat her and thrash her to your heart's content. I'll give you a hand if you like.
Sganarelle: No, I don't want to.
Mr Robert: Ah! That's different then.
Sganarelle: I'll beat her or not as I choose.
Mr Robert: Very good.
Sganarelle: She's my wife, not yours.
Mr Robert: Undoubtedly.
Sganarelle: I don't take orders from you.
Mr Robert: Of course not.
Sganarelle: I don't want your help either.
Mr Robert: Well, that suits me.
Sganarelle: You are an idiot to interfere in other folks' business. Remember what Cicero said about not putting the bark between the trunk and your finger.
(*He beats Mr Robert and chases him out*)

With Punch and Judy, there is a frisson of horror that removes it from the category of pure cartoon and the Molière can be explored to see if it, too, says anything about the nature of marriage. A full-scale attempt to improvise and establish the offstage circumstances with the thoroughness of Stanislavsky is too obviously inappropriate, but an investigation of the relationship in a naturalistic manner, without the licence of comic violence and gesture, can help bring out what grounds for audience sympathy or revulsion there may be. It is useful for pupils to discover for themselves whether portentousness will stick and whether or not the episode provides a case study of a battered wife.

In *Tartuffe*, a parasitical and pious hypocrite establishes himself in the household of a wealthy and gullible bourgeois, Orgon. His objective is to secure power and wealth and as the play develops, he reveals, also, a lusty desire both for Orgon's daughter and for his wife. Orgon is invincibly determined to believe in Tartuffe and this causes problems for the other members of his household, his wife, his daughter, his son and the maid, all of whom see through the hypocrite and are desperate to find a means of converting Orgon to the truth. Orgon proposes to marry his daughter, Mariane, to the hypocrite and as he begins, in Act II, Scene i, to tell her his plan, the maid, Dorine, comes in and interferes, both pleading on Mariane's behalf and attempting to stir the girl to resistance and rebellion. The situation as presented is near to the Commedia dell'arte but needs to be seen in the context of a basically serious drama. Pupils need to experiment with what the scene seems to offer and discover the alternatives for the actor, the meanings it holds for themselves and for an audience.

With characters so simplified, a search for Stanislavsky's 'objectives' can be rewarding. Pupils might find it useful to formulate an aim for Orgon, for instance, along the lines of: 'I wish to complete the persuasion of Mariane', while Mariane's may be a wish to avoid complying without upsetting her father in the process. There is, in fact, room for variation here according to the individual intuitions of the actress.

Work in threes can test out the helpfulness of these simple orientations. In the first part of the scene, Dorine keeps interrupting her master and his lines show him getting more and more annoyed. Pupils playing Orgon can experiment with motivations to see which feels right. Is he, for instance, annoyed merely because Dorine stops him completing his aim or is it possible that he unconsciously knows she is right? Could it be that Orgon feels guilty about having so much when Tartuffe professes poverty? Will the scene and the play take this approach to character? Whatever we decide, a 'reason' can be a useful springboard for emotion. In exploring Orgon's obsession, pupils are learning something of the personal consequences and dangers of an inflexible psychological stance.

Mariane has nothing to say at all. What contribution does this actress feel she should make to the impact of the scene as the group is developing it? Should she look tragic and woebegone? Should she communicate with Dorine in any way? How useful to the actors will it be if she is the one to divert Orgon's attention constantly back to Dorine by a quizzical or a deprecating glance, say? Where is the best position for Dorine? Behind Orgon? On the opposite side of Mariane?

In the latter part of the scene, Orgon forbids Dorine to speak and she makes do with gesture. The effect this can have on a stage can be conveniently explored by the teacher himself taking a selection of Orgon's speeches and addressing them to a Mariane while behind him the rest of the class (as Dorines) perform gestures either rude to him or encouraging to her. They can push inventiveness to the limits as the text allows liberty here also. When Orgon (the teacher) turns round, they must either freeze or convert the gesture into something innocent. Their aim is not to be caught out by Orgon. Then some of them can become an audience and the Dorines invited to see how far they can go in raising a laugh at Orgon's expense without making Orgon's blindness incredible. Pupils acting Orgon in this episode are told, in the text, to aim a blow at Dorine while she ducks and makes her exit. If Orgon is given a rolled up newspaper and allowed to make free with it throughout the foregoing part of the scene, the possibilities of the specified blow, by contrast, as a genuine physical expression of venom can be tested.

In Act III, Tartuffe gives himself away to Elmire and Damis, who are Orgon's wife and his impetuous and immoderate son. Elmire arranges an interview with Tartuffe to discuss marriage to Mariane. Damis hides and eavesdrops, probably behind a screen. We are in a room to which there are at least three doors, one to outside, the other two to other parts of the house. The position of these can be provisionally agreed and such furniture as might be suggested by the action — possibly a settee and chairs, or just chairs. There would also be a table.

37

Scene iii of this Act involves onstage only Elmire and Tartuffe. The meaning of the encounter emerges partly through the discrepancy between what Tartuffe is saying and what his body (and particularly his hands) are doing. In some classes this scene might cause embarrassment and there might be a case for calling for volunteers to perform it on behalf of the rest. At first, Tartuffe is his respectable self but towards the end he comes out into the open and admits his lust verbally. The class can help by suggesting appropriate business (such as the closer and closer approximation of Tartuffe's chair to Elmire's) where it is not stipulated in the text. The actor's big problem is that of style, because the style of playing determines the tone and meaning of the play. In the abstract, Tartuffe's actual deeds sound like a catalogue of villainy. Is a comic interpretation possible or desirable? Should he be played as a monster? Can he be played for laughs? Students might be encouraged to try the early part of the scene as though his social mask has slipped without his intending and then to try it as though he is in full control and is cynically nudging the audience with his elbow. The playing of Elmire is also very important. Try playing her as though she is genuinely distressed and then as though she is manoeuvring as cleverly as Tartuffe. What difference do you expect this will make to your audience's reactions?

Scene iii contains some very long speeches by Tartuffe in which he attempts to persuade Elmire to comply with his desires. As before, it might help the actor to attempt to formulate an objective for this character in this scene. This can help him sense the direction of the arguments and the ongoing drive can be further reinforced by inviting the pupil to underscore and detach those lines which carry the main thread. Take this speech for example:

Saintly, yes, but a man as well. At the sight of your divine beauty one does not ask for reasons, one surrenders. That may surprise you, but, dear lady, I am no disembodied spirit. If my humble confession offends you then blame not me but yourself for being so desirable. The beauty of your body dazzled me and I was your slave; you looked at me with those gentle eyes and my heart melted. You overwhelmed me: I forsook everything, my fasts, my prayers, my tears. Your face was always before me. Surely my looks, my sighs, have told you so a thousand times. Now I am bold enough to speak. If you deign to look with pity upon the suffering of your unworthy slave, if you could bring yourself to give me ease of body and mind and come down to my base world, I would give you, O fairest of women, my undying devotion. Your good name will be perfectly safe with me — you need fear nothing. All these womanisers at the Court — how unsubtle they are, how coarse! They brag about their conquests and their loose tongues dishonour the altar where they pretend to worship. But *we* can love and not tell; nothing will be said, nobody will suspect. The lady of *our* choice knows we must protect our good name. With us she will find love without scandal, pleasure without fear.

The direction of the argument can be indicated by the following statements:

Saintly, yes, but a man as well

If you deign to look with pity upon . . . your unworthy slave . . . I would give you . . . my undying devotion

Your good name will be perfectly safe with me

We can love and not tell

These lines could be tried in isolation until they become familiar. The very baldness of their appeal under these circumstances has a certain appropriateness, as Elmire is in no doubt about the speaker's intentions, however much he may wrap them up. On these pegs could be hung the actor's improvised embellishments and finally the original (translated) links.

Elmire traps Tartuffe and is now in a position to blackmail him. Either he forgoes his claim on her daughter or she blows the gaff to Orgon. Unfortunately Damis bursts in from the closet and threatens to do that very thing himself. Damis's immediate 'reason' for losing his temper is the revelations he has just overheard which reinforce the anger which is his individualising trait throughout the play. Pupils should push the immoderate behaviour to the limits allowed by the context. The context includes the pupil playing Elmire and the pupil playing Tartuffe. What degree of anger will be needed to disturb this Elmire's composure? How will Tartuffe react to this intrusion? The actor playing him will need to experiment to find where he feels most comfortable on the stage if he is to get his due share of the audience's attention. He will also have to decide how he should look and whether there is any business (e.g. fumbling with some beads) that he might be doing.

Orgon's entrance follows quickly on Damis's and he remains dumb while Damis tells his tale and Elmire tries to apply the salve before leaving. Orgon's reaction will obviously be at the focus of attention and it will be conveyed at first in purely visual terms. The expressiveness of the grouping can be emphasised by having the actors experiment in groups with freezing into a tableau (or a sequence of tableaux) for a publicity photograph. Work on the face and posture of Orgon helps the actor decide how to say his first line: "What have I heard? Great Heaven! Is this true?" Is he, for a moment, persuaded that Tartuffe is the villain Damis accuses him of being or is he hoping for a denial?

Tartuffe now calls himself "the basest scoundrel that has ever lived", playing on Orgon's religious susceptibilities. Orgon rounds on his son with vehemence and utter conviction. The usefulness of formulating an overall 'objective' for Orgon can here be tested. What effect does it have on the tone of the episode if Orgon behaves in an exaggeratedly machine-like and predictable way? Is there any room for inner psychological conflict in the playing of him? Is Tartuffe in full control despite the adverse twists of fortune or is there room for the audience to laugh at him? Pupils should be encouraged to experiment with the business suggested in the text, particularly the constant kneeling in which Tartuffe and Orgon indulge. Will it take more kneeling than is specified? If Tartuffe is panicky, does this rob him of the menace the action asks us to believe in? If he knows what he is doing, do his exaggerated postures inevitably make us laugh at him or can they be performed so as to make us laugh rather at Orgon's extreme credulity? Experiments are also in order with the pace of the action, the speed with which the developments follow each other. The faster they are played, the less opportunity the actor has to linger over effects. Students of mine who have played the scene with non-stop vigour have emerged exhilarated rather than morally moved. Could it be that the play allows us to enjoy Tartuffe's sheer cheek as well as condemning his hypocrisy?

Whether a pupil needs any help with understanding and empathising with this kind of hypocrisy, the teacher must judge for himself. He may not have directly encountered the religious, puritanical kind and the teacher may find it advantageous to draw parallels with political hypocrisy (or even with certain religious observances in school Assembly). It will be useful, though, to rivet the actor's attention on the material gains Tartuffe hopes for and possibly to remind him of various con tricks which have been perpetrated in living memory.

The Second Shepherds Play

As a play, *The Second Shepherds Play*, from the Wakefield Mystery Cycle, can appeal to pupils of all ages; but whether all pupils can tackle the script in the classroom is another matter. The language, although intended for popular consumption, is archaic and the rhyming verse, while preserving a necessary formality, can create difficulties for children new to scripted work who are wrestling with the sense. A version such as David Holbrook's, which retains the vigour of the original while making it comprehensible to the modern actor, has much to recommend it. John Bowen's adaptation serves the actors well but loses something of the weight.

However, the play was 'popular' theatre and it creates broad effects, has clear and simple situations and the movements required of the actors are usually obvious. The kind of acting it encourages is what Russell Brown calls 'primitive', or 'emblematic', calling for clarity of statement and an emphasis on the group picture. Three shepherds, carefully individualised, are joined by Mak, whom they know to be a thief. While they are asleep, he steals a sheep and takes it home to Gil, his wife. Then he returns and lies down with the others so that when they wake up they are not at first aware that anything is amiss. Mak says he has had a dream in which his wife has given birth to yet another child and that he has to leave. The shepherds discover their loss and set off for Mak's cottage. Mak hides the sheep in the cradle and his wife gets into bed. The shepherds search the cottage but in vain and start to leave. Returning to give the child a present they discover that the proposed recipient is really their sheep and they toss Mak in a blanket. After this, they sleep, and an angel appears to them, directing them to Bethlehem to honour the baby Jesus.

The play had a doctrinal purpose, enacting a mock nativity against which the real nativity could be seen, and the comic outcome, where Mak is tossed rather than hanged, establishes an appropriate mood of Christian forgiveness. The parallels may not be so obvious to our pupils and Mak's lust and covetousness not so immediately recognisable as Deadly Sins. But the script retains the potential for seriousness. The shepherds are distraught at losing part of their livelihood, superstitiously afraid when they see the animal-looking baby, angry when they realise how they have been tricked. Mak and his wife are desperate to keep the theft a secret and terrified of the consequences of being found out. Without an awareness of danger, actors might trivialise the comedy or lose that poker face without which any comedy ceases to be funny. The teacher's problem is to enable his pupils to experience both elements to the full without losing a sense of the ambivalence of the tone.

Supposing the class are working on the last part of the play, from, say, where the shepherds visit Mak to find their sheep. If the class are capable of reading the episode with at least the minimum of expression and comprehension, this does give an initial 'feel' of the type of play it is or could be. With younger and older pupils alike, giving them direct access to the obvious physical life of the action pays dividends, not least in allowing them to dispense immediately with the script but also in emphasising how visual an impact a Mystery play needs to make. In fact, a visual stimulus can give a clue to the relevant style of mental image the pupil needs to form. In this type of play, pictures of stained glass windows, for instance, can help. With Ionesco, a painting by Magritte might convey a useful sense of realistic detail in an incongruous setting. With Molière, Restoration Comedy or melodrama, drawings of contemporary actors might help the pupil shake off any alien preconceptions, providing they are not allowed to encourage the self-conscious imposition of purely external mannerisms.

With *The Second Shepherds Play*, in the first instance, the pupils could concentrate on the moves that are definitely stated in the lines, filling in the intervening bits with silent actions which follow the general direction indicated by the dialogue. This technique can be used with any play which depends on this kind of action or which offers this kind of explicit help. (Shakespeare's dialogue is larded with cues for action.) As well as galvanising the body into the kind of physical expressiveness that ought to accompany the words, this method is a way of standing back from the words and getting a general sense of direction. When the movement work is fed back into the play, it can also remind the pupils of the need for movement to be continuous and not just something which spasmodically punctuates reading. Educationally, one would hope the pupils would become more aware of the importance of paralanguage, not merely in drama but in life, and more adept in their use and interpretation of it.

Our young actors will also need to organise their available space, setting up a cottage and an 'outside'. They will need a 'bed' and a 'cradle' and can adopt other items such as a table, stools and a cupboard as and where they deem the action requires them, according to the help, for example, that these things give the 'shepherds' in carrying out their search. Entry from outside is by an imaginary door. Groups can also experiment with the various comic possibilities not specified in the text. For instance, when the three shepherds appear to have departed, might not Gil be tempted to leap out of bed chortling with triumph? What will she do when the shepherds suddenly return? What comedy can be made out of Mak on the one side and the shepherds on the other side of a non-existent door? Are there advantages in having one actor play the sheep?

If the teacher wishes further to emphasise the comic, and especially the visual element, he might challenge the groups to do a silent film version of the episode. He can suggest that they try to perform the mime they have just rehearsed in half the time they took. It can be useful to impose a time limit by using a perky piece of music such as the Badinerie from Bach's Suite No. 2, which lasts about ninety seconds. He can play this to create the mood and suggest a time span before the groups begin work on the exercise or to accompany presentations. At this stage, judgements can be encouraged as to the neatness and economy with which comic effects can be achieved. Although the situation obviously gives scope for invention, pure self-indulgence on the part of the actors might diminish the impact. One group of second year pupils I took had the shepherds haul Gil out of bed as they searched for the sheep and then had them haul her out again when they realise she hasn't had a baby after all. One might defend this brutality by referring to the fact that Laurel and Hardy get away with showing scant respect for the sick and injured, but in our example the repetition of the deed might be criticised on the grounds that it is inimical to dramatic variety and that it weakens the comic climax.

The serious potential of the action can also be explored in mime. There needs to be some initial preparation of the minds of the actors so that they are aware of what things annoy or terrify the characters. Everybody will have experienced the fear of being found out or the pain of loss, but few will have personal acquaintance with consequences as dire as hanging or starvation and this dimension will have to be built up. This background is common to all the characters and the actors will be working here on common drives. They will next be asked to base their performance on this set of assumptions. A cast capable of handling the reading can work with the scripts at this stage as the activity required of them is less frenetic. Casts are often surprised at the weight some of the lines can carry.

1st Shepherd: Mak, — as I wish to avoid Hell — think it over,
    'He soon learns to steal who can't say nay.'

or

3rd Shepherd: Fair words there may be, but love there's none.

43

When Gil says if she has been guilty of deceiving them she'll eat the child, the effect is quite ghoulish, as it emphasises not merely the joke that it is a sheep but the travesty of motherliness she has become.

Some features of the script, though, will resist solemnity and the ending is not the tragic one that the solemn approach implies. The appropriateness of solemn treatment at particular points can be discussed when groups present their versions.

To complete the process, pupils must be allowed to work on the script given a free hand to treat it as it seems to them to require. With poorer readers, the teacher might begin with or even settle for a small section such as that immediately after the return of the shepherds. They have some idea of the type of fun to be had and have had some experience of being involved in the characters. What is demanded of them now is that they fit the word to the action and discover an appropriate tone for the line.

3rd Shepherd: Mak! We forgot the child's gift — come and unbar.
Mak: (*Aside*) Ah, now they'll rumble the theft — I thought we were clear!
3rd Shepherd: The child mustn't be bereft, the little day-star.
       Mak, by your leave, let me give the little dear
       But sixpence.
Mak: No! Get away! He sleeps.
3rd Shepherd: I think, yes, he peeps!
Mak: When he wakes up he weeps
       I pray you get hence.
3rd Shepherd: Give me leave to kiss him and lift him out.
       What the devil is this? He has a long snout!
1st Shepherd: Something's gone amiss: lets not wait about.
2nd Shepherd: Ill spun weft like this always shows in the suit.
       (*They go in. He recognises the sheep*)
       Ah, I thought so.
       That child's like our sheep.
3rd Shepherd: Now Gil, may I peep?
       I thought kind might creep
       Where it might not go.
1st Shepherd: This was a quaint gaud and a far cast,
       A really smart fraud.

Pupils might preserve any business with the inevitable door, if they so wished, allowing the third shepherd to burst in after "But six pence". The covering and uncovering of the 'child' implied by the rhythm of the next exchanges may by now mean only the disciplining of business already invented. The rhymes, far from being an experience only for the reader, can be seen to encourage the actor to ritualise the sequence in a comic way. At least they will know that their aim is to recover the vigour of their mimed performances. If Mak has

44

a touch of genuine fear and the shepherds are genuinely concerned, the effect may not merely be more portentous but paradoxically more funny than if the episode is played with 'knowing' comedy.

The journey of the Shepherds to Mak's house anticipates their journey to Bethlehem. Perhaps this parallel might have been obvious from the start to the original audiences and have guaranteed that the performances didn't veer off into unadulterated farce. John Bowen, in his adaptation, interpolates the groans of Mary throughout the scene as a constant and simultaneous reminder of the real issues at stake that night and with an amenable class a device of this kind could be exploited. In any case, some work on the final section of the play can help reinforce the basic seriousness we have been trying to bring out.

The end of the pageant changes in mood and adopts a ritualistic aspect. Where before we had three individual shepherds travelling in search of their sheep and of the thief who stole it, here we have representatives of the lower orders presenting gifts to the Son of God. The ritual and ceremonial acting faces the pupils with new challenges and the teacher with problems of motivation. Doctrinal belief cannot be assumed and familiarity with the story may have bred contempt. How do we enable the pupils to perform it with conviction?

It is important in this particular play that the ritual be firmly linked to the earlier comic section and be seen as a natural extension of it. What remains of the individual characterisation must be stressed and preserved. The Third Shepherd, for instance, is still the leader, the optimist, jollying along his gloomier comrades. After tossing Mak in a blanket, all three lie down to sleep. An Angel appears 'above', sings, and delivers his command. When the three awaken and discuss their common dream, the unusualness of the coincidence can be enough to provide a believable psychological motive for following it up. Their abortive attempt to rival the divine harmonies of the Angel could be omitted in classroom performance and the story-line taken up again. A journey round the room in groups, fitting in at agreed moments the speeches which express the shepherds' appreciation of the privilege accorded them by God, will work with some classes. With others it will be enough to mime the walk, picking out those gestures which individualise the shepherds but also exploring their progressive common fatigue. Suitable 'mood' music could reinforce the sense of ritual in this.

The revelation of Mary and the child is easy enough in a drama studio, where a spotlight can create the effect. Even in a classroom, though, it needs to be felt as an 'event' and it may be brought about by a concerted and stylised reaction on the part of the group of shepherds as they simultaneously 'notice'. The problem can also be offered to the class to solve. Groups can next work on the presentation of gifts. The similarity of the speeches encourages repetition of action and the actors should concentrate on working together, watching each other, producing a group effect. They should experiment with movement. What are the shepherds representing here? How can the pupils show that they are working men without making the characters laughably clumsy? What makes for dignity in this context? Formal timing of actions with words is very important here and needs working on. So also does the tableau round the cradle. What effects are possible at this point? What can the Shepherds as a group legitimately express? Try abasement. Try kinship. Which is consistent with the shepherds we have come to know? Visual, pictorial detail must be clear and right, if it is to be effective, and the tableau must be seen and commented upon. Will there be any advantage in attempting to suggest a visual similarity between this grouping and the grouping round the cradle of Gil?

The Angel and Mary have a more obvious didactic function, but it should be stressed that they, too, have a contribution to make to a group performance. The actors can experiment with the effect different manners of delivery can have upon the three actors playing the shepherds. How will Angels and Maries simultaneously ensure that the audience takes in their important message? Are there places to pause while the listener absorbs the sense?

Mary: The Father of Heaven, God omnipotent
That the world has given, his son has sent:
My name could he name even, and laughed as if he knew his father's intent:
I conceived him through God's might, even as He meant
And now he is born.
May he keep you from woe:
I shall pray him so,
Tell the world as you go
And remember this morn.

The teacher may decide to do the Angel himself, with the class in groups reacting as shepherds. Mary, though, has functions other than delivery of a speech and a pupil actress needs to work on significant, non-distracting gestures in the context of an ensemble. Her speech

46

must be judged to trigger off an appropriate reaction on the part of the shepherds before they officially withdraw. Once they have withdrawn, where do they withdraw to? If, when presenting, they join the audience, what does that seem to signify, if anything? What does it make the audience feel?

There is a doctrinal message in the play, but its success with modern pupils need not depend on their acceptance of this or their willingness to push it. I would challenge them to explore the coherence and consistency of the work as a whole and the contrasts and comparisons within it. Next, I would build on the comic sympathy which the shepherds earned earlier, the potential seriousness in the comic interlude and the common social and religious background of the group and later exploit any opportunities for identifying the pupils with the psychology and situation of the shepherds. This may involve a reference to familiar analogous experience or a simple invitation to try the 'magic if'. The status accorded to the shepherd might even have implications for democracy that are worth considering.

Brecht

The plays of Brecht have much in common with plays of Shakespeare or mystery pageant plays such as we have been considering but they also have features which qualify them to represent a distinctive style of their own. For teaching purposes and for the purpose of the present discussion, *Mother Courage* and *The Good Woman of Setzuan* have a convenient structure which allows scenes from them to be treated as self-contained. Both at times sacrifice the prime attraction of narrative suspense, *Mother Courage* in particular. Both aim at the Brechtian 'openness' which encourages the audience to alienate itself from its own stock responses and consider fresh possibilities for the behaviour of the characters. These characters are what they are at least partly because of the society in which they live, and this needs to be remembered. As in the Medieval Mystery plays, the acting needs to be clear and vigorous and to some degree emblematic, with the contribution to a group effect a high priority. But Brecht's purpose at best is not didactic as the Mystery plays are: it is to allow the audience to contemplate an idea rather than be carried away by an emotion. The style, even in a translation (such as Bentley's), comes over as non-sentimental and we are not invited to identify with heroes and heroines. Nevertheless, as anybody who has produced

47

Brecht's major plays will testify, individual psychology may absorb the actor or actress as much as social motivation and terrible is the temptation to get involved. Workshops on both *Mother Courage* and *The Good Woman of Setzuan* will need to test the extent to which the temptation can and should be resisted.

Scene Eleven of *Mother Courage* presents some particularly tricky problems for Brechtian purists, but has on the face of it some attractive qualities for youngsters: action, suspense, climax. At a superficial reading it seems to portray a heroine performing a heroic self-sacrifice, some cowardly and treacherous peasants to throw this into relief and some villainous soldiers. The action of the play takes place during the Thirty Years War. Mother Courage, a canteen woman, who makes a living from the war by selling food, drink and equipment to the soldiers involved in it, has been bereft of her grown-up children one after another, until only one remains, Kattrin, a dumb girl. Mother Courage has gone into the town before Scene Eleven begins and Kattrin has been left at the farmhouse with the wagon. Some soldiers arrive on their way to the town and demand of the peasants to be shown the way. After threats to the livestock, the peasants agree that the son should act as a guide. While the old couple pray, Kattrin takes a drum, climbs up a ladder onto the roof of the farmhouse, pulls up the ladder and begins to drum a warning. The soldiers return furious and a succession of threats is made in an attempt to persuade Kattrin to give up drumming and come down. They fail and the soldiers are driven to shooting her. The Protestant town is roused and the soldiers lose their mission as Kattrin does her life.

Group work on the bullying of the peasants by the soldiers should aim at exploring possible reactions to the peasants and the soldiers. Are the peasants simply cowardly, the soldiers brutal by nature? If pupils are made aware of the pressures on the old couple threatened with a loss of their only means of survival and on the soldiers threatened by their absent Colonel, it can produce a more committed approach to the acting of the parts and at the same time a more considered one.

When the soldiers and their young peasant guide have departed, the old peasant climbs the ladder to see what is happening around the town. The dialogue is entirely between the peasant couple, and work on this can be done in pairs, exploring possible viewpoints. The old woman asks "There's nothing we can do, is there?" and shortly

afterwards repeats it as a statement: "No, there's nothing we can do."
If the section is taken as far as this last line, it gives the line a climactic
importance and makes urgent a decision on how to play it. The pairs
can explore the possibility that there is in fact nothing that can be
done and the possibility that this is an attempt on the old woman's
part to convince herself and get her husband's connivance.

An important factor we have temporarily left out is Kattrin's
reaction to all this talk, but this can be effectively explored during
the peasant woman's prayer.

(*To Kattrin*): Pray, poor thing, pray! There's nothing we can do to stop this
bloodshed, so even if you can't talk, at least pray! He hears, if no one else does.
I'll help you. (*All kneel, Kattrin behind*) Our Father, which art in Heaven, hear
our prayer, let not the town perish with all that lie therein asleep fearing nothing.
Wake them, that they rise and go to the walls and see the foe that comes with
fire and sword in the night down the hill and across the fields. (*Back to Kattrin*):
God protect our mother and make the watchman not sleep but wake ere it's too
late. And save our son-in-law too, O God, he's there with his four children, let
them not perish, they're innocent, they know nothing — (*to Kattrin, who groans*)
one of them's not two years old, the eldest is seven, (*Kattrin rises, troubled*)
Heavenly Father, hear us, only Thou canst help us or we die, for we are weak
and have no sword nor nothing; we cannot trust our own strength but only
Thine, O Lord; we are in Thy hands, our cattle, our farm, and the town too,
we're all in Thy hands, and the foe is nigh unto the walls with all his power.
(*Kattrin, unperceived, has crept off to the wagon, has taken something out of it,
put it under her apron, and has climbed up the ladder to the roof.*)
Be mindful of the children in danger, especially the little ones, be mindful of the
old folk who cannot move, and of all Christian souls, O Lord.

The exploration can be done on a class basis. Each member of the
class finds a space and closes his or her eyes, a ploy which allows
each pupil to insulate himself from both embarrassment and the
example of others. The teacher himself now reads (affectingly) the
long prayer speech and the others do their versions of the actions and
reactions of the dumb girl. A sequence of movements is, of course,
laid down, but I have seen it performed most effectively in these
circumstances with a considerable variety of interpretation. The
teacher is using the speech for the benefit of the Kattrins in this exercise but there are qualities in the speech itself, the detailed explicitness about the children, for instance, which show that Brecht was
concerned to give the actress playing the listener something to bite
upon. Nevertheless, the singleness of emphasis here should be made
clear to the pupils, as the audience reaction to the episode eventually
may be to take a critical view of the peasants at this point, the
peasants preferring, as they do, to pray rather than act themselves.

49

Some detachment from Kattrin herself can be experimented with by the teacher's having volunteers perform the actions in isolation while he describes what they are doing in the third person or possibly by having them say aloud what they are thinking.

When the peasants and the soldiers try to persuade Kattrin to stop drumming, a succession of suggestions, threats and appeals is made. The old peasant suggests that they knock her down with a tree trunk; the first soldier suggests they offer to spare her mother and the offer is made; the Lieutenant suggests and experiments with the possibility of making an alternative noise; he then suggests setting fire to the farm; the peasant woman suggests that they should threaten to smash the wagon; and finally the musket arrives and accomplishes its purpose. Groups can take a section each and work, each with their own Kattrin, on that. As a class, the sections can then be performed in the proper sequence. They could be linked by having one volunteer 'representative' Kattrin explore the appropriate and changing reactions of the girl as evidenced by her manner of drumming. In fact, all those not performing at any one time can be Kattrins and all (to cut down the noise) mime the drumming.

As a class or in groups, the pupils will eventually have to decide how the scene as a whole should be presented to an audience and audience reactions need to be tested if possible in the classroom. Should Kattrin be played as someone making a heroic decision and sticking to it through thick and thin or should she be played as a reluctant heroine, 'made' by circumstances? The legend in the text at the beginning of the scene gives away the outcome. Should the sequence of attempts at persuasion, then, be played as though the outcome is a foregone conclusion or should the actors try to create anxiety in the audience on Kattrin's behalf? Does a growing tension seem demanded?

Of course, an audience watching a performed version, however ragged, will have actual intentions and possibly achievements to comment on. They can compare and evaluate the behaviour of the old peasants, the young peasant and Kattrin in terms of acceptable ways of playing the roles.

The Good Woman of Setzuan also contains a heroine with whom youngsters readily identify and it has psychological subtleties and a complicated plot which further remove it from Brechtian theory. However, the play is a fable and many of the characters have a caricature or cartoon-like quality and serve an obvious emblematic or representative purpose. Scenes are also units of meaning and repay individual attention. Shen Te, the prostitute, given money by the gods to start a business, almost ruins herself by her 'goodness' and generosity and is forced to adopt the persona of a male cousin, Shui Ta, who has ruthlessness enough to deal with the parasites who batten on her. Shui Ta is eventually able to open up a tobacco factory, employing the former thieves for a pittance. Shen Te has fallen in love with an unemployed flier, Yang Sun, who also sets out to extort from her the money to pay his fare to Peking and fly again, but is frustrated by Shui Ta. Mrs Yang, Sun's mother, persuades Shui Ta to employ Sun in his factory where, through selfishness and callousness, he rises to be foreman. The scene shows his transformation and the effects of accepting the values of a dog-eats-dog society.

Investigation of the style of the scene will need to examine the presentation of Shui Ta, raising such questions as whether he is just a mask or whether there are lingering traces of Shen Te and her motivation in the way he advances Yang Sun. It will also experiment with the presentation of Yang Sun to discover the behaviour which will create the appropriate 'gestus' for the scene. Mrs Yang presents the scene as her story and, while she fulfils some of the functions of the legend in the scene in *Mother Courage*, her smugness and sycophancy and connivance are important elements in the total effect. The families, 'huddled together' and slaving away, say nothing and the opportunity occurs here for eloquent business.

Work on the tone of Mrs Yang's address to the audience can be done with the teacher rendering different possibilities and asking for preferences, or trying out variations as suggested, or by pupils doing the same thing.

There's something I just *have* to tell you: strength and wisdom are wonderful things. The strong and wise Mr Shui Ta has transformed my son from a dissipated good-for-nothing into a model citizen...

Some of her narrative can work like dance-drama, directing the actions of the characters. The teacher as narrator can control the work of the pupils while allowing them to interpret Mrs Yang's words as they think fit.

Actually, honest work didn't agree with him at first. And he got no opportunity to distinguish himself till — in the third week — when the wages were being paid...

or this:

That evening I said to Sun: 'If you're a flier, then fly, my falcon! Rise in the

51

world!' And he got to be foreman. Yet, in Mr Shui Ta's tobacco factory he worked real miracles.

Groups of the appropriate size can perform while the teacher steers the narrative. A queue of workers, Shui Ta, Yang Sun and the existing foreman (the former unemployed man) are required for both these episodes. The groups will have to decide what they will be doing when the narrative helps them mentally to detach themselves from their roles and relate their behaviour to the point being made. Shui Ta is often played in a mask and a simple mask can help the actor adopt the persona of the cruel slave-driver. A mime of the dismissal of the former foreman for cheating (Is he hang-dog, resentful, truculent? Can he afford to be truculent?) and of the promotion of Yang Sun should concentrate on showing what happens to both characters as a result of the events. All pupils could work first on bodily postures to express the contrast between the layabout Sun and the posturing official, dressed in his brief authority.

Threes can work on the cryptic interchange between Yang Sun and Shui Ta when the flier accepts the job. (Mrs Yang watches.)

Yang Sun: So it's the factory or the jail?
Shui Ta: Take your choice.
Yang Sun: May I speak with Shen Te?
Shui Ta: You may not.
    (Pause)
Yang Sun: Show me where to go.

Is this to be played for psychological subtlety or clarity of point? Shui Ta has beaten Yang Sun at his own ruthless game and presents him with a choice of horrible alternatives. His only way out seems to be to soft-soap Shen Te. Does he expect to be allowed to do this or is it a forlorn hope from the start? What does the pause express? A deep subtext or an obvious reluctance to accustom his mind to the idea of uncongenial work? The lines are simple and easily learned and can be toyed with until an acceptable mode of playing is arrived at.

The episode where Yang Sun impresses himself on his boss again calls for clarity of statement:

    (Shui Ta has a bag of money. Standing next to his foreman — the former unemployed man — he counts out the wages. It is Yang Sun's turn)

Unemployed man: *(reading)* Carpenter, six silver dollars. Yang Sun, six silver dollars.

Yang Sun: *(quietly)* Excuse me, sir. I don't think it can be more than five. May I see? *(He takes the foreman's list)* It says six working days. But that's a mistake, sir. I took a day off for court business. And I won't take what I haven't earned, however miserable the pay is!

Unemployed man: Yang Sun. Five silver dollars (*To Shui Ta*) A rare case, Mr Shui Ta!
Shui Ta: How is it the book says six when it should say five?
Unemployed man: I must've made a mistake, Mr Shui Ta. (*With a look at Yang Sun*) It won't happen again.

The queue of payees can be as long as desired and some individual variation can be achieved by each recipient deciding whether or not he is one of the foreman's friends, a beneficiary of the fiddling. Mass participation is thus possible here. Is Yang Sun's honesty at this point genuine or is he merely greasing round the boss? Which makes more sense in terms of the meaning of the scene? Is Yang Sun himself a gullible victim of the system? What will the others try to register when he makes this declaration? When Yang Sun becomes foreman he becomes like a prison guard standing 'with his legs apart' and yelling orders, visually adopting a new social role. The scene requires the setting up of a tobacco factory and research can be done to discover the stages of the process of cigarette making. Then different parts of the process can be carried out by different sections of the class, possibly to the accompaniment of a record of machinery or to the teacher's (or Yang Sun's) clapping. The former foreman is given the task of singing a work song and he sings of the Seven Elephants lorded over by the Eighth Elephant, who has his boss's favour and a gun. Stylised action is suggested and the cigarette making can be made to fit the rhythm of the verse as spoken. Setting up the song as a musical event in the classroom is too much to expect, but a useful aural stimulus, in the form of the recording of Brecht himself singing the heroine's song from *Mother Courage*, would provide, in its Germanic attack, an indication of a possible manner of delivery. On this occasion, the teacher himself might even be justified in doing the recitation and steering the responses. If, as Yang Sun and Shui Ta (in pairs), the pupils can act out the progress of Sun from being 'chosen' to guard the others, to sitting 'on his big behind', to receiving rice and to brandishing his gun and being laughed at, the relevance of the song to the situation in the factory is immediately appreciated as is the function of the song in pointing out the meaning of the situation by focusing on essentials. The scene as a whole can be put together and can employ the whole class at once if the teacher so wishes, letting the factory workers be a participating audience, taking in the manoeuvring of their betters. The experience might also enable the pupils to gain insight into both the sufferings and the helplessness of the oppressed.

Chekhov

Chekhov works within a naturalistic mode which reproduces in detail the observable surfaces of life. Settings are prescribed and actors are required to interact with furniture and properties and to give attention to the details of stage business. It is possible, as Stanislavsky did, to encumber actors with too much of this kind of help. Carefully selected, actions, sounds and images may take on poetic overtones. While trivial events occupy the audience's attention, important events may be occurring. For the actor, the problem will be that of discovering what is not included in the text as much as what is. Characters in Chekhov may be preoccupied with their individual problems, but the author allows us to see those problems in relation to each other. The audience homes in on individuals and also embraces them as a group. Consequently the teacher must find methods of alerting the pupils to the sense of continuous life in particular characters, while at the same time reminding them that the real significance of a character is in his contribution to the total effect.

We are at present looking for methods of working directly on a text mainly from the point of view of the actor. The stage directions prescribe a setting for him to operate within rather than against and the imagined position of the audience is in front, all looking at him from the same direction. It is difficult for long to separate what an actor does from the way people will see it and, in deciding how to use the available classroom space, a pupil should be encouraged to investigate what kind of orientation is going to help him, for instance, to make best use of small, significant gestures. He will also be concerned to determine how he wants to relate to his audience, whether he wants them to accept him as a 'real' person and to what degree he wants them to sympathise with him. This will lead him into the controversial area of the play's atmosphere. Is Chekhov inviting indulgence in an experience of unrelieved gloom and boredom or is there anything in the selection of traits, the interrelationships or the structure which makes it possible for the actor to detach himself and solicit an audience's connivance at a more critical appraisal?

Where a play relies heavily on a subtext, the initial impact on a stage will depend on the clarity with which actors are able to suggest the existence of this subtext and this in its turn depends on their sense of the characters as pre-existing creatures. The feeling of identity will have been built up over the rehearsal period. But before a student can do meaningful practical work on, say, the first episode in *Three Sisters*, he will need to build up some kind of dossier on the characters involved. A class reading of the whole play is important preparation for this. Pupils in groups then work on each of the three sisters, clarifying feelings: their longings, their hopes, etc. Next they perform the episode in threes or a volunteer group of three works on an agreed set, to be replaced by another three as required. They should find themselves investigating the significance of Irena's stillness and half-attention, of Olga's marching about and marking of books, of her short temper with the obviously non-working Masha, who sits reading, of Masha's whistling which so annoys her elder sister. As actors they will appreciate the essential isolation of the characters (even though Olga and Irena share a wish to leave for Moscow) while, in watching others perform, pupils should gather an impression of the common dissatisfaction among these characters. The three main characters, Chebutykin, Toozenbach and Soliony, who enter, can be introduced into the exercise. They must at least appear to be preoccupied, but improvising a detailed conversation which bursts through with the appropriate remarks at the right moment is virtually impossible and somewhat pointless. The weight of the past is not heavily upon them at this stage as it is upon the sisters. If they try a conversation, however, and let it burst through on cue with whatever they are saying at the time, the ironic appositeness of what Chekhov supplies is thrown into relief. This is a sample of the original:

Olga: . . . Oh, Heavens! When I woke up this morning and saw this flood of sunshine, all this spring sunshine, I felt so moved and so happy! I felt such a longing to get back home to Moscow.
Chebutykin: (*to Toozenbach*): The devil you have!
Toozenbach: It's nonsense, I agree.

Again, to get the full effect of the way the two groups are counterpointed, the class must be allowed to see a cast of six perform it, with the sisters in the foreground occupying one space and the men in the background in another area.

By the end of the first act, both cast and audience will be in possession of relevant information as a result of living through the action. The party scene is useful for practical work, as it legitimately allows a number of characters to sit round a table or in a circle without bothering much about problems of movement and orientation. To make assurance doubly sure, the teacher will probably need first to invite the pupils to remind themselves (in groups) of the circumstances of each individual character, any intentions or objectives the character might have and his or her attitudes to the others, and to quiz them about these. He might proceed by taking an individual speech such Koolyghin's, which goes:

Irena, you know, I do wish you'd find yourself a good husband. In my view it's high time you got married.

He then fires this at the group who have worked on Irena, asking how she might react, or asking for a volunteer to show a reaction. He then might try it on groups who have worked on other characters and see if they could have any reaction. The group representing Toozenbach, the character who has recently declared his love for Irena, should have something interesting to say on this score. The aim is to alert the pupils to the reverberations an innocent remark can set up. Group work on the whole episode can now be attempted. A class capable of doing it might be given time to learn the lines, at least of the first part of the lunch scene, as some characters have only one short speech, some two and only Koolyghin three. This frees the actors' faces to experiment with means of conveying the unspoken, or reinforcing the spoken, with hidden emphasis. Work on a scene such as this can help pupils understand an important aspect of the language both of a play and of life.

In Act II of the same play, there is a scene where the main focus is on a group as a whole and the individual boredom and inertia are submerged in the impression of a spiritless society. Atmosphere seems more important than psychology, and the construction of dossiers therefore inappropriate. It is the general fluctuation of hope and frustration that the pupils need to experience. In fact, Masha contradicts herself, saying at one moment:

I think a human being has got to have some faith or at least he's got to seek faith

and at the next:

'It's a bore to be alive in this world, friends', that's what Gogol says.

What she says seems more important than the fact that she says it. Following Raymond Williams's lead (in *Drama from Ibsen to Brecht*), a method I found worked well was that of reallocating the lines. In turn, the students take a speech — or even part of a speech — irrespective of who says it and are asked to emphasise the mood, to feel for changes in tone. They are then asked if there are lines which only one character could have said. They are investigating the extent to which a group of people can be both victims of and responsible for a common response to life. Here is the dialogue minus its ascriptions:

Think of the birds that migrate in the autumn, the cranes, for instance: they just fly on and on. It doesn't matter what sort of thoughts they've got in their heads, great thoughts or little thoughts, they just fly on and on, not knowing where or why. And they'll go on flying no matter how many philosophers they happen to have flying with them. Let them philosophise as much as they like, as long as they go on flying.

Is't there some meaning?

Meaning? Look out there, it's snowing. What's the meaning of that? (*Pause*)

I think a human being has got to have faith, or at least he's got to seek faith. Otherwise his life will be empty, empty . . . How can you live and not know why the cranes fly, why children are born, why the stars shine in the sky! You must either know why you live or else . . . nothing matters . . . everything's just wild grass . . . (*A pause*)

All the same, I'm sorry my youth's over.

'It's a bore to be alive in this world, friends', that's what Gogol says.

And I feel like saying: it's hopeless arguing with you, friends! I give you up.

Balsac's marriage took place at Berdichev.

Must write this down in my notebook. Balsac's marriage took place at Berdichev.

Balsac's marriage took place at Berdichev.

In the immediately following section the company disintegrates into small groups and isolated conversations take place. Nothing, in an obvious dramatic sense, happens. Is the episode, then, formless? Have we just a slice of life with no significant comment being made? The teacher might investigate this by casting the pupils and sitting them down with their appropriate interlocutor(s). He makes sure that if they perform their conversations in sequence it is not in the order prescribed in the text. He sets the process in motion starting at one end. A pair with two sections in the scene take the first one first. An effect of purposelessness is almost unavoidable, and useful critical discussion can centre on whether Chekhov has managed to maintain significant links with the unfolding action of the play or whether the audience is left with the feeling that the play itself has become purposeless. Is there an irony, for instance, in the placing of this conversation between Toozenbach and Irena at the end of the section?

Toozenbach (*picks up a box from the table*): I say, where are all the chocolates?
Irena: Soliony's eaten them.
Toozenbach: All of them?

Shortly before, Soliony has said if he had Natasha's little brat he

57

would eat him. Is Soliony now behaving as if he were a child? And then there is Vershinin's speech:

I've just been reading the diary of some French cabinet minister — he wrote it in prison. He got sent to prison in connexion with the Panama affair. He writes with such passionate delight about the birds he can see through the prison window — the birds he never even noticed when he was a cabinet minister. Of course, now he's released he won't notice them any more . . . And in the same way, you won't notice Moscow once you live there again. We're not happy and we can't be happy: we only want happiness.

Is this oracular statement capable of being taken as a valid comment on the aspirations of the futile people around him? Is it best placed at the end of the section, before the progressing action slips once again into gear? Would it spoil the effect of trivial boredom if it occurred too soon? The juggling of material is a method that can be applied to other plays, particularly where there is no strong plot to afford the student an easy way out. The student is discovering the necessity for the form for himself. Finally, if the form of the original is accepted and the play as written ready to be tried, one useful experiment is to try the scene with the conversations overlapping. From the point of view of the actors, the most likely effect will be to create a feeling of self-absorption and, from the point of view of the spectators, it will reinforce the sense of the disintegration of a society.

Overlapping cuts out any pauses at all, but the pause elsewhere in Chekhov is as important as it is in Pinter and can be the means whereby the subtext as conceived by the actor is allowed to express itself. Take, for instance, the famous scene in *The Cherry Orchard* where Gayev addresses the bookcase:

Gayev: My dear, venerable bookcase! I salute you! For more than a hundred years you have devoted yourself to the highest ideals of goodness and justice. For a hundred years you have never failed to fill us with an urge to useful work; several generations of our family have had their courage sustained and their faith in a better future fortified by your silent call; you have fostered in us the ideal of public good and social consciousness.
        (*Pause*)
Lopakhin: Yes . . .

The pause before 'yes' can speak volumes. Students should be allowed to try the section in pairs or possibly with the teacher feeding the last line of Gayev's speech to selected students in turn. Their own conception of Lopakhin as a person and particularly in relation to what Gayev represents will determine whether they say the "yes" with indulgent embarrassment, with impatience and a quick glance at the watch, with the bitterness of the ex-serf etc. Naturally, such

58

work needs to be done in the context of work on the scene as a whole to be fully meaningful.

I have touched before on the problem of translation. Ideally, students should refer back to the original text and make their own translations, but this is rarely possible. It is useful exercise, however, to make the students aware of what effects a translation can have and of the grounds on which the layman can make decisions about the translation he prefers. This is naturally work for advanced pupils. It can be done quite neatly and practically with *The Cherry Orchard* by taking a section such as that between Trofimov and Anya in Act II, or between Trofimov and Liubov Andreevna in Act III, dividing the class into pairs and allowing them to 'produce' the duologues for themselves, first in a translation such as the Penguin version for Elizaveta Fen and then in Trevor Griffiths's avowedly political 'adaptation'. The problem is to see if the predilections of the translator make a difference to the way the actors feel impelled to perform. If, for instance, Griffiths gives Trofimov prophetic authority, can we then square this with the fact that shortly after leaving Liubov in Act III he falls downstairs, causing hysterical laughter?

The Caretaker

Some modern plays discard a number of traditional features, and teaching approaches have to take account of this. A play like Harold Pinter's *The Caretaker* does contain characters with comprehensible motives and the action does show a distinct development, but the author forgoes many of the opportunities for creating obvious suspense. Indeed, he seems intent on frustrating some of the expectations we might bring to a play in a naturalistic setting. The dialogue, far from being an instrument of communication between the characters, is often a means of avoiding communication and for some of the time it deliberately mystifies the audience. It may be possible for actors to construct a coherent subtext but parts of the action, at least, will defy attempts to discover simple explanations. Linking present events with causes in the past is made difficult by the impossibility of being absolutely certain whether past events really happened. This is particularly true of Davies, the tramp. The characters may have 'intentions' but they may not be aware of them and, further-more, they may only acquire them as the action proceeds. The

59

atmosphere sometimes seems unable to make up its mind whether to be funny or frightening.

To establish a meaning for the play, the student has to look not simply at and between the words but also at the actions as described in the stage directions. Sometimes it is carried solely by movement and gesture. The very opening of the play consists of the following sequence:

Mick is alone in the room, sitting on the bed. He wears a leather jacket.
Silence.
He slowly looks about the room, looking at each object in turn. He looks up at the ceiling, and stares at the bucket.
Ceasing, he sits quite still, expressionless, looking out front.
Silence for thirty seconds.
A door bangs. Muffled voices are heard.
Mick turns his head. He stands, moves silently to the door, goes out, and closes the door quietly.
Silence.
Voices are heard again. They draw nearer and stop. The door opens. Aston and Davies enter, Aston first, Davies following, shambling, breathing heavily.

How the teacher tackles this in practical terms depends on whether his pupils have read the rest of the play or not. If this is their first encounter with the text, they will need to discover what, if anything, can be inferred from the actions as given. The teacher will probably need to help them build up a sense of place, but Pinter himself gives very specific indications as to the precise location of objects. One way is to use one of the class as stage manager and let him read out the names and destinations of props in turn, while others place them or pretend to place them in a demarcated area. Volunteers can then try out various Micks for the audience or, with the memory of the communal construction to prime their imaginations, pupils can work as individuals or in pairs (alternating as performer and spectator).

The range of possibilities open to the actor when it comes to gauging the relationship of Mick to the room and to the people who enter is best discovered by experience. Why is it important that Mick should look at the objects slowly and that his face should be 'expressionless'? Pupils can be invited to see what difference it makes when Pinter's injunctions are ignored. They might try looking around at various speeds and be then asked to describe the different 'feel' of each variation, in other words to account for an action done in a particular way. Let Mick, during his thirty-second silence, change his position and the direction of his gaze and invent motives that might account for this behaviour. Then try to imagine what kind of circumstances might allow a person to remain expressionless.

Now the actor must react to the stimulus of the banging door and the voices. What to do is clear enough but the problem is how to do it. The actor might choose, instead of merely 'turning his head', to leap up and, instead of moving silently to the door, to stride noisily and aggressively and then to fling it open and leave it open. What might decisions such as these imply about Mick's attitude to the new-comers and his intentions? Now let the pupils explore the actions as described, try different ways of turning the head and of moving to the door and ask the same question.

Actors and spectators will both be involved with the question of what kind of actions and what style of playing seem to harmonise with other elements in the sequence. No clear and positive motives are indicated in the text. If the actor betrays clear and simple inten-tions to the audience at this point, does this fit the 'expressionless' Mick of the thirty-second pause? If Mick marches towards the door and then, as we gather from the indifference of the arrivals, obviously fails to confront them, how acceptable is the march? If our Mick has indicated clearly that he has sinister plans for the new arrivals, the overstatement will probably become evident when we are allowed temporarily to switch our attention to Aston and his guest.

So far we have started with the actions and Pinter's description of them. Pupils who have read the play through already will, as actors, have Mick's subsequent words and deeds to call upon when deciding how to play the opening. Perhaps Mick is laying claim to the room when he gazes slowly round it. Perhaps he does not react violently to the banging door and the voices because his brother is in the habit of collecting things and his acquisition of a visitor is no surprise. The actions can be tried to see if motivation such as this makes sense. An awareness of objectives, even limited ones, may help an actor feel secure but we are still faced with the problem in this play of how clearly these objectives should show. Pupils can be invited to play the reactions to the voices deliberately betraying their feelings. If they are not surprised by Aston's arrival with Davies, let them indicate to the audience that Aston is 'at it again'. They should then repeat the sequence disguising these feelings and spectators should be allowed to decide which approximates more closely to their sense of the play as a whole and possibly to comment on the kinds of dramatic interest created by the different versions. If the teacher wishes to focus on audience-reaction here and is adept as an actor himself, I see no objection to his demonstrating these alternatives to the class and calling for their comments.

It is convenient with *The Caretaker* to start with movement work because the play itself begins with a movement sequence. There are other plays where a silent episode can be detached from the body of the action and used for introductory rehearsal. Pupils are thus freed from holding a script at the earliest possible moment and their powers of physical expression are called into early service. They can individually explore the despair of Falder, alone in his prison cell, in Galsworthy's *Justice*. In groups, they can rehearse the coke-stealing episode in *Chips With Everything*, by Wesker, so that it completes itself in the duration of a chosen piece of music. The more neatly it is done, the easier it is to understand the airmen's admiration for Pip, who devised the scheme, and the nature of his responsibilities as a natural leader.

So far, in our work on *The Caretaker*, no reading of dialogue has been required. It comes when Aston and Davies enter and it looks deceptively easy, but careful control has to be learned and exercised. Actions and gestures continue to be very important, supporting or modifying the meaning carried or implied by the dialogue. Much can be learned from straight production work by the pupils themselves. I have found that habit can make them instinctively perform actions in a manner alien to the style of the text and this is fruitful ground for the teacher to help them explore. When offered a seat by Aston, the actor playing Davies is strongly tempted to sit but Davies does not actually do so until a couple of pages later. The instinctive action and the prescribed one show us two slightly different Davieses. It is also a temptation for Davies to over-react to the sight of the Buddha, even though the words do not refer to it at all, and this would give the teacher another opportunity. But instead of relying on an alert response to such phenomena as they occur, the teacher may prefer deliberately to set up an experiment in which Davies sprawls in a chair when invited to do so and Aston, whom the text requires to sit on the bed absorbed in rolling himself a cigarette, moves around ministering to him, offering him tobacco, listening intently to his opinions, etc. Pupils doing this can be in a better position to assess the importance and meaning of actions as stipulated.

The dialogue is as non-revealing as the initial mime. With the mime I suggested that actors could be encouraged both to declare and hide their intentions. Peter Hall, in an interview in *Theatre Quarterly*, claims this as an important feature of his rehearsal method, when producing Pinter. The actors expose the hidden feelings and then adopt a metaphorical mask. Supposing, when Aston offers Davies the job of caretaker, one feels that Aston's enthusiasm is outstripping his desire or his power to carry the project through and that Davies appears to be hedging again, behind his grudging acceptance. Are they both playing a game, one might ask, and, if so, do they secretly know that they are doing so? Are they putting on a show for each other's benefit? The problem can be investigated in the manner Hall suggests. In pairs, for instance, the pupils can try out the scene as though each character admits that the whole thing is a bit of a joke and doesn't care if the other knows it. Then, afterwards, the joke can be submerged and the pupils asked to comment on whether this gives an acceptable meaning to the apparently meaningless exchanges. When Mick rejects Davies perhaps his bland politeness seems to disguise the threatening violence which erupts when he smashes the Buddha. Bring Mick's aggression to the surface and then see what this does afterwards to his playing of the politeness. Discoveries made in this exercise might lead to a discussion of the crudity or subtlety of Mick's underlying motivation and to the credibility of his creation as a character. In the cases of both Mick and Aston there is a certain amount of background material for the actor to build upon in individualising his character, whatever the effect of this might be. Davies, though, is akin to characters in other Pinter plays insofar as simple causes for given effects are difficult to pin down. Some drama teachers experiment with motivation by letting the pupils choose from a list of specific identities. They might end up, for instance, playing Davies as though he were a criminal and Aston as though he were a social worker collecting 'case studies'. The aim is to see what this does to the play. I think there might be some value in this where the facts are not yet known or where they are deliberately vague. But it seems to me that to alter the premises merely to see what this does to the meaning does not have to be the same as a serious search for a meaning that will hold. In other words the list of 'identities' must be carefully chosen and the application of the exercise skilfully and relevantly made.

In any play the pace at which actions are performed and at which words are released has an important effect on the construction the audience places on them. In many dramatists the placing and duration of pauses depend on the actor's instinct, but Pinter not only writes them in for us but grades them as well. Sometimes they appear as three dots, sometimes as four and the longest pause is described as a 'silence'. Pauses may imply that the mind is working though the words are not being spoken. In *The Caretaker* they may imply that the character has no more to say or that he doesn't want to continue speaking. A simple and obvious experiment for the pupil is to try a section full of graded pauses without the pauses in the first place. Done like this, the episode where Aston offers Davies the job can seem simply ludicrous; with the pauses, the personal rhythm of each character (Aston's shyness, Davies's evasiveness) is starkly highlighted. The validity of Pinter's system can be tested by juggling with the lengths of pause to see if this in fact makes any difference.

There is a close relationship between pace and rhythm. The beginning of Act II shows an alternation between Mick's staccato interrogations of Davies and his long speeches full of rambling irrelevances. The contrasts may be funny, but whether Pinter achieves a unified effect should also be investigated. Are the surprises here sprung on us in Mick's manner related to something surprising in human experience or are they a stagey manipulation by Pinter? On the stage, some continuity would be provided by Davies's persisting anxiety and wariness but the producer would still need to ask himself how far he should or could keep the suspenses going. Pupils can investigate what is gained or lost by taking the interrogations slowly instead of quickly or by introducing further hesitations where they are not prescribed. The long speeches, too, could be delivered giving weight to each full stop and portentousness to the statements.

Waiting for Godot

Beckett's *Waiting for Godot* seems to offer a picture of the human condition itself. The impression it conveys to some people is of meaninglessness, of the inevitable failure of human beings to communicate or take positive action; to some it shows humanity capable of a heroic if limited achievement. The mood is complex, containing both tragic and comic elements intermixed, and the precise nature of the tone is difficult to pin down. Some see the play as an exercise in self-pity; others as a romp in which the vigour of the fun dispels the clouds; others see the comedy as an escape and a trivialisation, a great deadener, like habit. Can the tramps really carry the burden of being symbols for humanity? Does our laughter endorse their ineffectuality or do we laugh at it?

The 'style' of *Waiting for Godot* has some things in common with that of *The Caretaker* and of *Three Sisters* and some of the teaching approaches used for them are applicable here. The play is different enough, however, to face the pupil with different priorities. Not a great deal happens in either of these other two plays but the action does move forward, albeit slowly, and in both of them it takes place in an identifiable social setting. Place in *Waiting for Godot* is unspecific, and like his classical counterpart the actor has to relate his body much more to 'pure' space. The time element is deliberately confusing. Although his background provides an unreliable explanation of his behaviour, Davies in *The Caretaker* is a genuine tramp and Aston's experiences in the hospital directly link with and possibly account for his preoccupation with electrical devices. Similar 'given circumstances' are not discoverable for Estragon and Vladimir, Pozzo and Lucky, and although the characters have certain distinguishing features for the actor to hang on to, both actor and director may need to find a different tack. More than in plays relying on individual psychology, the director is going to have to pay more attention to the contribution his actors make in the general scheme of the play. Charles Marowitz defines the problem well:

> For the actor, it means a radical adjustment to the idea of motivation. Instead of playing subjective reasons, he has got to start playing objective ideas. He has to stop insisting on credibility in terms of human behaviour and concentrate on credibility in terms of the writer's version of reality. And since that version is sometimes inverted, or abstracted, or consciously rearranged for effect, the actor has to learn to give way.
>
> (*The Method as Means*, p. 152)

Even the characters in *Three Sisters* (as we saw) sometimes find themselves helping to create the rhythm of a general mood but Vladimir and Estragon frequently seem to represent the two sides of a single mind. Structurally, the second act of *Godot* repeats much of the first but makes significant modifications. The two sets of characters, the tramps on the one hand and Pozzo and Lucky on the other, while contrasting insofar as Pozzo and Lucky bring in a social relationship of master/servant, have much in common (for example, their interdependence) and the actors need to know in what ways they are reinforcing such an impression. For much of the time they are alone together, the tramps engage in all kinds of role play, from resembling a married couple to acting as parent and child. They also play games such as name-calling.

Some of the playing is directly to the audience, deliberately breaking the illusion and implicating the spectators. The piece may sometimes seem to be more like a series of music-hall turns than a developing action. The dialogue is colloquial yet stylised and rhythmical, making use of pace and pause as Pinter and Chekhov do but providing no easy psychological clues as to pointing and emphasis. A passage from *Godot* may contain no core of sense, no sustained argument, no clear 'through line'; and the characters may, as in Pinter, be talking past each other. It may not be possible to discover and know the 'real' intention behind pronouncements; there may be no clearly decipherable subtext. As Charles Marowitz puts it: 'The innumerable folds of the play constitute its essence, and it is *that* which the actor is obliged to convey. There is a modicum of action and a thread of narrative, but it all exists for the sake of its *intimation*; for what the play suggests and implies rather than for what it appears to state.' (*The Method as Means*, p. 148.) The language of the body, gesture and movement, is also accorded high priority by Beckett, but stage directions indicate a grotesquerie of style in the performance.

Practical work, important with all scripts, is vital with *Godot*. Emphasis is less on the sense of the words than on the behaviour of the characters and on the rhythm and timing of the action. Pupils need to experiment with tone and mood and effect, to discover what coherence there might be. Insofar as they sense for themselves the range of delivery which is permitted, the different ways of relating one section to another; insofar as they test upon the pulses the attitudes which the situation and personal interactions encourage, they will be embarked on a valuable critical and educational enterprise.

Let us suppose the teacher decides to work on a section from the first Act of the play, pages 16–21 in the Faber paperback edition; a section involving only the tramps. Estragon falls asleep and Vladimir wakes him. Vladimir refuses to listen to Estragon's account of his nightmare and Estragon proposes that they part company. Soon he is offering to tell Vladimir a joke and Vladimir exits rapidly to urinate. He returns and the two tramps discuss suicide. They decide against it and agree to wait for Godot. A conversation begins about how they stood with Godot and they discover they are in a poor case. The conversation is complicated by the addition of the subject of a carrot, which Vladimir gives to Estragon. Our section ends with a 'terrible cry, close at hand' which heralds the entry of two new characters.

At intervals, there are strong visual statements in terms of pose and posture with which the students could legitimately begin their workshop. These are moments towards which a director can build. When the tramps are dejected at the thought of Godot's aloofness, there is silence and 'they remain motionless, arms dangling, heads sunk, sagging at the knees'. Almost immediately 'they listen, grotesquely rigid'. Then comes some music-hall business: 'Estragon loses his balance, almost falls. He clutches the arm of Vladimir, who totters. They listen, huddled together', and after sighing with relief, 'they relax and separate'. Just before Pozzo and Lucky come on 'Estragon drops the carrot. They remain motionless, then together make a sudden rush towards the wings. Estragon stops half-way, runs towards Vladimir, who is waiting for him, stops again, runs back, picks up his boot, runs to rejoin Vladimir. Huddled together, shoulders hunched, cringing away from the menace, they wait.'

Work on these sequences in pairs can be fun in itself and fun to watch. Perhaps the fun, one might ask, is a necessary part of effect? The behaviour of the tramps here is a result not so much of inner psychology as of choreography described by the author and interpreted by a director. Is it possible, in this mode, to express genuine desolation or deeply-felt fear? Experiment may show. Starting with actions such as these, the actor can get some feel of the mode of the play in general.

By attempting to discover how best to say the lines, the student is forced to consider the whole question of motivation. In the first part of the dialogue, up to Vladimir's exit, Estragon proposes to leave Vladimir. The suggestion reminds us of a marriage partner trying out the move on his spouse. Is there genuine feeling involved or is this just another game? Does 'marriage' here offer any hope of salvation? Both versions can be tried.

Estragon: That would be too bad, really too bad. (*Pause*) Wouldn't it, Didi, be really too bad? (*Pause*) When you think of the beauty of the way. (*Pause*) And the goodness of the wayfarers. (*Pause*) (*Wheedling*) Wouldn't it, Didi?

The subject changes abruptly:

Vladimir: Calm yourself.
Estragon: (*Voluptuously*): Calm ... calm ... The English say cawm. (*Pause*) You know the story of the Englishman in the brothel?

Students might ask whether Estragon has any 'reason' for changing the subject here, or is it habit reasserting itself? What impression should the actor try to give the audience? Should he make them despise Estragon? Laugh at him? Laugh with him? Pity him?

Shortly afterwards, Estragon tries to embrace Vladimir.

Estragon: (*Step forward*): You're angry (*Silence. Step forward*) Forgive me. (*Silence. Step forward. Estragon lays his hand on Vladimir's shoulder.*) Come, Didi. (*Silence*) Give me your hand. (*Vladimir half turns*) Embrace me! (*Vladimir softens. They embrace. Estragon recoils*) You stink of garlic.

In the context of the play as a whole, this could be viewed as one of those significant moments where genuine compassion is tried. Does compassion work? Should this embrace be stressed as a positive affirmation? What is the effect on actor and audience of Estragon's recoil? Is it just that he is embarrassed and inadequate as an individual? Does the abruptness of the recoil reduce the gesture to a joke? Is it possible to play the speech in such a way that Estragon retains his fondness in spite of the smell of garlic? Is it possible to carry out the stage-by-stage embrace so as not to get a laugh? What happens to the meaning if you play the embrace in a mechanical way? What interpretations, in other words, will this episode carry?

Some transition must be found to the next section, where Estragon proposes that they hang themselves "while waiting". The class, in pairs, or as a communal production, would be best to explore the section itself, first, and then see how it can be made to follow on. Vladimir suggests that Estragon takes precedence but Estragon protests that, since Vladimir is heavier, the privilege should be his. A lightweight Estragon, so the argument goes, will be dead, while a heavy-weight Vladimir, having broken the bough, will be left alone. The tables are turned by Vladimir when he points out that it is Estragon, in fact, who is heavier, but this has been evident to the audience from the start. Are we concerned with a serious revelation and exploration of character, a definition of the relative intelligence of the participants; or are we in the presence of a music-hall routine? Certainly, the sequence can be tried with Estragon showing serious intent and then with his knowing that his 'logic' has no foundation. It can be improvised as a music-hall sketch with the punch line being anticipated and savoured as a gag. Once the class or group has decided how the 'hanging' episode should be played, some work can be done on the 'silence' that separates this from the preceding episode

68

and actors can experiment with the physical gesture and facial expression that will make the transition acceptable.

Having rejected suicide, the tramps decide to wait and see what Godot 'has to offer'. They have already asked him, according to Vladimir, but Estragon can't remember what they asked for.

Estragon: And what did he reply?
Vladimir: That he'd see.
Estragon: That he couldn't promise anything.
Vladimir: That he'd have to think it over.
Estragon: In the quiet of his home.
Vladimir: Consult his family.
Estragon: His friends.
Vladimir: His agents.
Estragon: His correspondents.
Vladimir: His books.
Estragon: His bank account.
Vladimir: Before taking a decision.
Estragon: It's the normal thing.
Vladimir: Is it not?
Estragon: I think so.
Vladimir: I think so too.
     (*Silence*)

This is a section where pace and timing can make all the difference to the meaning, and students can experiment in pairs with this. Godot operates here in a particular social milieu. Are we meant to take this as a serious clue to the nature of Godot and a useful guide to the 'real' past of the tramps, or are the tramps merely finding excuses for him to make their frustration more bearable and incidentally offering the audience some recognisable social satire to laugh at? A slow delivery, giving thought and weight to each item, should give a different impression from a rapid delivery where one item is much the same as another. Perhaps within one particular speed-range there are alternative tones that are possible. Another experiment can be tried, this time aimed at measuring the importance of 'character'. Estragon's faulty memory is a recurring factor and it is this which triggers off the present exchange. But with our extract, the pairs of students can reallocate the lines and see if this makes any difference to meaning.

The next piece of dialogue can vary in import according to the use of pause.

Estragon: (*Anxious*) And we?
Vladimir: I beg your pardon?
Estragon: I said. And we?
Vladimir: I don't understand.
Estragon: Where do we come in?

69

Vladimir: Come in?
Estragon: Take your time,
Vladimir: Come in? On our hands and knees.

Pauses slow up the pace and could here suggest a note of creeping terror, making the last line wry and sardonic. On the other hand, we might still be in the music-hall routine and the last line could be hilarious. Students need to experiment with both the placing of pauses and the playing of them. How does one manage the 'silence' which separates this section, also, from its predecessor? One way of *following* it could be to do a little circular dance, ending up with both 'comedians' extending a palm to the audience, as though signalling the end of a gag and inviting complicity. Or thoughtful stillness might be preferable. Again, experiment will clarify the alternatives. We have, now in fact, arrived at the grotesque postures we rehearsed earlier and should have a clearer idea which style of playing those seems best to fit our individual impression as to the way the play should go.

After a moment of explicit fear, Estragon has some comic business with a carrot. In effect, a non-discussion takes place with two conversations vying with each other, one about the carrot and the other about a subject already broached before the moment of fear occurred: that of whether the tramps were in any way 'tied' to Godot. The strands can be disentangled and rehearsed separately. The carrot routine can be given full rein as a comic act, then the Godot discussion sampled as a serious attempt to sort something out. Words like 'tied', in fact, must have sufficient weight in the performance to stay in the audience's mind when a character (Lucky) who is physically tied to another (Pozzo) enters. When the dialogue is played again as written it will be found that the comic affects the serious:

Estragon (*His mouth full, vacuously*): We're not tied!

But the students will be more inclined to experience this and less inclined to anticipate it. When an audience watches the performance, it can comment on the kind of response that seems to be demanded of it at this point; whether it rejoices in the comic failure to carry on a serious discussion or whether it feels inclined to blame the tramps for shirking responsibility. The range of responses will, of course, legitimately be conditioned by who is playing the tramps on any particular occasion.

Radio drama

Scripts of radio plays seem more naturally suited to sedentary reading than stage or television scripts. The imagination is required to register a sense of space and spatial relationships, but the body of the actor need not physically experience them and the audience will not see them. Direct exposure to the temporal aspect of a radio performance, though, is still important if its meaning is to be understood; and methods must be found of alerting the class to the play as a sequence of sounds and silences unfolding at a particular rate and in a particular manner. The voice will be required to do a great deal more work not simply in describing what a stage or TV audience would immediately see but in filling silences unaided by facial expression and gesture.

It may be possible to act (or improvise) some episodes from radio scripts as though they were stage scripts. One justification for this, particularly with younger children, is that it provides a familiar and actual experience of space on which, as radio actors and producers, they will be able to build their purely imaginary effects. Unless they have heard radio plays — on local or national schools transmissions, for instance — a sense of what the medium can and cannot do will need to be acquired through experiment. In their own improvisation work, they will have learned how a change of place can be signalled without elaborate settings; but there are some conventions for which the stage has no direct or adequate equivalent. For instance, a change of voice from that of a young woman to that of an old woman, such as Ellen makes in Pinter's *Silence*, can instantly create in the mind of the listener both a real old woman and the idea of old age. Sometimes sound effects not only act as an economical means of establishing location but also provide a witty link between one scene and the next, as when, in *Unman Wittering and Zigo* by Giles Cooper, time is called in a pub and an alarm clock goes off announcing time to wake up for the young teacher who was drowning his sorrows seemingly no time before. A quick succession of scenes, a 'montage' effect, can create the impression of the school at work as the listener is whisked from room to room; the sound 'fade' is something peculiarly 'radio' and can signal, for example, 'etc., etc.', allowing the audience to withdraw as the sound recedes.

If, as I am recommending, the teacher tries to enable his pupils to

SCRIPTED DRAMA

engage in activities proper to the medium of radio, the same question
arises as arose with stage plays, namely how far along the road to a
polished performance he wishes them to progress. The problem is
posed most acutely if he decides to commit the performance to tape.
Professional production of radio plays can be discontinuous and can
be done out of sequence. So, at the rehearsal stage, can a theatrical
production; but with radio the final sequence can be arranged by an
editor and the actors need not in fact experience the play as written
at all. The editor can also select the best 'bits' from a number of
takes. It seems to me there are educational arguments for allowing
young actors to perform a radio play in its proper sequence and dispense with the editing. Similarly, I would dispense with the luxury
of 'mixing' facilities where the actors are confronted with a silent
waterfall while the sound of it is added later or with the luxury of an
echo chamber to put the characters in an underground cavern. I
would also have music over which a voice is laid played so that the
speaker can hear it. The important thing is that the imagination of
the participants should receive full benefit from these stimuli, even if
we risk a loss of 'polished equality'. If a microphone is to be used, I
should let pupils experiment with the ways an actor can relate to it,
particularly spatially. The director should be asking where we, the
spectators, are or whom we are 'with'; with whose point of view, that
is, we are most closely identified. It is possible to create some sort of
impression of a radio performance by having the actors behind the
audience or behind a screen of some sort. The off-mike effect which
signals the subordinate importance of the speaker or simulates
physical distance can be achieved (as in a studio, sometimes) by
having the actor turn his back or head.

A script which can be enjoyed by many ages is *The Nosebag* by
Louis MacNeice. It is based on the Russian folk tale about the dis-
charged soldier who kindly gives his last three biscuits to beggars and
is rewarded by the mysterious third beggar with a magic pack of
cards and a nosebag. Anybody playing with the cards cannot lose and
if the soldier wants anything he has only to command and it will
jump into the nosebag. The nosebag proves its worth in a pub where
the soldier produces three geese from it to pay for his fare. Here he is
told that the Tzar's palace is haunted by devils and he goes to see the
Tzar to offer to remove them in return for a large sum of money. In
the palace at midnight, he meets and plays cards with the devils who,
losing, accuse him of cheating. Before they can attack him he com-

mands them to jump into his nosebag and gets two blacksmiths to beat them to death with hammers. The play shows goodness and cunning rewarded, but it is set in a real world of landlords who are sycophantic towards those with money and of Tzars who treat peasants as dirt unless they see something in them which can be turned to their own advantage. The soldier himself is a reluctant saint, who succumbs, like certain Brechtian characters, to the terrible temptation to do good.

The dialogue is graphic and rhythmical but colloquial. The structure is episodic, with the soldier being the only link character. This makes it easy for groups to work on separate sections to be linked into a final sequence, as the soldier is the only change to adjust to. Some of the earlier episodes can be acted, as I suggested, as stage scenes, so as to provide a rewarding dramatic experience, but episodes like the showdown with the devils contain effects which are of the essence of radio. The soldier has just won at cards:

Soldier: Looks as if the game is over.
Captain: On the contrary, soldier, the game is about to begin. Devils! Where are your pitchforks?
    (*Hubbub*)
Little devil: Aw, why did I leave my pitchfork at home!
Captain: Now then, before we destroy him — aren't you afraid, soldier?
Soldier: Afraid? Of what? A Russian soldier . . .
Captain: Russian soldier or no Russian soldier you've cheated at cards and you're going to pay for it.
    (*The devils growl, warming up*)
Soldier: Stand back, devils, see this?
Devils: A nosebag?
Little devil: A dirty old, empty old nosebag.
Soldier: Dirty. Maybe. Empty? We'll see about that.
    (*More growling*)
    (*With sudden authority*) Devils! In the name of Heaven — in with you into my nosebag!
    (*Screams. Music*)
    That's right. One — two — three — four — five — six —seven — eight — nine — ten — eleven — twelve — thirteen . . .
    (*His voice is drowned in rising music*)
Soldier: Now then, smith, you and your mate get hold of this bag and lay it there on the anvil.
1st smith: Right.
2nd smith: Right.
1st smith: Oh, heavy!
2nd smith: Heavy. Aye. What you got in her, soldier?
Soldier: Never you mind. Just lay that bag on the anvil and beat it hard, the pair of you — in the ancient manner of smiths.
    (*Clanging music: the devils shriek*)

This is music, this is. Bling, blong, bling, blong. Harder my friends, harder!

(*The clanging rises to a peak, then slowly fades away*)

Pupils as actors will have to experiment with ways of playing the soldier, the devils and the smiths, and of concentrating their intuitions into purely vocal expression. The folk tale convention may create certain expectations and there may be no real doubt as to the narrative's outcome. But to this outcome there may be a variety of routes in the play. What kind of play does it become if the soldier is smug and the devils comic caricatures? What if the soldier is genuinely apprehensive and the devils seem to have hidden resources of evil power which might threaten the soldier's success? Does the presence of the Little Devil allow of this? How much tension is there, or could there be, in the sequence of exchanges leading up to the bagging of the devils? In what terms, in short, can the outcome be made convincing?

Younger pupils especially, but older ones too, will benefit by exploring spatially the menace which the devils represent. The pupil playing the soldier may be surrounded with a crowd of jabbering devils closing in on him and may afterwards be asked to reproduce the voice that occurred spontaneously then. The devils may try contorted physical movement accompanied by vocal expression so that the resources of the voice can be tested unself-consciously. Eventually they, too, will be asked to confine themselves to sound. The classroom itself will doubtless contain sufficient echo to add the hollow quality required. As devils, the pupils can try ad-libbing their comments and comparing the effects with that produced by the lines selected and ordered by MacNeice.

If the pupils are using a tape recorder, they can experiment with the placing of the actors relative to the microphone. If we place the soldier near to it, we will find ourselves sympathetic to his viewpoint. If we place the Devil Captain near to it, we may find it alters the balance. After all, in a sense the soldier *has* 'cheated at cards'. The bagging of the devils is difficult to act physically in a convincing way. The imagination is asked to accept that all the devils can be compressed into the space inside the nosebag and that they should disappear from view. Pupils can experiment with ways of producing this effect in terms of sound only. Perhaps a succession of screams ending in a muffling of the voice will do it. Perhaps a concerto of screams gradually diminishing as numbers are depleted will be more acceptable. Music is recommended in the text to drown out the soldier's voice as he counts. Is this music indispensable and if not what kind should it be?

One use it might serve in this context is to allow the soldier time to adjust to a new setting. If a tape recording is being done in a classroom, pupils might query the wisdom of allowing the echo effect to persist. Does it sound as if the smiths are in the haunted palace? Does this matter? If it does, are there ways of muffling the echo? The passing of real or imaginary weights from smith to smith may help with the rendering (if the words are said at the same time) of "Oh, heavy!" and "Heavy". In any case, the test will be the success with which the verbal effort of saying the word conveys the effect of appropriate physical effort. Is the soldier triumphant? Still anxious? Or what? Is music necessary at the end? Is there an acceptable alternative? How can pupils produce the effect of the smiths' hammering?

Pupils may not have heard radio plays but they will have seen television plays. Scripts of these are available and in use in schools. The Longman editions contain long 'stage directions' which are descriptions of effects such as the camera would produce. In my experience both dialogue and directions can sound terribly flat in the reading. The writer is writing with the knowledge that his words are appropriate to low-key acting and that his directions will require creative interpretation by camera men. The memory of particular actors playing the roles may help readers give colour to their reading (just as, of course, it may also restrict the possibilities for them); and familiarity, from the viewer's angle, with the conventions of television presentation may give the directions a better chance of being understood. Some help may also be derived from the pictures of the original performances with which Mr Marland sprinkles his Longman editions. But the experience of performance is nothing like as accessible in school as it is with radio plays. Schools with the necessary equipment may subject a few pupils at a time to the severe discipline of television acting, but for other schools, the problems of reproducing the effects of television performance in the classroom are formidable. There are some scenes, it is true, which can be related to an acting space and presented in the same way as a stage play. There are others, though, where this is not practicable. For example, in the scene of David's dream, in *David and Broccoli* by John Mortimer, the experiences of the character as he dreams are

75

impossible for the classroom actor. David's waking and sleeping life are made a hell by a bullying teacher, Broccoli Smith.

> (*Stars, planets, and comets are swimming in outer space. A rocket goes past in which are David and other boys in space helmets. David is talking down the intercom.*)

David : Saucer to earth! Saucer to earth! Are you receiving me, earth? This is Captain Golansky. Are you receiving me? Am just about to make descent on Mars. Planet now visible, will lead landing party on arrival. THERE IS NO SIGN OF ANY LIVING CREATURE!

> (*Shot of Mars approaching camera. The rocket lands. Swirling mist. David is leading the other boys. The music is slow and rhythmical and gradually merges into the sound of heavy footsteps approaching through the mist.*)

Keep together, men!

> (*David is alone. He looks round desperately as the footsteps get louder.*)

I think . . . there may be life here after all!

> (*He looks up in terror. Slowly the immense face of Broccoli appears through the mist. His great tentacled hands are stretched towards David. David screams.*)

Some of the stimuli are available only for the television audience and not for the actor who, as the character, is supposed to be reacting to them. A professional actor can use his technical expertise to turn on a sufficiently convincing effect, but our concern in the classroom is with experiential knowledge. Sound effects can be produced, music and slow footsteps, but the approaching planet, the swirl of the mist and particularly the gigantic face of Broccoli which needs the frame of the television picture to create the boy's obsessive terror are strictly for the screen. One might retort that modern pupils have sufficient sophistication to transform a mere reading into a performance in the mind, and I have admitted that there is something in this. I feel, on balance, though, that since the words in a television script carry less of the burden than those in a stage or radio play, they are less well equipped to stand on their own.

Setting a problem

We have looked at ways in which the acting problems thrown up by different styles of play can best be turned to educational account when it comes to establishing meaning. The teacher will have been exploiting opportunities as they arise, observing the possibility of alternatives as different personalities engage with the text. He will also have suggested experiments on the grounds that, although the first solution to a problem might well be an acceptable one, there might be others that the pupils would benefit by considering, even if they end by confirming their earlier decision. Examiners, too, often suggest and indeed create dilemmas. In both cases, if the motive is to provoke the pupil into clarifying his thoughts and feelings even if it means his rejecting the proposed dilemma as irrelevant, a valuable educational end will have been served. Indeed, 'acting out' an answer to a question may lead the pupil to the conclusion that the whole nature of the question needs to be changed. In the scene where Hamlet advises Ophelia to go to a nunnery, is he genuinely mad or is he merely putting on an antic disposition? Pupils might investigate the effect when Hamlet is played as mad and cruel; when he is played as sane but putting on an act for the benefit of the eavesdropping Claudius and Polonius; and when he is played putting on the same act but attempting to convey the fact to Ophelia at the same time. Does Macbeth really see the ghost of Banquo or is it a figment of the imagination? Tried with and without the ghost onstage, the question the experiment is actually trying to answer may turn out to be: 'what is the effect in terms of dramatic logic of actually giving the supernatural a visible and memorable presence in the theatre?'

It seems to me, though, that the teacher should beware of creating the feeling that a scene from a play is a problem to be solved rather than an experience to be felt upon the pulses. In the interests of avoiding this, it might be wise to steer clear of some of the more extravagant premises which can be put forward. Is it likely, in the context of *The Winter's Tale*, that Hermione is genuinely flirting with Polixenes at the beginning of the play? Might it really profit a class to try the scene in one way with Hermione as a self-betraying adulptress and in another with the whole affair being a figment of Leontes's imagination? Or might it not be more relevant to explore the ways in which the jealousy manifests itself, testing firstly the hypothesis that the seeds of it are already in Leontes's mind and secondly the hypothesis that it is born before the very eyes of the audience, mysteriously and spontaneously? I have found the latter exercise the more rewarding, and I ended the lesson with the Marlowe Society recording of the scene, inviting students to see where this version stands on the issue.

With a fourth year class working on *Henry IV Part One*, I found that a great deal of controversy grew up around the nature of Falstaff's contribution to the play. However, experiments to solve the age-old problem of whether Falstaff is a coward or not will end, with luck, by seeming less important than the more realistic problem of how to present him to an audience. The Gadshill robbery scene and the subsequent scene in the Boar's Head tavern are of interest here. Is Falstaff, when he lies about his fighting prowess in the tavern, a lovable wag, or are his lying and hypocrisy to be deplored? I tried the scene two different ways. I set up the whole room as the pub and involved those not playing named parts as imaginary clients. In one version, the clients tacitly conspire with the Prince and Poins to lead Falstaff on; in other words, he thinks they all believe him. Encouraging remarks by the Prince and Poins to egg Falstaff on can be made with a wink at the audience of clients.

In another version, the audience are allowed to jeer and mock as each outrageous claim is made, thus signalling clearly to Falstaff that he has been seen through. In the first version, Falstaff is exposed and discomfited, outwitted and disgraced; in the second, he carries on despite the opposition, rides the storm with enjoyment and remains in control of the situation. In my particular procedure, we have the reactions of the student in the hot seat and the impressions of the 'pub' audience as a basis for working out our opinion. Which Falstaff seemed right to us? Did either of them seem completely acceptable? Did we have to find Falstaff entirely sympathetic or entirely reprehensible?

We may conclude with the editor of the Arden edition of the play that the 'multiplication of buckram men does not mean either on the one hand that he expects to be believed or on the other hand that he has recognised his assailants and is pulling their legs: he is putting on the expected enjoyable show' (xliv). It may be that, although the best way to play the joke is for Falstaff not to be in the know, the stage vitality of his excuses is something which makes the audience criticism irrelevant and is something which the Prince and Poins looked forward to anyway. Practical work of the kind I have described throws up a question more fundamental than the one we posed, namely the question of function. What does Falstaff do in the play? What kind of consistency must the actor try to establish? Is his consistency one of comic function or must what he does be psychologically consistent? Is Falstaff a wit who must be expected to triumph or is he sometimes a butt? Can we really treat him as a 'person'? What 'facts' has an actor to build upon?

The 'clients' in my experiment were purely to stimulate the performers and throw their reactions into relief, and my way of organising it is of course only one among many. Other versions can be tried in groups with only Falstaff, the robbers, the Prince and Poins, thus opening up opportunities for more Falstaffs. But the prior statement of the actor's dilemma and the subsequent explorations can serve as a productive stimulus to further investigation.

3
Exploring further

The director's angle

So far, even when a class as a whole has been 'producing', the emphasis has been on the actor's intellectual and intuitive response to the text, to other actors and to an audience. The pupils have become the raw material of the play itself. The director's function that the pupils have mainly been carrying out is that of encouraging the actors and advising them on the playing of their roles. From time to time, though, they have been called upon to make directorial decisions of another kind. The director is in a better position than the actors to envisage the ultimate impact of the whole performance on an audience. He will be concerned with where the focus of attention is likely to be, what kind of focus, whether it will be shifting or steady, narrow or broad; and what precisely causes an audience to be mentally isolated on a stage or to identify with a particular group or to be lying under a cape with Caliban while Stephano and Trinculo poke at them and puzzle over them. He will be interested in the meaning the actor's position implies to an audience. He will take into account the relationship of one actor's voice to another's, the varying rate at which the events follow one another and the conflicts and contrasts which need bringing out. The character you play may not exist for the audience until you appear and a director is better placed to assess the likely effect of your appearance on the impression so far gathered. The director must, in fact, have regard to the likely impact of all the elements of an event working together and simultaneously.

We need to look, then, for methods of enabling the pupils not merely to home in on acting problems but to take a step back and start unifying. Where before we were concerned that the 'audience' should have their turn with the acting, now we must try to ensure that the guinea pigs who are living the stage events for us have their turn to see what they look like. It is worth stressing that we are really talking about a shift of emphasis. The acting process must be thought (and felt) through willy nilly. If, in the early stages, we allow our cast to concentrate on that, it is not because we believe that expression can be divorced from communication. We couldn't remain long in that delusion anyway, since, to give an elementary example, some scripts require actors to address the audience direct.

The most convenient way of organising a class so as to be able to alert them to directorial issues as they arise is that in which the class 'produces' a volunteer cast. Group work can follow, with pupils selecting from or adding to the alternatives suggested. Even then, as I suggested earlier, wielding a director's power requires more maturity and responsibility than most younger pupils are able to muster. Certainly there will have to be somebody extra to the number required for the cast if only to keep notes of group decisions and step back to check the audience viewpoint every now and then. If the group is experimenting with thrust, traverse or arena production, a number of 'directors' of this kind can be useful, ensuring that the orientation covers all relevant angles. Questions of focus sometimes arise naturally when a group which has been almost wholly preoccupied with acting presents its work to spectators. Perhaps the main character couldn't be seen at a crucial moment and spectators will complain. The teacher should watch for such opportunities to extend awareness of the importance of the appearance and shape of the action. Some teachers believe in operating with autonomous groups from the beginning and letting all the principles of directing emerge from practice. If there is world enough and time, this procedure has its educational attractions, but it seems to me that to remind pupils of some of the things they could be looking for doesn't necessarily have to preclude their finding others and can give them a degree of confidence and a sense of purpose. The mobile teacher, of course, can unobtrusively oil the workings, even though, in any other respect, the group is autonomous.

Let us examine the problems which arise for the director in working on part of Act II of *Arms and the Man* by Shaw, a play which can go well in the fourth and fifth years, and discuss some of the activities a classroom director might find useful. The scene is generously supplied with stage directions which the director is at liberty to accept or reject; and although in some ways the manner is naturalistic, a careful contrivance of effect and a careful composition of picture may be necessary, if the appropriate note is to be struck. The situation of the play is briefly this. During the war between the Bulgarians and the Serbs, Captain Bluntschli, a Swiss officer fighting for the Serbs, is sheltered by two Bulgarian ladies, Catherine and her daughter Raina. Neither of them at that time learns his name and Raina, who feeds him on chocolate creams, christens him 'the chocolate cream soldier'.

Act II takes place in the garden of the house. Two entrances/exits are required, one to the house via the terrace and one out through the stables. Onstage we see a table and chairs, where people have been having breakfast, and a bench. The war is over. In the house are Major Petkoff, the man of the house, and Sergius, Raina's intended husband, who have come home from service in the Bulgarian army. A quick read-through by the better readers gives a useful idea of the general content and a feel of the style. It can be tackled in class in sections conveniently determined by the entrance of a new character. Next, a setting is agreed. It is best to start with the type of setting chosen by the author, that is to say a proscenium setting and with the recommended location, that is to say the garden. The class will need to decide where to place the table and bench and how to create the raised terrace leading from the house (rostra or tables, for example). They may want to move these later but let them find out for themselves whether they are conveniently placed or not.

The opening section shows Catherine in the garden joined by Louka the maid. Louka brings a card which announces the arrival of Captain Bluntschli.

Catherine (*Reading*): 'Captain Bluntschli'? That's a German name.
Louka: Swiss, madam, I think.
Catherine: (*With a bound that makes Louka jump back*) Swiss! What is he like?

The stage direction giving Catherine's reaction may or may not be of any help to the actress, and pupils should experiment to see if the action can be done. Pair work would be possible here and the lines are so simple that the books would not be needed and the actresses — or actors if the class is mixed or all boys — could concentrate on physical expression. If the specified reaction does not feel right or look right, perhaps the stage direction gives a useful clue to the *kind* of reaction Shaw expects in Catherine and the effect he hopes to produce on the audience. The audience will have realised who the visitor is before Catherine does. The class can be asked whether the audience should feel sorry for Catherine or should laugh at her. If, as is likely, they decide she should be laughed at, how would they advise Catherine to play the incident and how should they (as director) pace it so as to help? The actress might be asked to try a double-take or an exaggeratedly loud rendering of "Swiss!" They might put store by a pause that Louka might introduce before "Swiss, madam, I think" or ask her to try various tones of voice and volumes of delivery to provide the right contrast with Catherine and so trigger the laugh more effectively.

After this, Catherine becomes panic-stricken and the comic contrast of behaviour between the two women can continue to be emphasised. The class could at this stage be divided into twos or threes (depending if a separate 'director' is required) to experiment for themselves with the various directorial suggestions as to the means of producing the appropriate (comic) mood. When Bluntschli enters, the 'director' should be asked to gauge the effect on the audience of his new smart appearance. What inferences about his motives (and his changes with Raina) might they make? Catherine's reception of him makes amusing reading in the stage direction. How can you produce the effect in action? In what ways can the particular people acting be deployed to create the incongruity between what formality requires and what we get? If you have two different actors does it work the same way or do you have to make adjustments? If it doesn't work, what is missing? Catherine's speeches seem to demand the same anxious delivery. Would she move about? How? What use can you, as director, make of the contrast between her movement and Bluntschli's? Up to the next arrivals, we have another duologue, then. This, too, can be done in pairs. Although a director might have to interfere to regulate the atmosphere, he would be able, even on a proscenium stage, to allow a couple of actors to create their own pattern of movement, since masking is no great problem. A couple of actors, then, with the benefit of directorial advice behind them, can work for themselves on problems both of interpretation and presentation.

The entrance of Petkoff and Sergius realises Catherine's worst fears, especially as they are maddeningly hospitable. Warmth in Petkoff will contrast with the build-up his wife gave him as 'a lion baulked of his prey'. Retrospectively, the 'directors' may see that the line will need subtly 'pointing', that is to say the actress should make sure the audience remembers it. The attention of the class or group could be drawn to the relationship of Catherine to the audience. They may, as we have suggested, have decided the audience should laugh at her, but if she alienates too much sympathy the audience will not share her anxiety and the particular humour of the episode may be lost. Her fears derive from her respectability and she is fighting against the inevitable, but is Shaw cruel to her? Wrestling with production problems, we are wrestling with meaning. Is the pupil who 'sends up' Catherine not merely in danger of killing the joke but of being less kindly than the text, perhaps, allows?

Suppose it is decided that the focal centre of interest is Bluntschli. The 'directors' should be watching what happens here, not reading the text. What factors do, could or should keep the audience's attention on him? The 'directors' might comment on the dress he could be wearing. (Would his uniform be violently different from the others?) It might be that he is the most interesting character anyway and that the audience would look at him wherever he was, in the same way they look at Hamlet even while Claudius is kinging it in the most prominent position. Perhaps the actor we have needs help, though. How can you arrange the characters on the stage so that he draws your eyes? (He might be put between Petkoff and Sergius, for instance, with Catherine at the side.)

They are all heading for the house when the entrance we have been unconsciously waiting for occurs. Raina comes on, meets Bluntschli and nearly spills the beans.

Raina: Oh! The chocolate cream soldier!
> (*Bluntschli stands rigid. Sergius, amazed, looks at Raina, then at Petkoff, who looks back at him and then at his wife.*)
Catherine (*with commanding presence of mind*): My dear Raina, don't you see that we have a guest here? Captain Bluntschli: one of our new Serbian friends.

Shaw's stage directions here imply an almost posed tableau and the 'directors' should try composing this. Experiments can be conducted to see what variety of effects are possible without losing the comic importance of the moment. Shaw's description of the way the characters glance at each other is like passing a ball which finally reaches Catherine. This can be most effective on the stage as it takes the audience's eye with it and the ball, in another sense, is now in Catherine's court. There are other ways of producing the same effect but it definitely requires a director's-eye view if it is to work properly. How would you suggest Catherine says her line "Captain Bluntschli: one of our new Serbian friends" so as to make it clear to the audience what she is up to? Perhaps the entrance of Raina should look as if it is 'held' for a snapshot. If so it may be necessary to look again at where the steps down from the rostrum are placed and even to move them or re-angle them. The very least one requires of a set is that it should enable the actors to create the play, and changing the shape of the space can give relevant insights to a class.

Yet another comic entrance follows soon. Nicola, the phlegmatic and sycophantic servant, arrives with the bag which Catherine asked him to bring.

> *He descends; places it respectfully before Bluntschli; and waits for further orders. General amazement. Nicola, unconscious of the effect he is producing looks perfectly satisfied with himself. When Petkoff recovers his power of speech, he breaks out at him with):*
> Are you mad, Nicola?

The dialogue continues:

Nicola (taken aback): Sir?
Petkoff: What have you brought that for?
Nicola: My lady's orders, major. Louka told me that —
Catherine: (*Interrupting him*) My orders! Why should I order you to bring Captain Bluntschli's luggage out here? What are you thinking of, Nicola?
Nicola: (*after a moment's bewilderment, picking up the bag as he addresses Bluntschli with the very perfection of servile discretion*) I beg your pardon, Captain, I'm sure . . .

Again, there might be a way of positioning Nicola to reinforce the fact that, although unconscious of it, he is of great interest and importance. The comedy can be explored by experimenting with different ways of dropping the bag (which he does) — even whether he drops it on Petkoff's foot or not.

Having worked through the scene like this, the pupils will have had experience of the ways in which the elements of a scene can be made to work together and of the implications for meaning of a director's decisions. It so happens that the entrances and exits of characters, although convenient markers of sections for rehearsal in this scene, signal a contrast or change of mood while also adding to what has already been established. Such contrasts keep alive an audience's interest and need to be emphasised. If the same guinea-pig cast has explored the whole scene under the class's direction, the scene could now be farmed out to groups according to 'section' and put together again at the end, or all groups could work on a chosen section and results be compared. Somehow there must be a complete run-through after the workshop or the vital feature of rhythm will be lost.

In considering *Arms and the Man* we have discussed the desirability of regarding the shape of the acting space as susceptible to experiment. Alterations, though, remained within the confines of the proscenium stage on which we had agreed to mount our classroom 'production'. A further development from this can be to let casts experiment with the scene or a section from it in different kinds of auditorium. If one has the audience on three sides, the table will need to be moved for a start; although the entrances could remain where they were at the sides of the upstage area. The grouping should be pulled out three dimensionally, although inexperienced actors may still attempt to play out front. If the teacher asks the actors to go to the extent of playing in the round, playing out front is denied to them and the posed moment is difficult to contrive and perhaps is not even desirable. An audience needs to be dispersed all around the arena to watch a rehearsed episode played out before any relevant observations of the efficacy of this kind of staging can be made. Students of mine have found that, when the spectators are forced to look at the actors and not see them against a set or a wall, and when the picturesque possibilities of the proscenium grouping are no longer available, the characters 'feel' more human. Such a suggestion leads into a very interesting consideration of the 'humanity' of Shaw's characters and the 'natural' qualities of the dialogue. The social poses are more obviously something donned and adopted. A class, of course, may conclude that it makes no difference and agree with Marowitz that the liveliness of performances matters more than where the actors and the audience are. Even this can lead to relevant discussion of the nature of communication.

It can be enlightening to perform a play in another medium altogether than the one for which it is intended. A group of Sixth Formers of my acquaintance worked on a TV version of the death of Antony in *Antony and Cleopatra*. Handling the cameras and doing the mixing themselves, they discovered a preference for close-up shots, giving an intimate feel to the action. They were then in a good position to decide whether the original text allowed of this interpretation or whether the public feel of a stage performance of this scene was truer to its spirit. A different medium, like a different kind of stage, can reveal an unsuspected potential in the material, just as it can show, by the resistance it encounters, that the material cannot be used without distortion of its meaning. We are attempting to discover what can legitimately be done by a given group with a text as written rather than to reinforce any preconceptions about the authenticity of a particular mode of presentation or about the 'nature' of a stage, radio or television play as such.

Music and effects: the director experiments

Music and effects can both stimulate actors and convey meaning to the audience. A director doesn't have to create the effects himself but he needs to decide what is required and to instruct his functionaries clearly. Pupils in the classroom can be involved both in making the decisions and in experimenting with the practicalities. Given the fact that pupils will mostly be carrying books and that most classes in scripted drama will be conducted where there is no stage lighting available, music and sound effects are likely to be easiest to manage. The necessity to read makes slow fades or infernal gloom an unlikely luxury. If stage lighting is available, overall 'mood' lighting for a scene requiring none of the more stylised changes can help the imagination, but time has got to be allowed for the insertion and possible rejection of filters and the angling of lamps. If the pupils are able to learn by heart a section of the play, then this makes possible more adventurous flights of expressiveness, such as the use of lighting to give shape to space, perhaps limiting attention temporarily to one or two people or indicating the size of locale. But how manageable a sophisticated presentation will be depends on how conveniently one is able to organise the operation. When pupils are 'producing' simultaneously in groups, this cuts out the simultaneous setting up and working of the lighting. If groups are allowed their turn, other rehearsal rooms are indicated and this can be a tall order. Sometimes a teacher can capitalise on the normal classroom lights, especially if they can be switched off some at a time. A 'blackout' can be suggested by merely dousing some of them and certainly lighting can be very effectively simulated.

Musical and sound effects, despite the blackout, can, more easily than lighting effects, be experimented with in groups. Music can be integral to the action in the sense that it is written in, as with the *Song of the Eighth Elephant* in *The Good Woman of Setzuan* or the brass band in Ayckbourn's *Ernie's Incredible Illucinations*; or it can be added to accompany ritualistic movement or, as in Victorian melodrama, to reinforce a mood. It might be acceptable solemnly to recite the Angel's song in *The Second Shepherds Pageant* but in *Roots* there is no substitute for the actual playing of *L'Arlesienne*. The excitement felt by Beatie Bryant and communicated to her mother cannot really be shared and understood by the audience until it, too, hears the music. Sometimes music itself and the manner of playing it can be the subject of experiment by pupils. When I have worked on *Uncle Vanya* with senior students, I have found it almost impossible to resolve the problem of the interpretation of the ending without some recourse to some such experiment, either in class or in groups. Is Sonia's optimistic pronouncement really the 'message' of the play or is it merely a dream, a wish-fulfilment for the character? Astrov, whom she desired, has departed; Voinitsky (Vanya) has also been disappointed both in love and in life. The scene is Vanya's room and he sits at his table trying to force himself back into his clerking routine. Marina, an unimaginative old nurse, sits knitting. Also there is Mariya Vassilievna who makes notes unconcerned with what is going on. Telyeghin, a local landowner, a sycophantic figure of fun, enters with his guitar which he quietly 'tunes', then softly plays. Chekhov does not say how he plays or what. If the director allows the actor playing Telyeghin to take his cue from Sonia, he will reinforce the wistful daydream. If the director acknowledges the necessary contribution of the passive old woman, he will probably present Telyeghin's guitar playing as similarly self-absorbed, according to the way of the world. If Telyeghin plays an unromantic tune, it will undercut the speech completely. It is quite difficult in reading to take all these alternatives into account but performing brings the director up against them and he is forced to make a choice.

'Noises off' give considerable scope for pupil ingenuity and expression. In *Rhinoceros*, by Ionesco, there is a scene in the law office. Downstairs a rhinoceros has destroyed the staircase. This animal is really one of the clerks who has been transformed and his wife is in the upstairs office with the other clerks. His trumpeting is a call to his wife but the stipulated 'tenderness' is only one of its possible qualities. Perhaps it could also be grotesque and revolting. Fourth, Fifth and Sixth Formers working on this episode as a class or in groups, exploring the implications of the different sounds, are exploring alternative meanings. With the voice they can try making noises which are simply plaintive, or plaintive and horrible, or simply horrible, and applying them to the action. Put onto tape and slowed down to replay, these noises can sound more monstrous. Pupils might also ask if it matters whether the noises are the authentic utterances of a rhinoceros or not. How loud should the explosion be in Act IV of *The Alchemist*? Should it be a completely outrageous bit of farce or should the sound-effects man aim at making the audience take in the fact that it can have a symbolic significance as well? Should the audience interpret it as signalling or reinforcing the impression that the schemers' 'plot' is starting to get out of hand?

What of the knocking in *Macbeth*? Are we 'inside' Macbeth, hearing it as doomladen and portentous or are we critically outside him, recognising its innocent practical intention? How does the bell sound, that calls the sleepers to witness the murder? When, in Act V of *The Wild Duck* by Ibsen, Gregers says to Hjalmar that he thought he heard the wild duck cry from the attic, is that what he really hears or would a director be justified in boldly making it into a cry from Hedvig, recognisable by the audience but too fleeting for the characters onstage? This would involve a decision to underline the symbolic identification of the girl with the bird.

The use of noises by Chekhov is extensive and Stanislavsky went to town on them, adding many more of his own to the wealth of sounds already specified. Pupils might be given the same free hand to do the same to other texts as well as Chekhov's, thereby declaring their own feelings and intuitions about it and testing the self-sufficiency of other elements in the performance, notably the words.

Reading to oneself

Some teachers choose to require their students to read a play text to themselves. This may be as preparation for or an extension of a fuller treatment in class, or it may represent not merely the first but the only impact the play is allowed to have. Conditions may force institutions such as colleges or Universities — particularly the Open University — to rely on private playreading, guided or otherwise, of some of its set texts. What excuse, though, for the teacher who sat my twelve-year-old daughter and her classmates on the floor of a beautifully-equipped drama studio, gave them each a copy of a riotous one-acter, told them to read it in silence and left it at that?

To be scrupulously fair, when she told me about it, it was not to complain but to say how much she'd enjoyed the play: the grief was mine. At all levels, there is pleasure to be had from reading certain texts to oneself, even if, for some, it is mainly at the narrative level. It is true, also, as we have repeated, that an artistic and educational experience must, in the long run, be personal. Playreading has undoubted attractions as a private activity. The reader can take the play at his own pace, savouring and clarifying at will. He can think of places rather than sets or stages and where there is talk of horses printing their proud hooves i'the receiving earth he can see them un-distracted by the man telling him to see them. A ghost can terrify him instead of merely intriguing him as to how it was made to glow like that.

If he has a certain amount of theatrical sophistication, he can pro-duce the play in the theatre of his mind. He can cast it from the best actors he knows or better still play all the parts himself; he can direct it himself and be his own audience. If something might not work, he can forget about it and ignore the consequences. He need not suffer like the theatregoer from the simplistic interpretation of another director or the inadequacies of real actors. In classroom terms, he is at the mercy neither of the egotistical group leader nor of the un-committed group. All this assumes, of course, that he can not merely read but can read a play!

In my view, the teacher who relies solely on a private reading for a play to make its impact loses more than he gains. Turning back may clarify, but since the play is an experience which exists in time, the reader may seek to clarify where clarification is not necessary or appropriate. Does it matter, for instance, if Peter Quince's original casting is not carried through or if Oedipus seems to forget why he really invited the servant? On the other hand some things are more easily clarified in rehearsal and the reader is likely to overlook them. To imagine a real place instead of a stage set or a stage may actually distort the experience. Read Brecht this way and you lose the necessary detachment; read *Godot* or *The Government Inspector* this way and you will be in for a rude jolt when a character addresses you as a theatre audience. Narrative has its appeal but, as Ron Hayman points out, the reader is more likely to psychologise than the actor, who will be more concerned with how to behave — unless, of course, he has been prepared by an unintelligent votary of Stanislavsky. Does Othello have to sound self-indulgent or self-glorifying on a stage, or does our sense of stage convention help us to accept his pleas at face value? Unless the reader keeps the stage pic-ture in mind he is likely to focus only on the speaker and dismiss the silent characters from the stage. Thus he forgets that when Hamlet says "To be, or not to be ... " he is in the presence of Ophelia, Polonius and Claudius and they will contribute to the meaning the audience receives. Indeed, it is hard, sometimes, to keep in mind who is actually speaking, as the eye goes for the speech rather than the attribution. By the same token, stage directions are skipped or skimped. Some plays in themselves are harder to understand on one's own. Fourth year pupils will be helped by the colloquial idiom of *Billy Liar*, but a Sixth Former wrestling with Ben Jonson will have difficulty following even what is happening. Jonson's plots are much more manageable with faces or persons to associate with the parts. Shakespeare often lets his characters speak the subplot, by letting them tell us their private thoughts, but Ibsen or Chekhov are helped by the contribution of the actor, who has the whole part in his mind. Either that or they require careful re-reading.

It may be a luxury to be one's own actors and director, but meaning in a play derives from a coherent interpretation and the artist who doesn't have to follow through the practical implications of his decisions detaches expression from form. He may escape what Shaw calls the 'greasy commonplaces of flesh and blood' but as actor he loses the vital stimulus of fellow artists which can open up ways of playing to him. The full potentialities of comic action, for instance, cannot be known until one comes up against an actual foil. As director he loses the vital struggle with plastic but resistant personality. As an audience of one, he misses the shared excitement which the text was intended to generate. Educationally he loses the benefit of other insights and having only words to look at he cannot exercise the bodily reactions and the empathy which contribute to his total impression.

It might be argued that both actor and director read privately at an early stage. But they have their experience to call upon. It would seem sensible for the student to be exposed to the text in this way after he has been exposed to the play in performance, on stage, tape or videotape. I concede the danger that a particular way of presenting the play then becomes fixed in the mind as the definitive version. But youngsters need the experience of theatre if their future play-reading is going to be duly complex and full-blooded, and a private reading for them is not a good teaching method anyway. For some, it may never even be a possible one. An intelligent Sixth Former with whom I went to see a Stratford *Coriolanus* found, on reading the play to himself afterwards, that he had no difficulty at all in rejecting the silly, clownish performance of the actor playing Menenius when he realised that the text suggested quite another kind of realisation. He had felt uneasy, anyway, even before checking. He also said it helped in reading the play to be able to fit a speech to a face. Open University students doing the drama course, far from swallowing uncritically the one (televised) version of some of their plays were, in my tutorials, often scathing.

If watching or hearing a performance is out of the question, then the teacher must contrive some means of alerting the private reader to what he must bear in mind, and to the totality of response required. If necessary, the student must be urged to read the play at least twice for different things, firstly to sort out the sense and the argument, secondly to include the other elements that will hit an audience simultaneously with the words. Possibly the most meaningful private reading comes when a student refers to the text in sorting out his own response during or after a practical exploration or at least a collaborative one.

Reading with others

Taking the picture as a whole, the sedentary class playreading is the most popular method of handling scripted drama that I have seen. Because of its convenience it is usually the method chosen. There is much less chance of the more spectacular manifestations of anarchy, such as fourteen-year-olds swinging on the lights or pulling out radiators horizontal, if students are safely locked in their desks. With examination candidates the teacher can at least feel he has time to cover the ground even if he isn't always touching it. The particular size or composition of the class may make this method inevitable. With the sort of mixed-maturity problem one gets in middle forms, it can be highly embarrassing for a super-sensitive girl to declare her love to a goofy, giggling boy if she has to do it face to face. An adult class containing the aged and infirm will not be too happy rolling about. I fondly dream of a situation, though, where the most (or only) valid excuse for sitting as against moving is that there is no space to move in.

The Open University rightly recommends its home-based drama students to take every opportunity to get together with others and read their texts aloud, and certainly this has advantages over the mere private reading. For the speaker there are both interlocutors and listeners, providing a particular human context for his utterances. In a sense, of course, they are not his utterances, but the choice of how to make them, what intonation to choose, what effect to try to produce and what meaning to give it are his and he will be stimulated to make an appropriate adjustment. He will also be able to pool insights with his classmates and benefit from the shared enjoyment that the play is designed to arouse. Poor readers, unable to make anything of a private reading at all, can at least get something from a group reading. Children read dialogue aloud more easily than a section from a novel because dialogue is designed to be said and if the play is in a modern idiom it is even more accessible. I heard a dreary rendering of a mediocre play about a mining disaster in Yorkshire by a low stream in a Yorkshire comprehensive school. It absolutely gripped their attention and they claimed to have loved it. Some of their fathers were miners, it is true, but the point is that as an exercise it had some success and teachers of this particular class had little enough of that to chalk up.

The possibility of stopping and re-examining the text obviously cannot here be adjusted to everybody's individual needs, but what a group can contrive more easily than a private reader is the experience of an event in time, where tempo is controlled and deliberate silences are felt rather than read about. For some scenes, the teacher may have to use his best readers to make this happen and he may have to star himself. He may be justified in feeling that the first impact of part, if not all, of a play should be as complete as he can make it. I remember the groan that greeted a mis-timed reading of Bluntschli's answer to Sergius's challenge in *Arms and the Man*, when, seconds later, the fourth year class tumbled to it.

Sergius: At six o'clock I shall be in the drilling-ground on the Klissoura road, alone, on horseback, with my sabre. Do you understand?

Bluntschli (*staring, but sitting quite at his ease*): Oh, thank you: that's a cavalry man's proposal. I'm in the artillery: and I have the choice of weapons. If I go, I shall take a machine gun. And there shall be no mistake about the cartridges this time.

I have always made sure I did the first reading of that myself on future occasions. Whether the 'good' reading comes early or late, the teacher must make sure that the rules of the game are known and that the class do not feel they have been relegated to the status of passive spectators. They should at least be given the opportunity to articulate their responses both to the play and the reading, and preferably be involved in the run-up to the reading or the development from it.

What I would stress is that the class playreading should never settle simply for a read-through. In school, the teacher should think all the time in terms of a sedentary workshop. The hypnosis of print is still the enemy and in this situation he is not able to move his actors in space. Indeed, creating a consciousness of the missing spatial dimension will be his hardest task. The whole visual aspect of the play will need to be made as vividly present as possible if the imagination is not to be overtaxed or misdirected.

Should the teacher be working with the whole class, he can judiciously insert open-ended questions at appropriate points in the reading. He might ask a reader who else would be on the stage at the moment he is speaking. What effect would the speaker expect his words to have upon the people he is speaking to? What would the speaker or his hearers be doing? How would these actions affect the way the lines were said? Where is the speaker positioned with regard to his hearers? Is he alone or in a group? Is he higher or lower? What impression is he or should he be trying to give the audience? Is the character's opinion of himself the same as the audience's opinion of him? With older students a greater degree of self-consciousness might be encouraged. An older actor might be asked how he finds that the audience, in the shape of the currently non-acting members of the class, affect the way he plays his role. What effect does it have upon his playing when different people play opposite to him?

These are all questions to the reader as actor, but one advantage of the sedentary reading is the ease with which functions can be assumed. Slip in a question about directing and the whole class are immediately directors. Both those involved and those not involved in acting can be invited to make a director's decisions. They can be asked what advice they would give to actors on how to speak or move at a particular point. On a given stage — one they might know, like the school stage — they can decide where the focus of interest might be for the audience and make suggestions about the deployment of actors. They can be TV directors and be asked which characters they would have in 'hard' and which in 'soft' focus at this moment or from which angle they would film them.

The student can also be addressed as a member of an audience in a theatre. How does what has been happening in today's lesson fit in with what happened previously? What would be the effect on him of seeing the figure of Bolingbroke standing silent during Richard II's deposition? What would be the effect on him (the spectator) of the sight of Bolingbroke's silent army crossing the stage before Flint Castle?

For students to imagine the effect on themselves and others of their physical relationships and orientations is difficult, and it is obvious that playreading would be greatly improved if the readers had at least the memory of spatial experiments or theatrical spectacles to call upon. There are things that can be done, however, even with the mainly desk-bound. Chairs, if separate, can be turned towards the centre of the room so that readers can 'locate' the person they are addressing and not be talking to somebody vaguely behind. If you are lucky, you might even see them, when animated, glance up from the book!

There is nothing startling or revolutionary in this suggestion, although I have rarely seen it done. H.S. Taylor was crying in the same wilderness back in 1955. In *A Shorter Shakespeare* (Ginn & Co, 1955, p. 44) he recommends the following procedure for the courtroom scene in *The Merchant of Venice*:

This scene is among the best known of all that Shakespeare wrote, and thus, we might say, in the world. Like all well-written courtroom scenes, it goes with a special vitality on the stage. Something of the tension may be had in the classroom if we arrange for the Duke to be at the back of the room, centre, with Antonio front, left, and Shylock front, right. When their names are called, the latter should stand up and turn round to face the Duke and the rest of the court, remaining thus throughout the scene. Portia, when she arrives, will take a seat by the Duke: of course, she will turn to Shylock and Antonio when talking to them. On the same side of the room as Antonio, and as near to him as courtroom etiquette permits, would be his friends and supporters: on the other side, it is not unreasonable to imagine, would be Tubal and various other Jewish supporters of Shylock.

A scene needs to be fairly static before positions can be fixed as permanently as this and, for a play in which there is a deal of traffic, the teacher will have to work out in advance which characters associate most frequently with which and place his readers accordingly. Paradoxically, this method shows up the limitations of a class reading as such, as one of the snags is that it makes the changing of readers more inconvenient.

If only a moment can be seen or felt to 'go' in the way it was intended, the theatrical imagination gets a shot in the arm. Use can be made of what even this classroom has got, such as a door. How *would* Malvolio enter when he had on his yellow stockings? How would Shylock appear when entering the hostile courtroom? Would he be guilty? Defiant? Dignified? Try it, David. Now you, Jayne. How would Brian make his last exit in *A Day in the Death of Joe Egg* as he walks out on the problem of his spastic child and on his wife? The whole room can be pressed into service in a play like *An Enemy of the People*, when Dr Stockmann is in front (on a platform,

95

officially) with a number of other characters addressing a hostile public meeting. Some plays, such as *A Day in the Mind of Tich Oldfield*, which I wrote for *Prompt One* (Hutchinson), have the classroom in mind as a setting.

The radio convention expects a cast to move only in imagination and radio plays are particularly useful for sedentary class reading. Recording is time-consuming and an instant feedback can better be obtained by merely locating the readers at the back of the room behind the audience or even hiding them behind a cupboard. They could also have sat and rehearsed a scene in groups beforehand. The rehearsed reading, under similar circumstances, of a stage play can even be 'performed' in front of the class like a radio play. One needs to establish the radio convention as applying to this exercise too. Anybody who has been a member of a BBC studio audience at a 'sound' recording knows how enjoyable the experience can be. The artificiality of the line of readers can be part of the appeal, especially with comedy. It also, with stage drama, allows the class to observe the effects of the separation of cast and audience.

Another way the visual component of a stage play can be made directly accessible to sedentary readers is by the use of pictures and drawings. In a play where the set is described in detail and seems important — in, say, Ibsen, or Chekhov or Shaw — a ground plan or chalked sketch could be put up on the blackboard, executed by the teacher or by a volunteer draughtsman from the class with the advice of the others. Or pictures of actual sets from particular theatres can be displayed. What is important is that this can serve as a reminder that although the place is declared to be a Norwegian fjord it is also a stage with all the expectations which that arouses and it can serve to help the teacher indicate the focus. When a class needs to be helped to register the fact that a location has changed (for example in *Uncle Vanya* where we move simultaneously and more and more intimately into both the recesses of the house and the lives of the characters) or that it remains significantly the same (for example in *Look Back in Anger*, *Journey's End* or *Ghosts*) reference to pictures can make the point forcefully.

The aural dimension of a play, sound effects and music, are as susceptible to experiment as they would be in a large working space, and there will be opportunities for creative conversation which the less able readers can tackle with equal gusto and confidence. In the context of communal research, they can also be called upon to try out yet another rendering of an ambiguous speech.

Discussion will naturally arise during a reading and the degree, kind and depth of it will, of course, vary with the class. A reading which is orientated towards performance is more likely to give rise to discussion that is relevant to the way a play works and to what words do as well as what they say. Appreciation of the play is likely to be more soundly based because it is faithful to the true nature of what is being appreciated.

4
Planning a production

Our direct work on the text as written has so far involved the processes of acting, directing and spectating, some of the activities of the designer and effects men, and sedentary reading. The developing shape of a production owes much to the interaction of the personnel with each other and with the physical environment, and directors sometimes admit that, if they were under less pressure, they would like to leave more of the exploration to take place this way. However, as it is, both actors and directors genuinely have a certain amount of homework to do and amateur directors, at least, feel safer with something concrete worked out in advance, even if they do depart from it.

In the classroom we are not necessarily mounting a production. If we ask our pupils to do preparatory work on a role or on staging, the test to apply is whether it stimulates intelligent and imaginative inquiry. We are learning not about acting and production but through them. Some of the preparatory work can be done as the artists themselves might do it, sitting at a table, and this will appeal to some teachers. The teacher who so desires and who has the option can test the practical implications in action.

A communal reading of a play will still probably be the most useful way to begin. Then, even if some of the preparatory work is done in groups with quicker readers hunting up references, the whole of the class will have the memory of a tentative performance on which to base their ideas and make their contribution.

Preparing a role

Much of what we see of an actor's performance, then, will have emerged and developed in rehearsal through contact both with the director and with other actors. But, granting that his decisions can only be provisional, one good reason for doing some initial preparation on his own is that his personal contribution is thus less likely to be swamped. Since the actor will be engaged in silent reading and with rehearsing in his head, it is, in the classroom, an exercise for a fairly sophisticated and advanced student. 'In the classroom' here means in an educational setting: homework would be a valuable extension of this particular activity.

What one is doing in educational terms is approaching a play through 'character' but this is not quite the same thing as doing a character sketch. The actor will be concerned not simply with 'tracing the development' of a character but with finding ways of bringing changes about on the stage. He will be concerned with effects, with what effects he should be creating at a given moment. He will be looking not so much for information as for stimuli; not just reading but interpreting signals. He will be inclined to think of character less as a static category than as a dynamic challenge.

As an exercise for the student there are advantages and dangers. He is forced to ask not so much what kind of a 'person' his character is, not even how it should be played, but how he, personally, can play it. He is forced to reach inside himself for an appropriate response, to think about how he defines the character and how the character defines him. Some teachers might argue that the opposite is the case and that this method will encourage the students, even more than a literary approach, to develop too elaborate a psychology for their roles. I see this as a result of faulty preparation rather than an inherent weakness of the method. Actors do, in the privacy of their own minds, sometimes invent their own motives for the actions their characters perform, but they do it in the hope of creating their stage effects with greater conviction. Our student can fairly be required to go further than the actor and articulate his findings either in discussion or writing, should the teacher deem it profitable. At this stage it can be made clear that for the audience it will be the effect that will matter, however it is achieved, and that it is upon what it sees and hears that it will base its interpretation. As I have said earlier, we are not training students to be actors so much as using the actor's incentives and practices to provide a relevant educational approach. A worse danger with working on a role is that, until the director gives him the benefit of his wide-angle view, the actor may concentrate too narrowly on those parts of the play that involve him; but this again is something that a teacher can foresee and build into the preparation work or can adjust in retrospect.

An advantage which the activity of preparing a role shares with the composing of a character sketch is that it allows all students to work on the same character and it avoids the problems of deployment which beset practical work when it seeks to accord the same privileges. Ideally, of course, students should be allowed to test their preparation in practice. If the teacher wants them to make this extension he can set them to work on different roles and find a scene in which all their characters are involved. But from the teacher's point of view, this is more easily handled with duologues, (Astrov and Yeliena, for instance, in *Uncle Vanya*) as these are less complicated for a critical audience to take in and comment upon and they avoid such production problems as complicated grouping.

There is no set way for an actor to approach his part, although there are established practices which, if he is a professional, his training may have encouraged him to venerate. The teacher may like to issue a check-list of things to consider or he may prefer to leave it wide open, allowing the student, once the nature of the task has been made clear, to find his own priorities. Educationally, the latter is appealing but the check-lisneed not be prescriptive and could consist of optional guidelines. I offer the following as an example of a possible procedure. It is based partly upon my own experiences as an actor, partly on what actors have said about their work (see, for example, the Actor's Notes given in John Fernald's book: *Sense of Direction*) and partly on my experience as a teacher.

(1) Read the whole play

A class reading would be preferable. The teacher can prod the theatrical imagination if it flags. At this stage, the role to be prepared need not be indicated.

(2) Re-read the scenes involving the chosen character

Clarify in your mind the circumstances in which you, as the character, find yourself; where you operate; with which characters you are involved onstage; what you say to them; what the action requires you to do. If you are Caliban in *The Tempest*, for instance, you will learn that you operate inside and outside your cell, near Prospero's cell and in various locations about the island. You relate directly to Miranda and Prospero, to Stephano and Trinculo, to Ariel and, at the end, briefly, to the assembled lords. You complain to Prospero, you adopt Stephano and discard Trinculo. You reject your god at the end and you promise to reform. You carry a bone, carry wood, hide under a cape, get drunk, creep up on Prospero, get chased by invisible dogs.

The student carrying out the above investigation will be acquiring some intimation of the ways he will be using words and what he will be expected to do with his body.

(3) Discover what, if anything, your character says about himself

Caliban reveals that he was on the island before Prospero came and that he got it from his mother, a witch called Sycorax. He claims that he loved Prospero, was treated kindly by him and showed him all the qualities of the isle. Now, though, he is under Prospero's stern governance. He claims to have an exhaustive knowledge of the flora and fauna of the island and that in digging for pig-nuts he uses his long nails as an animal would. He admits he is a 'sot' and that he has dreams of riches.

(4) Discover what other characters say about you

Before Caliban comes onto the stage the audience will have had a picture of him presented to them by Prospero and Miranda. According to them he is a "freckled whelp, hag-born — not honoured with a human shape", a slave who never yields them kind answer. He does domestic labour for them but does it sulkily. To Miranda he is a villain whom she does not love to look upon. During their first confrontation, Prospero reveals that Caliban once attempted to rape Miranda, while Miranda reminds Caliban that she taught him to speak. Stephano and Trinculo regard him as a 'monster', some sort of freak. When his plot to murder Prospero is in full swing, Prospero, who knows about it, is genuinely troubled. Ferdinand notes that Prospero is "in some passion/that works him strongly", and Miranda that she "never till this day/saw him with anger so distempered". Prospero (himself) delivers himself of a pessimistic view of Caliban's capacity for redemption: "A devil, a born devil, on whose nature/Nurture can never stick."

(5) Compare your own view of yourself with the views of the others

The student is now invited to discover what 'facts' both sides agree upon and where statements differ. For instance, on his first appearance, Caliban attacks Prospero for capriciously changing from a kind master into a bully. Prospero's version is that his kindness had no

101

effect on Caliban and that strictness was forced on him by Caliban's attempt to violate his daughter.

(6) See if the character has any long-term or limited aims or intentions

Stanislavsky claimed that a character was held together by a 'through line of action' which could be traced through a play, but the search for such a thing helps an actor best when the role he is playing is an integrated one. Finding a consistent aim that might help one play one of the tramps in *Waiting for Godot* would prove difficult and possibly dangerous. Even over a short distance the formulation of aims may force the actor to play too self-consciously or deliberately and give the student an unnecessarily simplified view of human experience. Not only that, but a character may have a variety of functions to fulfil. The actor playing Richard II will have to be careful how much of the 'old' Richard he attempts to show during his performance of the deposition scene. If he stresses the reprobate, the audience may get the message that he is now getting his just deserts whereas it could be that Shakespeare wants us to focus our attention on the consequences of the abdication to the king as a man. Captain Otter and Cutbeard, in *The Silent Woman* by Ben Jonson, are used by Truewit to torment Morose over his desire for a divorce. For this Otter is disguised as a parson and Cutbeard as a doctor of laws. Their only qualification appears to be that they both have the habit of spouting Latin. Nothing in the previous 'character' of Otter suggests that he is a natural impersonator and there is a case for believing that it is Jonson who is using him, partly as a device for the plot and partly to indulge in a little satire on pedantic clerics on his own behalf. When I played this part, it was almost like having two roles. My 'aims' in the earlier scenes were to placate my wife and to enhance my reputation as a hard drinker, but these ceased when the disguise was adopted. From an audience point of view, the transformation is easily acceptable. The new costume and manner herald a new identity — for the purposes of the scene. Yet actors do (as was said in my introduction) reappear in their own persons; and if they are playing the same name part, they may rightly feel a need to give some sort of consistency to their performances. I found myself, as rehearsals progressed, instinctively giving what weight I could to the two speeches where Otter gleefully congratulates himself at having outwitted his wife, a tiny example of a delight in intrigue. And there was, of course, the Latin. Generally, though, the only recurring element seemed to be my function as a source and butt of satirical humour.

The search for aims, as long as one is not determined to find them at all costs, can provide useful revelations about the role and the play. Supposing a student decides that Caliban does not waver in his desire to murder Prospero or to possess Miranda (even by proxy) and that even when putting his case in the first scene he is not apparently trying to soften Prospero's heart. A student who declared his intention to attempt, in the first instance, to build his portrayal on these basic motives could be asked to show in what forms they recur and to give some idea of the means he might choose to express them. How will these aims affect his playing of the comedy scenes with Stephano and Trinculo? How will he say his final speech where he declares he will be wise hereafter and seek for grace? If he discovers in Caliban an unwavering intention to murder, this could have implications for meaning. He may have discovered an implacable will to evil and this will have repercussions on the impact of the whole play.

If the actor/student finds the 'aims' approach in this case irrelevant, he can be asked on what he bases this decision and how it will affect his playing of each scene in which he appears. When he describes his isle, will he do it with the love of a native for his home? Will he deliver his famous speech, "The isle is full of noises/Sounds and sweet airs that give delight and hurt not", out to the audience in a voice of wistful longing? If so, how will he make the transition from this mood to the mood of "When Prospero is destroyed" which immediately follows? Are there identifiable drives at all in Caliban? Is there anything to help the actor hold the role together?

(7) How might you get into the part?

How an actor 'gets into' a part may be largely a mystery, even to the actor. His imagination may be triggered by a variety of stimuli (the text, observation of other people, a poem, a piece of music, sculpture, a picture, a picture of other actors, other actors' performance, movement, etc.). The exercise we are proposing for our sedentary student will inevitably restrict his speculations to those which are accessible to him in this capacity. He has, of course, the data to be found in the text itself. He can investigate Stanislavsky's 'given circumstances'. These may be personal and social but they will also be theatrical. The theatrical circumstances, more specifically the style of the play as a play, will determine the spirit in which he accepts and uses the personal and social information.

He will soon realise, for instance, if he is contemplating playing one of the tramps in *Godot*, that a study of the way of life of a down-and-out is not particularly relevant and that he might be better employed watching music-hall or silent-film artists. I heard a professional actor, playing the part of Mosca in *Volpone*, ask for help to explain why he, as Mosca, requested Bonario to come to Volpone's house. He was told, rightly, that there is no answer and that the question in this case was irrelevant. That kind of plot motivation is not required for a convincing performance of the scenes. Both 'Volpone' and 'Mosca' would search in vain for a 'past' life on which to build and the parts require an energetic playing of attitudes rather than a subtle suggestion of subconscious impulses. The past experiences of Gina, though, referred to but not acted out, in *The Wild Duck*, will be useful for the actress to bear in mind to enable her to give subtextual meaning to her interactions with her husband.

When Caliban encounters Prospero for the first time in the play, the encounter is, for the characters, one of a long series of such clashes, but for the audience it is the first thing they see. The student will need to imagine Caliban's sufferings at the hands of his master, his resentment at Prospero's usurpation and his lust for Miranda. He might be invited to investigate the text to discover how much detail he is given by Shakespeare. He might find out about Caliban's work-routine, his hunting activities, his foraging for pig-nuts with his long nails. Precisely how far this information, these mental images, will help in the playing of a given piece of action is hard to say in the abstract, but some enlightened guesswork is possible. At what particular moments, he could be asked, might it help him to recall this background? At what points might it obviously not?

The student can be invited to research around and outside the play in his quest for useful stimuli. Perhaps there are historical circumstances which might throw light on the part. Accounts of voyages to strange lands, poems such as Marvell's *Bermudas*, might be read. Specifically, knowledge so gained might help him to understand and subsequently reproduce the reverence that Caliban feels for Stephano and his bottle of magic liquor. He might be asked if he sees Caliban as the exploited native or at what points, if any, such a guise might be apposite.

The kind of background work which is not accessible to the teacher is the background of the student's personality. An actor might find an impetus for certain emotional effects in a personal experience, something, for instance, that helps him hate Prospero or reverence Stephano or despise Trinculo or appreciate the novelty of liquor with due reverence. A student doing this kind of preparation might, like the actor, fairly claim that the validity of the analogies he draws is something only he can appraise. By discussing with him the apparent similarities and differences, though, the teacher might help him at least to speculate on the likely effects. Suppose the student remembers a resentment he felt towards his father on account of an injustice done and he decides he could invoke this to help him understand Caliban's attitude to Prospero. Is the injustice of the same kind and seriousness? Are the rights and wrongs in both situations equally clear-cut? Is Prospero like a father to Caliban? Questions such as these can help to clarify both the nature of the personal experience and the range of possibilities that the role of Caliban seems to offer. They can lessen the danger that Bertram Joseph fears, namely that there will be 'confusion between the intellectual knowledge of what the character feels and wants and the technique whereby an actor can make himself feel and want what he knows are the emotions and desires of the imaginary character' (p. 193). An actor trying lines through silently in his head or aloud in the privacy of his own bedroom can get some idea of what they are likely to give him in performance. The student could be asked which lines in particular he is looking forward to saying and what it is about them that appeals. Admittedly, one really needs the full theatrical context to appreciate the qualities of many of the lines but our Caliban might look forward to calling down on Prospero's head imprecations such as these:

> All the infections that the sun sucks up
> From bogs, fens, flats on Prosper fall
> And make him by inchmeal a disease.

Perhaps the very sounds and emphases of the words and the ongoing rhythm of the sentence may help him to create an impression of hatred and violence. There are lines which may make the limbs twitch in anticipation:

> There mayst thou brain him,
> Having first seized his books; or with a log
> Batter his skull, or paunch him with a stake,
> Or cut his wezand with thy knife.

How much more will they twitch when Caliban has a Stephano to persuade! The choice of lines will be idiosyncratic but they will at least reflect a personal enthusiasm and an initial engagement, and they can lead to a useful examination of the basis of their attractiveness.

(8) What contribution does your character make to the scenes in which you appear?

We have asked the student to distinguish between his own stated views of himself and the views of other characters. A director will have to decide whether the audience should accept either version as 'true', but our actor, too, has some grounds for forming an early opinion. On the basis of his own reaction to the text, our Caliban can get some inkling of whether he would hope for an audience's sympathy or not. If, on trying through Prospero's speeches for himself, he deems that they have more dramatic authority than Caliban's, he will feel bound to find some way of showing the audience that Caliban is a brute. If he decides that a measure of sympathy should go to both, he will need both to become and to remain critically detached from the character. Precisely how the actor achieves these effects cannot be completely known until he meets the actor playing Prospero. If that man should be a rather cold fish, and if he feels that a relativist interpretation is the right one, our Caliban might have to emphasise the brutality more. In practice, also, the actor's own interpretation might change under the influence of the other actor's insights, but in the absence of actual rehearsal this remains in the realms of speculation. Here we have a built-in limitation of the method we are discussing and it should be recognised. What is possible at this stage is a statement of alternatives and tentative conclusions.

The student will also need to see Caliban in relation to Stephano and Trinculo. He might foresee, perhaps, that while his terror under the cape, his delight in discovering alcohol and his hero-worship of Stephano are essential ingredients in a situation comedy, he will have to set himself apart from the others in the mind of the audience. The actor will here be using other characters to help him discover the function of his own character, to provide, that is, comparison and contrast. When Ariel stirs up trouble between Caliban and Trinculo, our actor can say something about the effect the scene might have and how he sees his own contribution to that effect. Possibly he sees it as broad comedy and will exaggerate the exasperation; possibly he will have an eye to what the audience will see and will exaggerate the contrast between Caliban and Ariel, introducing a note of savagery. ("Bite him to death, I prithee.")

(9) How does your role fit into the play as a whole and what contribution do your appearances make?

This question invites the student to take a perspective view of the entire play, a view easily lost when rehearsals start. He needs to observe his impressions can link up in the mind of the audience to form 'themes'. He needs to look at the scenes which precede and succeed his entrances, watch for repetitions of action, contrasts of mood. Caliban's designs on Prospero, his relations with Ariel, his acceptance of subservience to Stephano in the name of 'freedom', link with the usurpation of Prospero's Dukedom and the threatened murder of the King. If the actor remembers that his first comic scene with Stephano and Trinculo comes immediately after the discussion of the commonwealth and Antonio's treachery, he might better appreciate the relief his appearance might cause and the zest with which he can afford to play the comedy. Later, when he is drunk, he will need to take note of the fact that Ariel is not merely a comic device, an invisible voice to stir up trouble, but an emissary of Prospero, sent to torment and frustrate him. He will need to jot down notes on how this knowledge might affect his performance. At the end, having been led astray through bog and briar, he has to play the comic scene where Stephano and Trinculo are diverted by the fancy clothes and frippery. In the context of the action, this follows the scene where Prospero says:

> I had forgot that foul conspiracy
> Of the beast Caliban and his confederates
> Against my life. The minute of this plot
> Is almost come. – Well done! Avoid! No more!

and when his daughter says she saw him "touched with anger so distempered". If Prospero is played with a suggestion of genuine anxiety, it might temper any temptation on the part of our Caliban to play the next scene in too frivolous a spirit, since he will have to justify Prospero's fear as well as illustrating his power. In the last scene, he is driven in by Ariel, and the actor will need to have some idea of the importance of the Ariel/Caliban polarity in the play. His final speech, where he promises reform, will depend for its interpretation on the meaning of the whole production. At this stage, though, the actor will have at least some intuition as to a possible

107

reading and he can make tentative jottings even though he knows they will be subject to modification in rehearsal.

There is some writing work an actor would be less likely to do but which might benefit both him and the sedentary student trying to gain imaginative insights into the nature and meaning of a role, and that is personal 'creative' writing. In the case of *The Tempest*, an introduction to Auden's poems on the subject (*The Sea and the Mirror*) might be a useful stimulus to a poetic statement of the student's own. David Self (in *The Use of English*) provides some impressive verse written by Sixth Formers studying *Who's Afraid of Virginia Woolf?* They, too, came about via the example of these Auden poems and record personal insights into individual characters in the Albee. Although much of our writing has been 'about' Caliban, it is, after all, with a view to finding a personal way of embodying him. Nor are sedentary students restricted to writing. They can design themselves a costume, draw ideas for make-up or embark on a freely imaginative expression of their intuitions about a character. A teacher who had, say, Ralph Steadman's 'visions' of Lear and the Fool (examples of which appeared in the *Sunday Telegraph Magazine*, 1 April 1979) might use them as a stimulus to the production of a pictorial 'poem' in the way Auden's might stimulate a verbal one.

Planning a production: the director

A student faced with the early decisions a director faces will be led into the very heart of the play and its meaning. A director will have to form a clear notion of its 'style'. As defined by Michel Saint-Denis, style is 'the perceptible form that is taken by reality in revealing to us its true and inner character' (*Theatre: the Rediscovery of Style*). It is not something which makes a historical play different from a modern one since modern plays, too, have style, although we are often too close to them to see it. Saint-Denis argues that a director must first of all examine a play in its own terms and find out what the 'perceptible form' is and how it came about before deciding how to present the play. This is not to pursue some illusory 'authenticity' nor to treat pre-modern plays as museum pieces. But it does advise caution before imposing a style in production that is at odds with the possibilities of the text, even though a bold experiment may sometimes enormously enlarge those possibilities. Naturally, a director has also to consider his audience, and the idiom and con-

108

ventions of a by-gone age may need modifying or re-thinking to make them palatable. A production I saw of *Macbeth* did the soliloquies, for instance, with a still figure onstage in a pensive pose while a 'voice-over' said the words through a loud speaker. I am not saying I personally found this necessary, but obviously the director did. A director like Charles Marowitz (according to his admissions in an article in *Plays and Players*) may go as far as selecting for emphasis those aspects of a play (he instances the violence in *Romeo and Juliet*) which seem to him nearest our present-day experience. The student, in deciding the manner in which the play should be acted and the way it should look and sound, is making a statement about the significance it has for him as an individual and as a person of the late twentieth century.

Individually, or working with others, the student can consider how to costume his actors. Companies usually have a specialist costume designer, but the overall conception is the director's concern and the detail also very much his business. As director, the student can describe in writing the general effects he will aim at and the details of individual dress. If he can draw, he can do coloured sketches. The teacher can usefully collect samples of material which illustrate a wide range of colour and texture and let the 'directors' feel and examine these and make their choice. Styles of dress may vary from historical 'period' accuracy to dress of a different period including modern dress, or to dress which expresses theme or mood rather than period. I have seen *Coriolanus* done in Roman costume, Elizabethan costume, First World War costume and a kind of science fiction outfit. The range of choices can be demonstrated first to the students by means of pictures of different productions which the teacher collects from sources such as theatres themselves, books or back numbers of magazines such as *Plays and Players*.

The implications of the choices the students make provide a fruitful topic for discussion. How *do* you costume *Coriolanus*? Is the Roman ethos of the actual story particularly important? Is the world of the play really Elizabethan? Can Macbeth be a gangster or Antony a Middle Eastern military dictator? If you set *Much Ado* in British India, does Benedick's cavorting in the mess with the chaps suitably prepare us for his serious role later in the play? Were doctors in the twenties incompetent and unscrupulous enough to make credible a transplant of *Le Malade Imaginaire* to that era? Is *The Alchemist*, with its money-mad gulls, timeless enough to justify costumes committed to no particular period? If you update *Lysistrata* by playing its female characters as modern women's libbers and dressing them accordingly, do you affect the comprehensibility of their desire for marriage? How important is it that the costumes should create a harmonious effect? Does it matter if Rosalind has a magnificent Elizabethan skirt while Touchstone is dressed as a boy scout? Are there different kinds of harmony? The implications of student choices may be carried through in detail.

As well as costume, a director will have to ponder the use of make-up. He may be a Grotowski and decide not to use such artificial aids, but for the purposes of the exercise our student can be one of those directors who do use them. We have already seen how an individual actor can play with make-up to create an image of his character as he sees it. A director will have to take a larger view and make sure that there is some uniformity of style and interpretation. He cannot have a member of the cast of *The Comedy of Errors* making himself up as a 'real' Ephesian while another decides he has the clown-like stylisation of the Commedia dell'arte — unless the director himself has some respectable artistic reason for accepting it. The director will have to show by his choice whether he thinks the play wants us to identify with Antipholus of Ephesus's psychological sufferings when his own home is barred to him or to laugh at him as a farcical victim. Pupil 'directors' can make notes on make-up for each of the characters such as they might give to a make-up artist or they might do a series of simple drawings.

Some plays were intended to be acted in masks; Greek plays, for example, or modern plays like *The Caucasian Chalk Circle* by Brecht or *The Happy Haven* by Arden. Some think the mask, in fixing social status, can be a poignant reminder, when circumstances change, of the glory that has been (as in *Oedipus*). Others, like Pirandello, think that the very fixity of the masks force the audience's imagination to supply the changing emotion that the mask fails to register. Whatever the case, a mask can be useful in emphasising function and to ask the students to design or think about masks is one way of focusing on character as a theatrical entity. The teacher might invent a plausible premise which will allow him to include other types of play. He might say that the play is to be performed in masks, since there is an inadequate number of actors to call upon; thus one actor will have to play several parts. He might then require the students to make drawings or notes to show the functions of the various characters, to expose their 'essences'.

The director has also to decide on the shape of the acting area and the visual impact of the setting. Even a bare stage will have a contribution to make, but if the setting is to be more than that, he may collaborate with a designer. Students, too, individually or with others, can profitably work on designing a set. They may be helped by an elaborate description in the text or they may have to infer details from the dialogue. Designing a set raises the same questions of style and meaning as does a choice of costume. Whether one aims at photographic realism or significant formality may be influenced by the mode and conventions of the play. Setting, too, can create a sense of place, create a mood or emphasise a theme — such as claustrophobia or orderliness — or an idea.

However the student/director decides to use the performance area, he will have to make sure that the actors are at home in it and can use it. However beautiful a set might look, too much clutter hampers the very people who embody the action. Whether he is designing for a scene or a whole play, the student will have to bear in mind the significant moments. This in itself involves an exercise in appreciation. It can be done by class discussion or individual choice depending on the ability of the class. We mentioned this already in connection with the entrances in the scene from *Arms and the Man*. Suppose the student is designing for Act I of *The Cherry Orchard* and wants to create a room on a proscenium stage. He will have to incorporate three entrances, one from outside, one to another part of the house and one to Anya's bedroom. If he wants the procession to stream impressively across the stage he will need to place his outside door at least upstage and possibly in the back wall. Since the characters talk a great deal about the cherry orchard and look out at it, the positioning of the window will be important. If the director thinks that should be located in the upstage wall, he will have to put himself in the position of the characters who stand there. Will they be in the best place to express their feelings with their backs to the audience? With a play such as *Me McKenna*, by Don Shaw (*Playbill 3*), which takes place in a barrack hut, a new recruit is tied to a stove and his tormentor ultimately takes his turn upon it too. Let us assume the student decides this is the object round which the whole action revolves. Can he design a barrack hut which gives the stove the most prominent position when the moment comes?

111

Ideally, the students need to have seen a large number of different stage sets in use, but failing this facility the teacher will need to rely on his own extensive memory bank and on a collection of pictures which he must have to hand. He should try to encourage his students to be adventurous. Do we need to see a cherry orchard at all? Is it sufficiently well established in the words and thoughts of the characters not to need a representation? What is gained by showing the walls of a room? What kind of interpretation of *Hedda Gabler* would be implied if the set was painted not in period colour but uniform red? What difference would it make if the attic in *The Wild Duck* was the auditorium? Or can you start with themes themselves? What is a particular play 'about'? How can you stamp this on the audience's mind? If you think *Richard II* is not so much about an individual as about kingship, will it help to suspend a massive crown over the stage?

The teacher may find it easier to begin this sort of work by taking the class to the school stage, pacing it out and making a ground plan of it. (Sight lines too.) Even though the scope is limited by this, the student's imagination is anchored in reality and for the teacher there is the advantage that at least some of the problems the class are wrestling with are the same for everybody, and there will be common ground for comparison. Designing for a different shape of auditorium needs experience of seeing such auditoria in use or using them oneself.

The students, then, could draw a ground plan of the set in position, draw an elevation (coloured) or construct a cardboard model. If they cannot draw elevations particularly well, they can describe in talk or writing the impact they hope to achieve. Alternatively, they can start with any old bric-à-brac to represent walls, chairs, etc. or they may work on an abstract level and arrange the objects in terms of heights and shapes. It is the educational aim that is the overriding one. The test is not so much whether the student has produced a design worthy of John Bury as whether the exercise has helped him form a valid concept of the play or scene. It will, or course, have to be possible to use such a set, and a teacher who has the necessary space will find it useful to check this by taking an example, setting it up using what is at hand, as one does in rehearsal, and asking volunteers to act out a page to an audience which is in the prescribed position.

The director and designer, of course, will have to analyse a play to see how many (if any) changes of location there are, even though he may decide in the end that they do not need to be supported or indicated by a change of setting. The student carrying out this analysis can learn something of the rhythm of a play. He can get an inkling of the compression of *Oedipus Rex* and it may be borne in upon him that the real action of the play is Oedipus's process of discovery, which takes place entirely before the palace, rather than the unalterable past events the King is trying to unravel. If he is examining *Antony and Cleopatra*, the opposition between the concepts of Egypt and Rome becomes apparent, as do the ebbing and flowing of Antony's priorities.

Design may include lighting and a director will have to do homework on that. The effects he has in mind will stand or fall by whether they work on the actual set, and the choice of filter will be influenced by the colour of both decor and costumes. The scope for the sedentary student, especially if he has had little or no practical experience of lighting, is very limited. There may be some useful 'preparation' he can do, however. If he merely thinks about the kind of emotional impact he, as director, hopes his lighting will have, about whether the mood he hopes it will evoke or reinforce should be 'cosy', 'cold', 'threatening', etc., the exercise can be a starting point for an investigation of meaning. If the teacher has a set of coloured 'gels' and the students are allowed to handle them and hold them up to the light, they may choose the ones that create the appropriate personal vibrations. A genuine lighting technician would, of course, blow a mental fuse, insisting, perhaps, that it is combinations that count, but it is the educational spin-off that counts for the teacher.

Choosing music presented fewer problems than lighting to pupils engaged in practical 'direction' in the classroom and the same is true at the 'preparation' stage. We have discussed how pupil directors can experiment with music and sound which are integral to the action or support it in some way. The sedentary pupil preparing for his production can also make such provisional choices, but in addition to that can take a broad view of the whole projected performance and consider the use of music to put his audience in the mood before the play begins, put them back into the mood or into another mood towards the end of the interval and ultimately to round the performance off. First, he may be asked to describe the kind of music he would like under such circumstances. The teacher then selects a range of specifications from the class and consults his musical colleague in the hope that he will supply him with a set of records. Record and request will, of course, not necessarily match, but there is a chance that at least some of the pieces will approximate to some-body's idea of what the play suggests. Even when they don't, they can help define more exactly what the individual would really like. The teacher will be able to make some inferences from the choices and rejections themselves, but if the class is fairly articulate he can ask them what it is in the play that they think they are trying to capture. He should encourage the pupils to consider a variety of functions that music can fulfil. It could be 'atmosphere'; it could suggest a historical period; it could be ironic. In a play full of ironies, such as *A Day in the Death of Joe Egg*, one might play a joke on the audience by prefacing the performance with a pop song such as Ken Dodd's blithe and thoughtless 'Happiness'. The tartness of the play's reality becomes more pungent by contrast when it actually begins. Not many people in the play understand the truth of what Bri and Sheila have to face with their spastic child and even Sheila is prone to self-deception; some just don't want to know. Dodd's song might ironically echo their wishes. At least it gives food for thought about the play. In this instance the music would probably be a song the pupils knew already and somebody in the class might have the record.

Another approach is for the teacher to select some music himself, ask the class to pretend that it is an audience waiting for the curtain literally or metaphorically to go up, play an extract and then ask the class what kind of interpretation it would lead them to expect. He can collect pieces actually used from the openings of recorded pro-ductions, for example. The music for a Stratford production of *The Winter's Tale* is available on a separate disc.

A radio play may rely as much on sound effects as on music to introduce the action. Again, the selection of the 'significant' sound is a critical exercise in itself. Where it is not a sound that is organic to the action, care will have to be taken to avoid the aural cliché. Is there, for instance, a way of signalling a seaside scene other than by using seagulls or night time than by using owls?

The pupils can be asked to decide where, as directors, they would have the intervals or even whether they would have them. A director may or may not need to decide until quite late in the rehearsal period but the pupil has no constraints at all and this exercise requires a prior grasp of the wholeness of the play if it is to be done skilfully. With a five-act play, one or two intervals might be considered reason-able and they need not coincide with Act divisions, which are often artificial in any case. Students should in the first place let the scenes group themselves in a way which seems most meaningful to them and then ask themselves if the resulting sections balance to a satisfactory degree. In *Richard II* there might be a natural break at the end of Act III Scene i, the first part of the play showing the folly and punishment of Richard the King and the second section the agony and death of Richard the man. The second section begins with the return of Richard after a long absence. The choice of interval here might be felt to contribute to an interpretation of the play as the tragedy of Richard rather than as a political play about both Richard and Henry.

Sometimes a play anticipates intervals. *Look Back in Anger* sends the audience to its coffee reeling from the sight of Jimmy Porter in the arms of Helena Charles, his 'enemy'. The pupils might query the health of that effect on the dramatic construction of the action and on the credibility of the turn of events as presented. In fact, choosing where to put the intervals should lead to a consideration of whether there really are breaks in the action of a play at all, whether a leap in time or a switch of locale justifies a hiatus in attention. Doesn't what follows depend for its effect on a contrast or comparison with what goes before?

Pupils engaged in practical class or group work may find them-selves naturally involved in deciding who should play which part and certainly will find themselves opposing or supporting somebody else's choice. It is possible to make a casting session the basis of an excursion into the text, but there is the danger in some classrooms of personal embarrassment on the part of both director and actor. A teacher can avoid this by using photographs and recordings of famous or at least 'outside' actors and inviting the class to make their choice from them. Which picture approximates most closely to their conception of this character? Are there any others which might prove interesting to try, even though they are not quite what the pupils expected? The class might be invited to imagine they are the kind of director who casts largely by voice. The teacher then plays versions of the same extract from a play by different recording companies and asks the pupils to decide which of the actors they would trust with the part in the play as a whole, bearing in mind scenes of a different kind which the actor might also have to en-compass. The Caedmon and the Marlowe Society versions of the scene between Macbeth and Lady Macbeth after the murder of Duncan, for instance, offer widely contrasting performances. Are

115

there any other roles you might ask them to read for, any other combination of these voices possible?

The teacher who is energetic enough could profitably collect on tape a series of recordings by his friends (thespian or not) of a long speech, and use these in the same way.

At some stage in the production, thought will have to be given to publicising and advertising it. The terms in which one chooses to couch one's inducements depends on one's conception of the play and assessment of the likely audience or the audience one desires to attract. Suppose a company decides to use photographs of representative moments from the production taken in rehearsal. The class or the groups will need to clarify which kind of audience their production will be aimed at and then, as individuals within the class or as members of a group working in concert, they can be invited to choose their 'moments' and say what effect they would hope to create in each picture and in the pictures as a collection. If the group can agree on the general style of production this could become an 'active' exercise, with pupils forming the appropriate tableaux, perhaps as suggested in the game *Clay Pigeon* (see pp. 163–4). They can then be asked to comment on each other's groupings and selections. With polaroid cameras there could literally be pictures available for display and discussion. Designing posters can be a valuable means for the individual to encapsulate a vision of a play's meaning. One is not after artistic brilliance, but if some students do feel embarrassed at their inadequacy, they could contribute ideas while a classmate executes the joint conception.

Many theatre programmes are lavish in their supply of information or help for the audience. As with publicity work, deciding on the content of such programmes can involve a careful assessment of the nature of the play, an exact description of the style of the production and a sensitive estimate of the needs of the reader. But where publicity work is concerned with getting the people in, devising programme notes may have an important effect on the meaning of the event, or at least may be thought to have. The pupil at his desk will not have the director's particular incentive, but furnishing notes even for a putative production and an imaginary audience can particularise and focus his thoughts in a relevant way.

What programmes include varies considerably and a collection of them is useful for initial display. Some give portraits of the actors only; some, a synopsis of the play; some, facts about the author, his life, times and theatrical fortunes; some, an account of past productions of the play; some, pronouncements by the author about his intentions; some, pronouncements (perhaps mutually contradictory) by critics on his achievement; some, a declaration of interpretation on the part of the director, perhaps with supportive quotations from authorities; some contain a director's justification or apology for the liberties he has taken in cutting, censoring or updating the text; some indicate the literary sources or, when the play takes a historical theme, insist on filling in the historical background to the events.

Almost any of these approaches involve the pupil in valuable critical activity. Which plays and which audiences will benefit from a synopsis? Would a family tree help in a production of *Richard III*? Does the audience need to know about our author's life? Is such knowledge likely to enhance its understanding of the emphases our actors will place? Will descriptions of past productions help to characterise the one we are offering? Does an author (Shaw? Bond?) have to be right about the effects his play will create? If you dig out extracts from the critics, literary and theatrical, can this help set up a mental dialectic through which an audience could arrive at its own assessment of the performance? How actually useful is historical information about events described in your play likely to be? Be careful, because the reader of your programme note will soon be in a position to find out. What benefit will an audience waiting for the curtain to rise on your production of *The Plough and the Stars* derive from knowledge about the Troubles? Will it clarify the play? Does the envisaged audience at *The Alchemist* need to be reassured that alchemy really was taken seriously at one time and that there have been con-men in all epochs? What does validate a playwright's vision and a stage artist's presentation? If you decide it would be a nice idea to set *Much Ado* in post-First World War England, try justifying this to an audience which has just paid its money to see one of its favourite Shakespeares or to see the play because it is a 'set book'.

The most important aspect of a director's work is his contact with the actors. For the purposes of organising a rehearsal schedule he will have to analyse the play according to the appearances of the characters. One way is to make a list of the characters on the left of the page, divide the page horizontally according to the number of pages in the script and rule across or shade in a narrow rectangle if that particular character is on stage at that point.

For the reader inexperienced in directing and even, sometimes, for

117

the director, an analysis can cause surprises. Students will find it hard to know, at times, who is in fact on the stage, as the character will have had nothing to say for ages. If the teacher asks the students to compare analyses, there will be disagreements on which he can capitalise by sending them back to the text. In Act II, Scene i of *Richard II*, the dying John of Gaunt, Northumberland and the Duke of York await the arrival of the king. When Richard enters he brings with him Queen Isobel, Aumerle, Bushy, Green, Bagot, Ross and Willoughby. An analysis of the scene, using the Penguin text, would look like the table below. Queen Isobel in fact speaks only one line: "How fares our noble uncle Lancaster?" and it is very easy after that for the reader to forget she is there. One might, however, ask the class if her presence on stage, she being a sympathetic figure, would in any way modify our unfavourable impression of Richard. In the play as a whole, it is arguable that, for the audience, the fact that she is able to love Richard contributes to a change in attitude towards him. Considering whether mere stage presence might be an important factor can direct attention towards the importance of action and away from an attempt to develop too elaborate a psychology for Richard and to look for facile consistency between the suffering man of the deposition scene and the callous dandy of the earlier scenes. It might also steer the class away from a too ready temptation to treat the play as a morality play. The growth of oaks from such little acorns requires an opportunistic teacher but it is the initial shock of discovery that starts the process. As the analysis shows, the 'caterpillars of the commonwealth' are also present during this episode. In

	79	80	81	82	83	84	85	86	87	88
Gaunt	—	—								
York	—	—	—	—	—	—				
Northumberland	—	—	—	—	—	—	—	—	—	—
Richard			—	—	—	—	—			
Queen			—	—	—	—	—			
Aumerle			—	—	—	—	—			
Bushy			—	—	—	—	—			
Bagot			—	—	—	—	—			
Green			—	—	—	—	—			
Ross			—	—	—	—	—	—	—	
Willoughby			—	—	—	—	—	—	—	

view of the fact that they say nothing at all, this, too, may cause the class to express surprise. This gives the teacher the excuse to ask them to visualise the effect their presence would have on the audience, especially following Gaunt's great speech on England and his earlier remarks on Richard. Aumerle comes in and goes out with them. Is he at this stage distinguishable? Ross and Willoughby come in as part of Richard's entourage but stay behind with Northumberland. What will be the effect of the contrasting groupings in terms of meaning? A view of the play as a whole in terms of a diagram will reveal things about the role of Bolingbroke or can be used to stimulate investigation of it. He, too, at times says little but contributes much, as in the deposition scene. Possibly the class may draw conclusions about his importance relative to Richard.

The physical relationship of actors to each other, to an acting space and to an audience, can be expressive in itself, even though, in a full production, the significance of the play derives from many sources of which this is only one. In a classroom, a consideration of grouping and movement in abstraction can at least awaken a sense of the relevance of theatrical factors and can be a starting point for useful discussion.

There are directors who can organise the movement and grouping without pre-planning but others prefer to go into rehearsals with at least some possible solutions in their heads. Some directors have a board or a marked table top which to them represents the stage area and then, using pegs, pepper-pots or what have you, they plot out the main traffic and tableaux of the play. Certain amateur directors plot the whole play in advance this way, detailed links included. In some cases it is because they are nervous and inclined to panic if faced with a large number of actors all waiting impatiently to be told where to stand. They feel more secure with a pre-arranged plan. The trouble is that real actors are not pepper-pots and unless the director makes allowances for change and modification due to spontaneous invention, the result will be a marionette show. There can be little harm, however, in a preliminary engagement with some of the problems, especially where the stage is full, when a tableau or set piece is called for, or when, as in *The Alchemist*, the plot taxes the director to keep in mind just who has gone off with whom and where.

Paradoxically, although this 'blocking' exercise precedes rehearsal, in a classroom the pupils will be better able to handle it if they have had experience themselves of moving and congregating in a theatrical space. This suggests that it is more suitable for senior pupils than for younger ones. Even here, the teacher may find it necessary to demonstrate the procedure by first inviting the class to tackle a small section with him on a chosen model. The exercise follows logically from the one described above where the class experiment with bric-à-brac to create models of a working space. All the pupil needs next is something to represent the actors (such as pieces of Lego). To 'block' the principal groupings in a whole play can be very time-consuming and the teacher may prefer to use the method for its novelty value on a selected episode or scene. When devising the setting in the first place, the pupils may need to be reminded that the scene they are tackling is part of an Act, or the episode part of a scene, and that the setting will have to be such that all the major events in the larger unit can take place in it.

A scene such as Act II, Scene iii of *Macbeth* (the discovery of Duncan's murder) is ripe for this kind of treatment. Macbeth and Lennox discuss the storm. Macduff enters and urges them to go and see Duncan's body for themselves. He raises the alarm and gradually the stage fills up, beginning with the entry of Lady Macbeth and Banquo, and continuing with the return of Macbeth and Lennox with Ross, and ending with the arrival on the scene of Malcolm and Donalbain. The student runs through the dialogue in his head, keeping his eye or finger on each character in turn as it speaks. Pupils could, of course, work in pairs, in which case they will find it easier if they take alternate speeches to read aloud while physically indicating the speaker. The 'director' need only at this stage relate the characters to each other. He should not worry too much about the mechanics of getting an actor from A to B. If he feels B is an expressive place for the character to be, he should simply move him there. In the *Macbeth* scene, he will be forced, in wondering how to relate Macbeth to Banquo and Macduff, to think about the atmosphere of suspicion that might keep these three apart and keep Malcolm and Donalbain together. As a character speaks in the director's head, the director should ask himself whom the character is addressing. Pairs can remind each other of this drill. Is Macbeth's speech when he returns from the scene of the crime strictly for public consumption or should he be isolated, thus allowing his words to be partly a genuine expression of regret? When he confesses to killing the grooms, whom is he trying to convince? If Banquo, move 'Macbeth' across to him, if Macduff instead or as well, make the equivalent approximation. It could be that ultimately the groupings we have contrived would be totally masked from some of an audience. Pupils may never become technically very expert at avoiding this, but we are exploring meanings, not mounting a full public performance. The teacher will have to decide whether it is worth his while progressing to a reconsideration of the blocking in the light of an ultimate presentation. What his pupils will gain is a fuller sense of the repercussions of events. Which characters must be seen, which must be prominent when a particular thing happens? How many reactions will the audience need to take account of? How wide or narrow is the focus at any point? Who moves when Lady Macbeth swoons? Do Malcolm and Donalbain occupy all our attention? They certainly do when the rest of the characters have gone, and this brings up another point. Actually sweeping off the model a number of pieces, or adding to their number, brings home quite vividly how the play is patterned in terms of the association of characters, which are events with a public significance and which pertain to the private ear. Pupils blocking for an audience now need constantly to ask themselves where the audience is looking. This kind of blocking is easier if the audience looks roughly in the same direction. 'Thrust' and 'arena' require a great deal of gratuitous redeployment and it is difficult in any case for the director seated at a classroom desk to make himself sufficiently mobile to take in all the angles.

The difficulty, though, about the whole exercise of blocking on a model is that there is a range of physical expression it is difficult to imagine when staring at a piece of Lego; for instance, the flashing glance, the unspoken signal. Ideally, somebody's blocking could be tried out with real actors to see what it feels like to do it or see it or both. The exercise then becomes a useful preliminary to class production work and still builds on each individual's engagement with the text.

Detailed work on a scene from a play often takes the form of asking the pupil to give a written account of the events, to say what he learns about the characters and to comment on its dramatic qualities. Such written work is valuable if it occasions disciplined thinking about the nature and value of particular experience. But the particular experience of drama is a many-sided thing and questions relating only to words ignore important evidence. Should we ask the pupil to put himself in the position of a director examining the scene for the purpose of conducting rehearsals on it, we cover the same

121

ground but automatically take account of the other relevant factors also. Like the actor, the director is only too conscious how theoretical and tentative his preparation has to be in the absence of those human interactions which will modify it, and perhaps modify it severely.

In the written exercise I mentioned first, the relationship is between one pupil, one text and some paper, but classroom organisation can be much more flexible than this. We could begin with a group reading, to help all pupils gain some idea how the scene could go, and then there could be individual, group or class preparation work which expressed itself not merely in writing but in heiroglyphics, diagrams, verbal explanations and discussion. In creating a prompt copy, of course, a director can write on the text itself and if a teacher can make this possible by duplicating the scene, the greater the freedom for the pupil. He may, though, have to content himself with numbered sheets which do duty for those a director would interleave with his script. There is an artificiality in the exercise insofar as the pupil is doing a director's preparation for the eyes of his classmates and the teacher rather than for the ears of a set of actors, a designer, etc.; and for this reason his prompt copy may need to be more explicit than a real one would. What the teacher needs to remind himself is that it is the personal response that counts, that it can express itself in a variety of ways and that his job is to make this expression as easy as possible.

A director, in his preparation, will have a number of questions in mind and may alternate in the attention he gives to them. This facility comes as a result of experience and we cannot expect it of schoolchildren, although senior pupils should have made appreciable progress in that direction given an enlightened syllabus. Hudson's book, *Shakespeare and the Classroom*, in recommending the preparation of 'Production notes', sees something to be said for both giving the pupil a totally free hand and offering specific guidelines. The one thing it repudiates is 'any attempt to impose a stereotype on the notes' (p. 64). In tackling a scene from *Julius Caesar*, the book suggests only three tasks, and one of these, 'to find all the information which the scene itself gives concerning the time and place of action', is especially angled toward this kind of text. Whether our teacher suggests the requisite tasks for all such exercises or whether he allows his pupils to choose his priorities from a longer list is up to him, but there is a case to be made for not expecting too

122

much at a time and also for allowing the pupils to decide on the order in which the tasks demand to be carried out.

As with 'Preparing a role', I list below what I think are the sorts of questions and issues a director might explore at the preparation stage which the teacher might turn to his advantage.

— What are the major events in this scene? Who enters and who leaves? Can it be divided into self-contained sections for rehearsal purposes and, if so, on what basis? What music and sound effects are required by the text, what lighting changes and what changes of costume, if any?

— What conflicts and contrasts of or in character might need clarifying for the actors?

— How do you expect the scene will look? What is required or is possible in the way of setting? What grouping or movement (including gesture) is specified? What opportunities do you foresee for movement to be added? What grouping or movement do you foresee as best emphasising the major 'moments' of the scene? (A complete 'blocking' on a model could help at this point.)

— What sort of things might actors be doing on stage when their characters are not speaking?

— What advice on the *style* of playing can one have up one's sleeve to offer to actors? (Perhaps it might help actors playing the family in *The Good Woman of Setzuan*, for example, to be urged to think of themselves as cartoon figures.)

— Is there one pervasive mood in the scene or are there strong contrasts of mood to highlight? By what means might a mood be produced? What effects do you expect the sequence of moods to have on an audience?

— What changes of pace, if any, seem to be indicated? (These might be marked directly onto a script with signs such as those denoting crescendo or de-crescendo in music.)

— In the context of the play as a whole, what major developments in character or action in this scene would you try to help the audience to register? For instance, does a character appear for the first time? What does his arrival contribute? Are there key lines or deeds which might be pointed out, and how can this be done?

123

5

Improvisation as invention

I made the point that the term 'improvisation' could be made to cover not merely the kind of exploratory, experimental work we have been considering so far but a more freely inventive approach to the text. In these freer forms of improvisation the pupil is able to make a much greater contribution to the shaping of an experience for himself. He may or may not have narrative or structural guidelines to work to but even if he has, the substance — the movements and the words etc. — will be his own. This is true even if he derives his narrative or structure from an existing play.

It may be that in some cases the teacher will settle for this, deeming that particular pupils will find it more educationally rewarding than attempting to internalise the words and actions given in the script. But generally speaking, if the teacher holds that there is some virtue in engaging with the experience of the dramatist, he will have to apply the test of relevance to his pupils' improvisatory activities. While remaining concerned that they should make decisions of their own, he will also be helping them discover the nature of the dramatist's decisions. The temptation to allow free invention to become an end in itself can be very strong. With poorer readers it offers the satisfaction of quick results and an air of busy excitement. Released into it too soon, even the more literate pupils are often reluctant to return to the discipline of the text.

The kind of improvisation we are discussing can be used both as an introduction to and preparation for the text and for remedial purposes, as a means, that is, of revitalising the flagging imagination. In approaching the text directly, we saw that account has to be taken of its mode and style. The precaution is even more urgent where improvisatory methods are chosen. Unless it has a recognisable and achievable purpose, a naturalistic enactment of a scene, from, say, a verse tragedy, runs the risk of over-simplifying and distorting. Improvisation needs to help the pupils accept and manipulate the conventions of the play. It also needs to focus not merely on character and event but on plot, theme, dialogue, imagery, symbols, structure, setting, tempo, pace and rhythm.

Inventing the lines

The most direct method of this kind is to try to 'invent' the text itself. What the pupil is trying to do is to discover the creative process that made the words of the text inevitable. A teacher may decide to start the procedure by himself abstracting the outlines of the plot, the succession of events, the broad traits of character, feeding these to the pupils and letting them make the play. The trouble with this is that they may not be starting with the premises with which the dramatist began and they could fail to take into account elements of the style of the play which are intrinsic to the meaning.

I saw a second year class working on David Campton's sketch *Do It Yourself*. The information they were given was that there were these two men, Percy and Arthur, that Percy was a Do It Yourself enthusiast and that Arthur was an interfering know-all. The sketch ends with Percy making a box to put Arthur in but with Arthur insisting on giving advice even in this matter. Arthur's blind pomposity is sharply exposed by the way Percy's lines both echo and add another meaning to his, while comic convention is what helps us to accept that Arthur would in fact be as blind as this.

Arthur: If only you'd told me it was a box to put me in, I'd have advised you.
Percy: I thought you would.
Arthur: Where are your air-holes?
Percy: I haven't got any air-holes.
Arthur: There you are. You're in trouble right away. And where's the wall-paper?
Percy: I haven't any wall-paper.
Arthur: You can't expect anybody to get into a box without wall-paper. And where's the lead-lining?
Percy: I haven't got a lead-lining.

The comic possibilities of that kind of dialogue may, for all we know, have struck Campton only in the writing and, if the situation is presented to pupils as a comic *idea*, the chances of its achieving Campton's particular comic effect can be fairly slim. The youngsters I saw achieved a generalised pomposity and a generalised irritation but had to start again from scratch when faced with the script.

Hodgson and Richards, in *Improvisation*, recommend that students should make contact with the text first and that constant recourse should be made to it, so that although structural ideas are again abstracted from the text and set up as signposts, the students have some experience of the context towards which they must build and the flavour of the style they must try to capture. Insofar as this method gives students a sense of the overall shape of a scene and of the structure of relationships, and insofar as it helps them to see roughly where they are going, it can be a great aid to comprehension. I found it worked especially well with a scene from Act II of Ibsen's *The Wild Duck*, where Hjalmar returns from the party and tells his family his version of events there. We had read and discussed the whole play first and there was plenty of information on which characterisation could be built. The dramatic logic of the scene quickly emerged and the actors were able to give attention to the reactions of their characters to events onstage and to the words of others — a particular necessity in performing Ibsen, as so much is buried beneath the surface and saying the lines without that awareness renders his plays somewhat meaningless.

In *Billy Liar*, another play in a naturalistic mode, Waterhouse and Hall capture the rhythms and idioms of colloquial speech and write about experiences, particularly the parent-child interactions, that are recognisable by and readily accessible to youngsters. A C.S.E. set, which I taught, read the scene where Billy arrives home late to be regaled by his father and subjected to a rigorous interrogation, not merely about his lateness, but about his whole way of life. Our first reading was gratifyingly expressive, but it had no 'shape'. We discussed the shifting relationships and reached some sort of agreement that somewhere the tide begins to turn and Billy is provoked into becoming the aggressor. What had to happen was that his father had to rile him beyond endurance and, with this premise in mind and the terms of reference for the characters clearly understood, we improvised the scene in pairs. Not only did we find that the style was remarkably easy to imitate, with many of the original lines creeping in quite naturally, but the climactic reversal of direction when it came was, in many cases, felt to be an inevitable result of the emotions the situation releases. For once, I was convinced that the improvement we noticed in the eventual performance of the text owed much to our indirect approach.

I also found the method of improvising the lines useful in tackling the scene described earlier from *Tartuffe*, the scene where Dorine interrupts Orgon's attempts to 'sell' Tartuffe to his daughter as a husband. Here the intentions are easily graspable and the stances relatively simple. But the very episode itself is based on an improvised form, that of the Commedia dell'arte, and actors in Commedia traditionally worked from scenarios. Gesture, facial expression and timing were given full and proper rein and valuable clues acquired to a valid way of playing the original. The text indicated that gesture should be timed with words and some crude attempt was made to take this into account in the pupils' own invented verbalising.

Generally, though, the more taut or poetic the script, the more difficult it is in improvisation to approximate to it. This is the reason given by Peter Hall for eschewing this approach in his rehearsals of Pinter plays (*Theatre Quarterly* Vol. 4, No. 16). I tried the method with Act I, Scene iv of *King Lear*, which includes the exchange between Lear and the Fool, just before Goneril makes her grudging entrance. Kent is also onstage, but he has little to say and is 'used' by the Fool as audience. The Fool taunts and irritates Lear, reminding him constantly of his folly and predicting disaster and also relating him to folly in the world at large. He contributes to the spiritual development of Lear but seems to have no personal motives, declared or undeclared, for doing so. There is no plot-development to hang on to and Lear now threatens, now encourages, his tormentor. The Fool seems hardly a character at all in the sense that the personages in the plays I have just been discussing are characters. Progress from one topic or riddle or proposition is often by *Godot*-like association or apparent whim. For the improviser of the Fool, then, the grasping of an inner logic to make the next step feel natural is fraught with difficulties.

With a group of senior students who had read the play, I did some preliminary work on the sense of the Fool episode, concentrating, though, as bidden by Hodgson and Richards, on 'the main elements of the structure' rather than on detail at this point. It was hoped, anyway, that some of the more intractable parts would become clear and deployable in improvisation. The episode can roughly be divided into sections according to the riddle, song or joke the Fool decides to introduce and we set up the recommended 'signposts'. This is the episode according to the Penguin edition:

Fool: Let me hire him too. Here's my coxcomb.
Lear: How now, my pretty knave! How dost thou?
Fool: Sirrah, you were best take my coxcomb.
Kent: Why, Fool?

Fool: Why? For taking one's part that's out of favour. Nay, and thou canst not smile as the wind sits, thou'lt catch cold shortly. There, take my coxcomb! Why, this fellow has banished two on's daughters, and did the third a blessing against his will. If thou follow him, thou must needs wear my coxcomb. How now, nuncle! Would I had two coxcombs and two daughters!

Lear: Why, my boy?

Fool: If I gave them all my living, I'd keep my coxcombs myself. There's mine. Beg another of thy daughters.

Lear: Take heed, sirrah, the whip!

Fool: Truth's a dog must to kennel; he must be whipped out when the Lady Brach may stand by the fire and stink.

Lear: A pestilent gall to me!

Fool: Sirrah, I'll teach thee a speech.

Lear: Do.

Fool: Mark it, nuncle:
Have more than thou showest,
Speak less than thou knowest,
Lend less than thou owest,
Ride more than thou goest,
Learn more than thou trowest,
Set less than thou throwest;
Leave thy drink and thy whore
And keep in-a-door,
And thou shalt have more
Than two tens to a score.

Kent: This is nothing, Fool.

Fool: Then 'tis like the breath of an unfee'd lawyer: you gave me nothing for't. Can you make no use of nothing, nuncle?

Lear: Why, no, boy. Nothing can be made out of nothing.

Fool: (*to Kent*) Prithee tell him; so much the rent of his land comes to. He will not believe a fool.

Lear: A bitter fool!

Fool: Dost thou know the difference, my boy, between a bitter fool and a sweet one?

Lear: No, lad; teach me.

Fool: That lord that counselled thee
    To give away thy land,
Come place him here by me;
    Do thou for him stand,
The sweet and bitter fool
    Will presently appear:
The one in motley here,
    The other found out — there.

Lear: Dost thou call me fool, boy?

Fool: All thy other titles thou hast given away; that thou wast born with.

Kent: This is not altogether fool, my lord.

Fool: No, faith; lords and great men will not let me. If I had a monopoly out they would have part on't; and ladies too — they will not let me have all the fool to myself; they'll be snatching. Nuncle, give me an egg and I'll give thee two crowns.

128

Lear: What two crowns shall they be?
Fool: Why, after I have cut the egg i'the middle and eat up the meat, the two crowns of the egg. When thou clovest thy crown i'the middle, and gavest away both parts, thou borest thine ass on thy back o'er the dirt. Thou hadst little wit in thy bald crown when thou gavest thy golden one away. If I speak like myself in this, let him be whipped that first finds it so.
Fools had ne'er less grace in a year,
    For wise men are grown foppish
And know not how their wits to wear,
    Their manners are so apish.
Lear: When were you wont to be so full of songs, sirrah?
Fool: I have used it, nuncle, e'er since thou madest thy daughters thy mothers; for when thou gavest them the rod and puttest down thine own breeches,
    (*sings*)
Then they for sudden joy did weep,
    And I for sorrow sung,
That such a king should play bo-peep
    And go the fools among.
Prithee, nuncle, keep a schoolmaster that can teach thy fool to lie; I would fain learn to lie.
Lear: And you lie, sirrah, we'll have you whipped.
Fool: I marvel what kin thou and thy daughters are. They'll have me whipped for speaking true; thou'lt have me whipped for lying; and sometimes I am whipped for holding my peace. I had rather be any kind o'thing than a fool. And yet I would not be thee, nuncle. Thou hast pared thy wit o'both sides and left nothing i'the middle. Here comes one o'the parings.

After an hour's work, running continually back to the text, three of the girl students performed this version (without books) to the rest and I tape-recorded it:

Lear: Kent, I'll hire you. Here's money for your service.
Fool: I'll hire him too. Here's my fool's cap. (*offers cap to Kent*)
Lear: Why do you give him your fool's cap?
Fool: If you don't know, you'd better have it.
Lear: Why?
Fool: Because — if I had two fool's caps, then I'd have one and I'd give him the other, but as I've only got one, he'd better get another one off his daughters.
Lear: Why?
    (*A baffled pause*)
Student playing Fool: Go on to the whip, that bit. 'Cos you didn't say why before.
Lear: I'll have thee whipped, fool.
Fool: You don't like to hear the truth, do you? And when you've found the truth you send her outside and when you send the truth outside, in come the lies through the door.
Lear: You're a pest to me, Fool.
Fool: I'll teach thee a speech:

129

Think before you act,
Think before you speak,
Don't run before you can walk,
Don't shoot your mouth off about things you don't know about.
And
Don't go off having a good time when you don't know what's going
on inside your own home.

Lear: This is nothing, Fool.

Fool: You say it's nothing. It's like nothing when a lawyer don't get paid for doing his job. *He* doesn't pay me anything. Do you take what I say as nothing?

Lear: I can make nothing of nothing.

Fool: Ah . . . (*to Kent*) You tell him, he don't believe me.

Lear: You're a bitter fool.

Fool: Ah, but do you know the difference between a bitter fool and a sweet fool? You see, you, you're the bitter fool, because you've given away all your lands, everything you ever owned and you haven't got anything left. Me, I'm a sweet fool, because I've got just what I started with, which was nothing.

Lear: You dare to call me a fool?

Fool: Oh, that's the only title you've got left. You've given the rest away.

Kent: That's not completely stupid, my lord.
          (*Blank reception*)
          That's not altogether foolish, my lord.

Fool: No, because if I was altogether . . . because I can't be all the fool, because people like him have plenty of foolishness . . . something like that . . . If I had two eggs . . . If you give me an egg I'll give you two crowns . . .

Lear: What crowns?

Fool: Because . . . if I've got two eggs . . . Right? And cut them down the middles and eat the white, you'd be left with two yokes, two crowns, and . . . you've given away your crowns, so you might as well carry your ass on your back, on the dirt . . . and . . . if you think I'm lying and speaking as a fool, then whip me, because I'm not, I'm speaking about you . . .

Lear: I'll have you whipped.

Fool: If I speak the truth, you whip me, if I lie, his daughters whip me, if I don't say anything at all, you both whip me, so I might as well shut up! Else I get caught in the middle.

Lear: You're lying.

Fool: No, I'm not. Look who's coming.

The discrepancies are apparent. Some parts are misunderstood and important points skated over. Images are devitalised, songs reduced to a summary, speeches structurally inverted so as to lose their punch. The actress playing the Fool tends to grab for a word like "because" to keep her going irrespective of what line she has been fed by Lear. Lear himself, in performance, sees his role more as a feed than as the centre of attention. All round, memory is as much in evidence as logic. This said, though, the audience was engrossed, impressed and highly amused. Although there is obviously still a fair way to go, the improvisation shows a remarkable grasp of the overall sequence and particularly, at times, of the *kind* of sequence it is. The actresses realise that the actual wording of the original lines is required to trigger off the next section, and Shakespeare is invoked because he is needed. I was thinking particularly of Kent's re-phrasing of "That's not completely stupid, my lord" to produce "That's not altogether foolish, my lord." Still not quite there, however, and this is what threw the Fool in his next speech. The songs may have been vandalised but the equivalent of the first aims at the proverbial *style* of statement. The image of the truth as a dog loses its physical force but the image-making procedure is preserved and a personal attempt is made to fill the bill. Speeches may be blunted but the Fool's penultimate one in the improvised version captures the manner of the original.

In all fairness, Hodgson and Richards see the effortless learning of the lines as the ultimate goal, and I didn't let it get as far as that. One would have to decide whether the amount of progress possible in the time available (in this case an hour) made this method preferable to direct experiment with the text. It could be argued that with this kind of piece it didn't. Certainly an early return to the text, whether to learn it or to realise it unlearned, is imperative and the provisional nature of our 'statement' must be clearly established.

There are scenes in some plays where the words given are relatively unimportant and mere approximation to them on the part of an actor does not make any drastic difference. This can happen even in Pinter! There is an episode in *The Caretaker* where Mick is cleaning the room in the darkness, with the Electrolux plugged into the light socket, while Davies stumbles about and backs away in bewilderment and terror. Students have admitted to me to seeing no comic potential in the scene at all until it was improvised in a darkened area with sound of movement and the sound of the Electrolux and with words themselves coming as sounds out of darkness and silence.

Davies: (*muttering*): What's this? (*He switches on and off*) What's the matter with this damn light? (*He switches on and off*) Aaah. Don't tell me the damn light's gone now.
> Pause
What'll I do? Damn light's gone now. Can't see a thing.
> Pause
What'll I do now? (*He moves, stumbles*) Ah God, what's that? Give me a light. Wait a minute.

131

> *He feels for matches in his pocket, takes out a box and lights*
> *one. The match goes out. The box falls.*

Aah! Where is it? (*Stooping*) Where's the bloody box?
> *The box is kicked.*

What's that? What? Who's that? What's that?
> *Pause. He moves.*

Where's my box? It was down here. Who's this? Who's moving it?
> *Silence*

Come on. Who's this? Who's this got my box?
> *Pause*

Who's in here?
> *Pause*

I got a knife here. I'm ready. Come on then, who are you?
> *He moves, stumbles, falls, and cries out.*
> *Silence*
> *A faint whimper from Davies. He gets up.*

All right!
> *He stands. Heavy breathing.*
> *Suddenly the Electrolux starts to hum.*

As long as he gets the sequence right (the switch, the matches, the kicked box, the knife, the falling over) the pupil acting Davies can concentrate on the fear and the pace, and the gains might outweigh the loss of Pinter's exact words.

In *Ernie's Incredible Illucinations* by Alan Ayckbourn, there is a scene in a boxing booth where young Ernie's Auntie May ('willed' by Ernie) challenges the boxing champion, Kid Saracen, to a fight and defeats him. Since many of the lines are throwaway lines and the physical action is of acknowledged importance, the whole scene cries out to be improvised. With a second year class, I organised some group work on the following section of it.

Ernie (*stepping forward*): And then suddenly I got this idea. Auntie May could
> be the new heavyweight champion of the world . . .
>> (*The bell rings. Auntie May comes bouncing out of her corner*
>> *flinging punches at the Kid who looks startled. Crowd cheers.*)

Auntie: Let's have you.
Kid Saracen: Hey, come off it!
>> (*Referee tries vainly to pull Auntie back but she dances out of*
>> *reach.*)

Kid Saracen: Somebody chuck her out.
>> (*Kid turns to appeal to the crowd. Auntie punches him in the*
>> *back.*)

Auntie: Gotcher.
Kid Saracen: Ow!
>> (*Auntie bombards the Kid with punches.*)

Ernie: (*Commentator style*) And Auntie May moves in again and catches the Kid
> with a left and a right to the body and there's a right cross to the head
> — and that really hurt him — and it looks from here as if the champ is
> in real trouble . . . as this amazing sixty-eight-year-old challenger

follows up with a series of sharp left jabs ... one, two, three, four jabs ...

    (The Kid is reeling back.)

And, then, bang, a right hook and he's down ...

    (Kid goes down on his knees. Crowd cheers.)

Auntie: *(to Referee)* Go on, start counting.

Crowd: One — two — three — four — five — six ...

    (The Kid gets up again.)

Ernie: And the Kid's on his feet but he's no idea where he is ... and there's that tremendous right uppercut ... and he's down again ...

    (Crowd counts him out. Auntie dances round the ring with glee. The crowd bursts into the ring and Auntie is lifted on to their shoulders. They go out singing 'For she's a jolly good fellow.' Referee and the Kid are left.)

The lines are clues to or appeals for action. I encouraged the pupils to use their own words first and they quickly grasped how this kind of dialogue works. Once *au fait* with the function, they did in fact adopt Ayckbourn's own words and used them unaided by the book as their own, a goal which, as we said, one doesn't have to insist on but is nice if you can achieve it. Some bits, I felt, asked for permanent alteration. The commentary on the fight is more natural if it follows the fight rather than steering it. Consequently, I encouraged the pupils to invent their own commentary according to the way the fight actually evolved. A bonus was the fact that this allowed for more than one Ernie in each group. Commentators, after all, could come from different radio stations and the verbal work-out was liberating. When the groups showed their versions to each other, the scope that was possible for individual expression within the guiding structure of the playwright's imagination became clearly evident. There are plays available which are only partially scripted, with the action of the intervening sections merely described in a scenario. One such play is *Ars Longa, Vita Brevis* by John Arden. Unfortunately, too much freedom can make a coherent whole harder to achieve and a fall between two stools a real likelihood.

Inventing the lines, as a teaching method, can have valuable effects in personalising a given experience. Introducing the lines before improvising is based on sound reasoning. A snag, in my experience, is that this can encourage students to see the exercise as a challenge to their memories and can produce the very kind of self-consciousness that Hodgson and Richards hope to eliminate. The teacher needs to divert attention by stressing that there are no prizes for remembering the words and that a lively performance is what is wanted. Another danger against which Hodgson and Richards warn the teacher is that of premature interpretation. Albert Hunt, when he tried the method with a scene from *The Caucasian Chalk Circle*, found that, left to themselves, the students adopted quite the wrong style of playing and thus distorted the meaning. He had to step in, so he says, with drastic remedial measures (*Hopes for Great Happenings*, pp. 8–9). When my own students performed their improvised version of the *Lear* scene, the audience were asked what they thought the exercise brought out and one of them commented: 'It showed that the Fool didn't need to be there — just wasn't there.' In both cases, discussion revealed itself to be essential to clarify or query opinions before they hardened. Hodgson and Richards recommend applying the approach to whole plays. Clive Barker (in *Theatre Games*) finds this leads to excessive verbalising. I found it a useful method with small sections, certainly, but it can be time-consuming. There are many methods available to the teacher and many different kinds of pupil to relate them to. Over the length of a play, a diversity of approach has a better chance of holding their interest.

Missing scenes

For the actor, it can help the continuity of his performance if he attempts to imagine the offstage life of his character. Often the play contains hints and descriptions and a director may invite the actor to improvise or act out relevant incidents or states of mind. An educationalist might gib at this, seeing it as a return to the worst excesses of A.C. Bradley. If scenes are missing, he could argue, it is because the dramatist has excellent reasons for leaving them out. Will not his students carry away a memory of the play with emphases in all the wrong places?

One can see some force in these objections, and I personally feel that strict discretion has to be exercised and the rules of the particular game made crystal clear to the student. Hodgson and Richards suggest that in order to understand the changes that have taken place in Leontes and Hermione in *The Winter's Tale*, the actor and actress should fill in imaginatively the sixteen-year gap in time. This has the worthy aim of preventing too flip and fairytale a manner of enacting the final ritual sequence. But the sixteen-year gap is partly a device to allow Perdita to grow up. The actors may find they will get enough help by surrendering to the lines in the last scene themselves. The student needs also to take into account the audience's broader view of the play, and for the audience other factors will contribute to making the changes in the principal characters acceptable. In the same play, Shakespeare omits to present the many reconciliations which take place before the final denouement, choosing merely to have a lord describe them. If one were to have students act these out one would be filling their heads with an experience Shakespeare did not intend them to have, since he wants them (as audience) to reserve their attention for the full force of the final scene.

One can merrily piece together the myth of Oedipus, arrange it in chronological order and have the students improvise their way through that. Whether this helps them grasp the significance of *Oedipus Rex*, though, is another matter. Sophocles seems more concerned to explore the hero's process of self-discovery. In fact, raking through the past to see if he could have avoided his fate is to pursue a notorious red-herring. If one were able to fill in with a simulation the experiences of Alison in *Look Back in Anger*, between her walking out on Jimmy and returning after the appropriate 'suffering', one might find it more difficult to arrive at a critical assessment of the play, since one of the points a student might consider should be the extent to which the play as given awards an excess of interest and sympathy to the hero. Shouldn't the student also be concentrating on the readiness of Jimmy for the change?

The hero of Bulgakov's novel *Black Snow* has written a play and given it to a director called Ivan Vasilievich. The director is closely modelled on Stanislavsky and the novel satirises his habit of seizing on insignificant details and giving them disproportionate importance.

The days passed in unceasing labour. I saw a great deal. I saw, for instance, a crowd of actors headed by Ludmilla Silvestrona (who incidentally had no part in the play) charge shrieking about the stage and then lean out of invisible windows. The reason was that in the same scene with the bouquet and the letter business, my heroine had to run to the window from which she had caught sight of the distant glow of a fire. This provided the excuse for a protracted étude, which was blown up to incredible proportions and which reduced me, I must confess, to a state of near-despair.

A director must ask himself what effects his experiments are having on the nature of the performance. Bulgakov's author suspected that, in his case, they were bad effects:

Sinister doubts began to creep into my mind as early as the end of the first week. By the end of the second I realised that the famous method was utterly wrong for my play. Far from getting any better at proffering his bouquet, writing a letter or declaring his love, Patrikeyev got more and more awkward, dry and completely unfunny.

Similarly, a teacher who accepts the limits imposed by the text and believes that an experience of the play in performance is educationally desirable must ask himself, in any individual case, whether this method of teaching (the invention of missing scenes and episodes), however 'creative' it appears to be, is making a relevant contribution to a valid realisation.

I believe it can. It worked for me when the actual pressure of the offstage experience was proportionate to the implied pressure of it onstage, where the contribution was in key with the style of the scene. In the scene from *Macbeth* which we discussed in detail, the experiences of Macduff and Macbeth in the murder chamber are obviously of crucial importance as factors in their behaviour when they appear. If, as I suggested, the actors might mentally rehearse them, why should they not go further and improvise them in terms of movement and voice? Whether, in the case of Macbeth, the teacher wishes to complicate the issue by introducing Lennox and Ross will depend on whether he thinks it helps the actor playing Macbeth to understand why Macbeth killed the grooms. By enacting the murder of Duncan, the actor is experimenting with feeling, testing its relevance and putting himself in a position to decide how genuinely appalled Macbeth should be. In *Henry IV Part 1*, the zest and commitment with which Falstaff spins his yarn might be explored by inviting the pupils to act out a slow-motion group performance of his imaginary fight with the men in Kendal green, to the accompaniment, say, of a pop-tune like *Albatross*, which is a leisurely piece played on electric guitars and punctuated with clashes on a cymbal. In *Antony and Cleopatra* we can try to understand why Cleopatra preferred death to public humiliation by improvising what she declares she fears, exposure to the 'shouting plebeians'. 'Cleopatras' take turns to walk the gauntlet between files consisting of the rest of the class giving vent to appropriate epithets. In *All My Sons*, by Arthur Miller, a tribunal has taken place before the play begins which determines the behaviour of some of the characters as we witness it. Can this be profitably reconstructed and the traumas made more real?

As Hodgson and Richards rightly suggest, a dramatist such as Chekhov is full of opportunities for this approach and one can understand his attraction for Stanislavsky. They instance the offstage scene in *Three Sisters* in which Toozenbach and Soliony agree to fight their duel, and it is true that this can help the actor playing Toozenbach to understand his air of preoccupation. Stanislavsky, to his credit, rejected Chekhov's suggestion that offstage reality be allowed to spill over onto the stage when he refused to allow Toozenbach's body to be carried on. The play seems to want the actress playing Irena to focus more on the character's concern to return to her engagement with the business of living. Ibsen, too, with so much of his action taking place offstage, strongly tempts the teacher to fill in the gaps. It can help, for instance, in *The Wild Duck*, to improvise in pairs the missing scene between Gregers and Hjalmar where Gregers tells Hjalmar the truth about his marriage. Certainly some adjustment of his frame of mind is necessary if the actor is to understand Hjalmar's new mood in Act IV and his behaviour towards his wife.

I agree with Ron Hayman that, in a sense, we are concerned in all drama not so much with psychology as with behaviour. Brecht specifically requires his actors to realise that the characters are not the way they are because of psychological determinism or because it is their 'nature' to be so. We referred earlier to the description by Albert Hunt, in his book *Hopes for Great Happenings*, of the improvisation he asked his students to do of a scene from *The Caucasian Chalk Circle*. It is the scene where Grusha asks the peasant for milk for the baby. The peasant claims he is short and blames the soldiers. Hunt found that the students were playing the peasant as typically miserly and Grusha as simply motherly. So he introduced the experience of the soldiers, delegating two students to vandalise the cottage before the arrival of Grusha. The peasant now became both indignant and frightened, as the soldiers were no longer merely an excuse but a memory. The improvisation served the purpose not of emotionally reinforcing the student's original conception but of modifying it. We have discussed Scene Eleven of *Mother Courage*, where Kattrin, the dumb girl, sits on a roof with her drum attempting to warn a nearby town of the approach of an army. Some soldiers attempt to persuade and force her to come down. It is easy, as we pointed out, to see Kattrin as simply a sentimental heroine and the soldiers as natural villains. What worries them, though, is the thought of their Colonel 'foaming at the mouth' if they fail. They, too, are what they are because of the circumstances they find themselves in. When I did this scene with a fourth year class, I asked them in groups to improvise the scene with the Colonel. Not only was there a greater urgency in the demands and threats made by the soldiers the next time round but a greater understanding of the soldiers' predicament.

137

Subtext and stage directions

As it can be useful to improvise unwritten scenes, so it can help to
invent for a character the thoughts and comments that a dramatist
leaves unspoken. A dramatist writing in a naturalistic mode denies
himself the use of soliloquy and aside, and in his case what we shall
be doing is temporarily changing the conventions of the play. The
subtext might be supplied either by the character himself or by an
'alter ego', another pupil standing behind him. In the film *Annie Hall*,
Woody Allen had a superficially innocent conversation with a girl
while subtitles showed his true thoughts. There, though, simultaneity
helped to achieve a deliberately comic effect. In our exercise the
result may indeed be unconsciously funny, but the benefits to the
class need to be confirmed by a subsequent return to the text as
originally written.

   We discussed earlier the performance of the lunch scene at the end
of Act I of *Three Sisters*. There I suggested the pupils worked from
dossiers they had built up on the individual characters. In the present
exercise they could either use such dossiers as a basis for their
invented asides or treat the invention of asides as the major means of
investigation. The action of the scene is fairly static, which simplifies
the problems somewhat. In the first instance the 'characters' should
be allowed to say what comes into their heads. If they want the rest
of the class — or the rest of the group — to be in a position to comment afterwards on the acceptability of the contribution, some sort
of sequence will have to be agreed when it is presented. It might
develop along these lines:

> *All are now seated at the table: the drawing room is empty.*
> *Koolyghin*: Irena, you know, I do advise you to find yourself a good husband. In
> my view it's high time you got married.
> *Irena (aside)*: I wish you'd shut up. I've just fended off the Baron and he's look-
> ing at me very significantly.
> *Toozenbach (aside)*: I agree with Koolyghin, it is time she got married. To me!
> *Chebutykin*: You ought to get yourself a nice little husband, too, Natalia
> Ivanovna.
> *Koolyghin*: Natalia Ivanovna already has a husband in view.
> *Natasha (aside)*: I have, but not everybody likes the idea.
> *Masha (aside)*: Trust my stupid, tactless husband to bring up that painful subject.
> The loathsome little upstart will be watching for reactions. I'd better
> create a diversion.
> (*strikes her plate with a fork. Says aloud*) A glass of wine for me,
> please! Three cheers for our jolly old life! We keep our end up, we
> do!

Koolyghin (aside): How embarrassing! What an impression she's creating. Better try to make a joke of it. (*To Masha*) Masha, you won't get more than one out of ten for good conduct!

Although in this particular episode Chekhov withdraws the audience to show them the group as a group, we can still justify ourselves in using this approach on the grounds that the individual reactions are 'in character' and the given remarks are subject to naturalistic logic. From an educational standpoint the attempt to articulate what you sensed was implied helps the students towards a clearer definition of the meaning of the experience.

Having an 'alter ego' for each of the characters in a group as large as this makes the exercise very complicated. Alter egos for a pair of characters such as one finds in *The Caretaker* is more manageable and susceptible to presentation. The Pinter play does in fact more nearly resemble a naturalistic drama than some of his other work but the psychological bases of the characters tend to shift a little under the feet. Having an alter ego speak out a subtext can be a useful means of investigation but it is fraught with dangers if the pupils feel they must find what they are looking for. Pinter may be more concerned to keep the audience guessing than to allow them to make precise inferences. We know that in the play as a whole Davies comes to want to establish himself in the flat and that Aston seems driven by a desire to 'collect' him as he collects bric-à-brac. But to impute Machiavellian subterfuge to either of them in an early encounter such as this could be premature or even invalid.

Davies: You sleep here, do you?
Aston: Yes.
Davies: What, in that?
Aston: Yes.
Davies: Yes, well, you'd be out of the draught there.
Aston: You don't get much wind.
Davies: You'd be well out of it. It's different when you're kipping out.
Aston: Would be.
Davies: Nothing but wind then.
                Pause
Aston: Yes, when the wind gets up it . . .
                Pause
Davies: Yes.
Aston: Mmnnn.

The Chekhov characters could be said to interlock at a subtextual level but these two are barely interacting at all. While an alter ego might fill the first pause with some secret wish that Aston will take the hint about poor old Davies having to sleep out, Aston's alter ego

will find it difficult to finish his sentence for him. He may just have
nothing to say. Even the Davies alter ego will have to distinguish
what seems clear to him and what is clear to the character.

For an actor, the most taxing time can come when there is a long
speech that the character he is playing must listen to and at the same
time register a reaction to. Davoren and Seumas in *The Shadow of a
Gunman* by O'Casey, are racked with anxiety to know whether the
Black and Tans are likely to search the whole house, since this would
involve finding the incriminating bombs in Minnie's room. Mrs
Grigson, another tenant, spins a long story about the way they have
just treated her husband, Dolphie.

> *Mrs Grigson*: Just to show them the sort of man he was, before they came in,
> Dolphie put the big Bible on the table, open at the First Gospel of St
> Peter, second chapter, an' marked the thirteenth and the seventeenth
> verse in red ink — you know the passages, Mr Shields — (*Quoting*):
>> "Submit yourself to every ordinance of man for the Lord's sake:
>> whether it be to the king, as sent by him for the punishment of evil-
>> doers, an' for the praise of them that do well . . . Love the brother-
>> hood, Fear God, Honour the King."
> An' what do you think they did, Mr Shields? They caught a hold of the
> Bible an' flung it on the floor — imagine that, Mr Shields — flingin' the
> Bible on the floor! Then one of them says to another — "Jack," says
> he, "have you seen the light; is your soul saved." An' then they grabbed
> hold of poor Dolphie, callin' him Mr Moody an' Mr Sankey, an' wanted
> him to offer up a prayer for the Irish Republic! An' when they were
> puttin' me out, there they had the poor man sittin' up in bed, his hands
> cross on his breast, his eyes lookin' up at the ceilin', an' he singin' a
> hymn — "We shall meet in the Sweet Bye an' Bye" — an' all the time,
> Mr Shields, there they were drinkin' his whisky; there's torture for you,
> an' they were laughin' at poor Dolphie's terrible sufferin's.

On the stage, the audience would be at least as interested in Davoren
and Seumas as in the speaker. To ask pupils to put into words the
thoughts of the two men is to remind them that the reactions are an
important part of the total experience. Seumas's thought would
probably be a simple extension of his oft expressed wish for self-
preservation. Davoren's would be more complex; he would be ridden
with guilt about putting Minnie in danger and horror stricken at the
scope for thuggery that the availability of whisky opens up for the
soldiers.

In Scene Eleven of *Mother Courage*, Kattrin, the dumb girl, is
prompted by the prayers of the unheeding peasants to take the ladder
and the drum and climb up on to the roof to warn the town of the
approach of the soldiers. Here again, her internal monologue, spoken
to accompany her actions, can help the clarity of her performance.

140

A danger is, though, that it invites the pupil to identify too closely with the character and read her actions as the simple result of heroic drives. A truly Brechtian approach would be, as I suggested earlier, to have her narrate her actions in the third person while performing them, in other words to speak out the stage directions. In a class, this could be done as a dance-drama with one person narrating what the rest of the pupils (as Kattrin) must do. Supplying stage directions where the playwright refrains from doing so can be a useful written exercise, forcing the pupil to visualise the play in performance. If he supplies them after acting an episode or seeing it acted, his observation will be to that degree sharpened.

Invented situations

Missing scenes, according to our definition, are scenes which are implied in but not provided by a text. The aim in improvising these was to improve the pupils' understanding of the onstage life of certain characters by allowing them to investigate their offstage life. Some directors try to ensure that the actors remain continuously and instinctively in character by encouraging them to act out invented encounters not directly suggested by the dramatist. A teacher following this procedure may be nervous of taking yet another step away from the text, and it is true that it remains important for him to remind himself firmly of his educational objectives. He needs to be clear in his mind just what he can achieve by this method. Some plays will be more amenable than others (how reliable is the offstage experience of Pinter characters?) and it will work better where characters have some sort of consistent psychology or an identifiable point of view.

Supposing a class is working on the trial scene from *The Merchant of Venice* and the performance lacks all sense of urgency. The Christians are not sufficiently concerned to dissuade the Jew from his projected course and Shylock seems unmoved by their attacks or his prospects. A remedial method I have tried is to divide the class into groups of, say, six and let them choose one to be Shylock. Then the teacher tells them that the rest are Christians and that they have asked Shylock to meet them informally (in a tavern?) to discuss the possibility of settling the affair out of court. The Christians are not adopting any particular role and can bring up any argument at all whether it is in the play or not. With a really stubborn Shylock, this

141

exercise can soon generate a gratifying exasperation or at least an intensity of commitment. It also works well with the teacher being Shylock and the class attacking him en masse. He may prefer not to wait until such remedial treatment is necessary and decide to use the method as a lead-in to work on the scene. As a guide to the tone and atmosphere of the scene itself, the exercise, however used, is too crude a device. What one could expect of it is that it will allow pupils to experience the concern the central conflict can arouse and to focus their attention on this as a conflict between people and on the words as something they use to achieve an end.

If the teacher wishes to use the tavern set-up to approach the play more directly, he will have to change the rules. He must allocate roles to those without them (e.g. the roles of Duke, Bassanio, Gratiano and Antonio – and also, if the anachronism doesn't bother him, Portia). It will be necessary to establish with groups of Bassanios, Antonios, etc., what type of person their name part is as defined up to the beginning of the trial scene and his frame of mind at that point, and to discover any identifiable objectives the character may have. The exasperation most will have felt in the earlier exercise will now probably seem more appropriate to Gratiano than to Antonio, who seems resigned to his fate. As a free improvisation, this could bring its own creative rewards but I must confess that, as an approach to the text, Fifth Formers with whom I tried it found it too sophisticated and difficult. A free improvisation can develop under the dynamic of the actors playing the parts and can go where it will: for present purposes, the mode by which the Christians can succeed is strictly determined, and, unless Portia artificially restrains herself, the improvisation can be over before it's really begun. It is the formality of the court procedure and the circumstances of Portia's disguise which allow the events to unfold the way they do.

Discussion between characters in pairs presents fewer complications, especially if it involves retrospective comment on events they have witnessed or taken part in. If Eisenring, the sinister fire raiser in *The Fire Raisers* by Max Frisch, gives an account to Schmitz, his partner, of his earlier encounter with Biedermann, their gullible prospective victim, the actor who plays him can clarify his ideas on his character's behaviour and his relationship with Biedermann and gain valuable insight into the subtext. It also forces him to react to the stimulus of a Schmitz as Eisenring might react. Ideally, of course, he is describing an actual encounter with a person playing Biedermann, explored in a classroom workshop.

There may be some objections that this encourages the pupils to identify too completely with a particular viewpoint and this seems to me to be an objection that can be raised to most improvised work of this kind. Eisenring may be satirising on our behalf, but suppose we improvised a discussion between the self-deceiving Biedermann and his compliant wife, Babette? Suppose the original play requires that the actor not merely present the character but conspire with an audience to ridicule or criticise him? To get too fond of Shylock might be to distort the experience of the drama. Presentation of the pair's conversation to an audience might be necessary to ensure that they retained the spirit of the play.

A method which allows the teacher to exercise some manner of control over this is the interview. Instead of having the characters quiz each other, he interviews them individually himself. I think for this to work, everybody needs to know where he is in the play at the time of the interview. In a film of a workshop on *Macbeth*, conducted with Fifth Formers at the Cockpit Theatre in London, a mike was thrust at various anonymous 'members of the public' and they were asked 'Who killed Duncan?' Some gave answers appropriate to a student of the play who knows all the secrets; some pretended they thought the grooms had done it; some said they thought Macbeth had done it because of his suspicious behaviour at the banquet. The exercise would have been more coherent and meaningful if the students had been asked to comment retrospectively, as observers, on the events of the scene where Duncan's murder is discovered (which we have looked at earlier). Better still, they could assume the roles of the participants and reply in character. This again is easier if they have made some practical engagement with the roles and it also allows them to incorporate the conditions of the performance into their answers. Pupils representing Malcolm and Donalbain could be caught before their 'characters' leave the country and asked what they fear and on what evidence. Macbeth might be asked to commit himself on the subject of his true feelings, the pupil representing Lady Macbeth to tell us whether she really fainted or merely pretended to do so, and if the latter is the case what it was that prompted the action. Banquo's comments might reveal what the pupil sees as being behind his controlled exterior. When Macduff said: "Wherefore did you so?", what did he mean exactly? There is, of course, a danger of indulging in academic speculation and motive hunting, but one might say in defence of the method that an actor would need to have an answer to at least some of the questions before he could play the part, or that it could help him to have an answer. The aim of the teacher should be to help his pupils not so much to learn 'facts about' the characters as to see how they work. If there is no answer in simple psychological terms to why an effect is created, it is up to him not to press for one. An actor might object to having to verbalise everything in any case. An actress playing Lady Macbeth might answer that the reason she faints depends partly on what the actor playing Macbeth does. The teacher needs to remind himself that the interview is not an end in itself.

The kind of interview we have been describing is in one sense private and in another sense public. What we have done is create a format in which useful exploration of the buried life of a play can take place. The characters think they are speaking in confidence and can tell all; the pupils know that what they say is open to the scrutiny of other pupils who are in fact getting the benefit of non-existent soliloquies. In acting as interviewer the teacher lends his authority to the rules of the game, but if he is satisfied that these are established he might delegate the job to a pupil. The interview format in itself has the advantage of being a ritual with which all pupils are familiar from their listening to radio and watching TV. The completely public kind of interview or the talk-back also have their uses. Supposing, after the trial scene in *The Merchant of Venice*, the participants are seated in a row and the class ranged in an arc before them. The 'participants' would preferably be pupils who have had some experience of playing the parts. The teacher or form compère welcomes them to Talk-Back, the programme where the audience asks the questions, and says they have in the studio the people involved in the trial whose result was reported in press and news bulletins recently. He introduces the characters by name and invites questions about their attitudes and conduct which the characters have to answer. He can build into the procedure the rule that only questions which can be answered from the play are permitted and only answers which can be made on the same basis. The public nature of the interviewing may make the characters hide behind a public mask, but probing can be done by allowing a certain amount of forensic interplay among the characters, barbed references to hidden motives. Another rule of the game is that the teacher can substitute other Shylocks or Antonios

144

etc. at will. The difference between the present exercise and that of straight discussion is that we are not here concerned so much with talking about character as with exploring the limits of attitudes and stances. If the interviewees perform with reasonable competence, Talk-Back can generate considerable imaginative excitement. The characters step briefly out of the remoteness of their imaginary setting into what is, for the pupils, a reassuringly familiar one; and if this makes them in the smallest degree more accessible it will have contributed something valuable. Once again the hope is that the benefits of the exercise can be fed back into future work on the scene, especially practical work.

Another format one might adopt is the tribunal. Four interrogators interview, say, participants in the scandalous events in Bohemia which take place in the early part of *The Winter's Tale*. They are encouraged to pin the characters down to what they actually did and said and witnessed, querying the value of hearsay evidence as it comes up. As each new victim comes forward, a new panel is substituted. The teacher, here, is arbitrator and stage manager. Once again he will be concerned to see that all the questions are relevant and can be answered according to the nature of the play. The legalistic framework is really a convention for stimulating searching exploration. This device also isolates the witnesses and allows them to tell the court what they might not want their fellow characters to hear. Needless to say, everybody must be crystal clear what point in the play they have reached. Keith Dewhurst's TV play, *Last Bus* (*Scene Scripts*, Longman) shows an incident involving violence on a bus and ends by having both the perpetrators and the witnesses interviewed. Here the teacher could ask the pupils to improvise the interviewing for themselves or use the original interviews as an inspiration for their own future work along these lines.

Analogies

Drawing analogies between the familiar and unfamiliar is something which teachers do for pupils and which pupils do for themselves as a natural part of the educative process. There is no pretence that the familiar is the equivalent of the unfamiliar in all respects; a degree of abstraction is accepted as part of the game. The reassurance of the known makes the unknown easier and more attractive to assimilate. Once this has happened, of course, the formerly unknown will modify the nature of the known.

In working with scripted drama, some teachers prefer to let the text make its own impact; some believe that it is valuable to draw parallels overtly and explicitly. Usually a teacher (and probably a director) will find it sufficient merely to suggest a parallel to a pupil (or actor) or to help him to find one for himself and then to leave it to germinate. A class may find it difficult to identify with Richard II when he suffers on account of his deposition. A teacher who had spotted the following cutting might use it to show that in one sense Richard wasn't unique:

Muhammad Ali's fear of losing again to Ken Norton has little to do with fighting. To him, being who he is outweighs even the possible reclamation of his world heavyweight title from George Foreman, and he knows that a second defeat by an opponent he has denigrated as a preliminary fighter would cost him not only his credibility, but his identity.

This is why Ali has driven himself to quite extraordinary lengths to recover, as far as the years will permit, the sort of physical condition of his early days as a champion. It is also why he turned angrily on the fight's promoter and a hand-ful of pressmen in the foyer of the Marriot Hotel here soon after his arrival and snapped: 'You all want to see me beaten. Once my black ass is whipped, you won't need me any more.'

The few non-Muslims close to Ali say he is terrified, after more than a decade as perhaps the world's most instantly-recognisable celebrity, of becoming an ordinary human being again. Losing to Norton at the Inglewood Forum on Monday would see him devalued instantly as a fighter and reduced to the ranks of the mortal.

(Alan Hubbard in *The Observer*, Sept. 1973)

Sometimes, though, the teacher may decide that it is useful for the pupils (as might a director for his actors) to act out their analogical element. For an audience, a director might try to engineer the shock of recognition by transposing the whole of a classic play into a modern setting.

Probably the most common procedure among teachers is to attempt to find a parallel for the dramatic situation: the characters, their dilemma and the events they take part in. Parallels are drawn with the actual or accessible personal experience of the pupil or with imaginable or reported contemporary experience. Of the two, the former would seem to be educationally more attractive, but there are difficulties and dangers with both. It is easy to get exclusively absorbed in the improvisation and then find that the text, when approached, fails to trigger off the emotions and thoughts that have been rehearsed. Indeed, the one may prove a distraction from the other. The analogical situation can too easily fall short of the original in dimension, or it can prove to be as remote to the pupils as the original seemed to be. If the teacher over-simplifies, the variables will assume as much importance as the common elements, and if he tries to make the analogy relevant at all conceivable points, he may end up producing something artificially complicated. Complications which were acceptable in the original because of the mode and conventions of the play can become a restriction and an intrusion in the analogical situation.

Another drawback is that the business of finding parallels can absorb a disproportionate amount of time and energy, especially if the teacher does the job properly and invites the pupils to share in the search. Should he decide to construct the parallel entirely on his own, it could be objected that he is merely challenging the pupils to discover what he, the teacher, has discovered already and not to go exploring on their own account. Certainly this is a fair objection to using the analogy as an introduction to a text rather than as a means of stepping back and taking a fresh look at it. Even when the analogy doesn't quite work, though, there is one consolatory recourse open to the teacher. He can ask the pupils to identify the inaccuracies and thus hope that the features of the original situation will become clearer. This is a somewhat cerebral exercise, but it must be admitted that unless the relevance of the analogy is in some way appreciated by the pupils the activity will have lost its point. As with all methods, the teacher must decide what he can expect from both the approach and the class, capitalise on his gains and cut his losses.

I was involved with some student teachers in conducting a workshop on the trial scene from *The Merchant of Venice* for a class of Fifth Formers. We wanted an exercise which would allow us to investigate the workings of Portia's mind and decided to look for a situation nearer home which would serve as a model. Let me confess at the outset that circumstances forced us to devise the exercise independently of the pupils and thus we courted the danger outlined above, namely that we would be doing the investigating for them. But we hoped that the improvisation would provide an inspiration to the participants to consider the available possibilities. The problem would be presented in terms of how to play the role of Portia — and, incidentally, how to play the role of Shylock.

What we had was a person in authority who knew something to an accuser's disadvantage and an accuser who was unreasonably anxious to bring a third to justice while deserving of punishment himself. We looked for a possible situation within the compass of the pupils' own experience. School was something they all knew something about and it had a recognisable structure of authority. What would constitute a serious misdemeanour in such a setting? Theft? Suppose, then, Pupil A steals a watch from Pupil B and weeks later it is stolen from him in his turn. Self-righteously he goes to the Head to complain and to urge that the unknown culprit be severely punished. What A does not know is that the watch has really been taken by B (in the changing room of the gym?) who was simply retrieving his own property. B has told the Head this, so that when A marches in demanding justice, the Head is forearmed.

In structure the similarities to *The Merchant* are fairly obvious. What is missing, though, is the whole build-up that the play enjoys. The psychology of A as it stood was difficult to grasp, and it proved easier to accept his self-righteousness if he had actually found the watch in the first place and only 'stolen' it in the sense of keeping it. But this does diminish his criminality and alter his deserts. In fact, a major difficulty with the whole operation was ensuring that the issues and penalties approximated in significance in the eyes of the participants to those of the Shakespeare scene. This is, of course, a matter of involving the pupils and making them care, an exercise in personal relations.

As a free improvisation, this school scene can work very well. The class is divided into thieves and Head-teachers, they are briefed separately and then put together in pairs. The Head has a genuine problem to solve and there are a variety of ways in which he can wield his authority. He may decide to give Pupil A enough rope to hang himself and he may not. The snag is that for the parallel with *The Merchant* to hold, he must. The teacher (and pupil) is faced with the further problem of finding a reason why the Head would delay which would appear 'natural' to the improviser. Even the 'Heads' that did manage this failed to touch on the notion of 'mercy'; failed, that is, to establish A's lack of mercy so as to tax him with it later. They became bogged down with other issues, as the following transcript illustrates:

A: Now the point is he deserves caning. That is the logical punishment for stealing. I want this lad caned.

Head: Are you certain it was the same person who stole the watch?

A: That is immaterial. The point is that this watch has been stolen by this lad and he must be punished for it.

Head: How do you know this boy has stolen the watch?
A: He has been seen.
Head: Who has seen him steal the watch?
A: I myself.
Head: I would like to see all the other people who say they've seen him steal it.
A: You will see them in time.

(Recorded by one of my students, Mr David Gregg)

Possibly I refined the analogy too far but unless the two parts touch at a sufficient number of points, the improvised situation fails to function as a model. From playing A, the pupils did have an insight into double-think and from playing B some of them became aware of the temptations (e.g. to indulge in sadism) that face a person in Portia's position, having, as she does, the Ace up her sleeve. But I feel that the labour of constructing the exercise was out of proportion with the gains. The analogy proved hard for the pupils to see. It didn't help the weaker pupils as it is often claimed analogies do.

Even with the roles the pupils can recognise and a situation they can envisage as existing, then, there is hard work to be done securing their emotional commitment and their awareness of the purpose of the exercise. The film I mentioned of the Cockpit Theatre's workshop on *Macbeth* showed a role-play exercise designed to investigate the forces that drove Macbeth. The pupils were divided into groups and asked to imagine they were members of a sports club, the kind to be decided by the group. They were also asked to designate two of their number to be captain and treasurer. The season had been a successful one, owing largely to the efforts of the captain who had enthused and disciplined everybody. It was now time to choose the captain for the coming season and although the incumbent could be re-elected, he was not forced to be. The treasurers from each group were then briefed separately. They had done all they could, they were told, to help and support the captain but their one ambition was to be captain themselves. Their problem was to persuade the other members of the club to elect them as captain. They could use any means, honest or dishonest: as treasurer, for instance, they might suggest that the present captain had been cooking the books.

In the group we focused on, a highly vociferous young lady skilfully managed to irritate and provoke her group into a vigorous argument by the sheer power of her personality. Whether this gave the pupils an insight into Macbeth's 'ambitions' is another matter. The analogy is in many ways an ill-fitting one. Macbeth is engaged neither in discrediting Duncan nor in persuading other people to elect him, himself. In the example we saw, the girl (in role) was impelled by ruthless self-interest. To impute such motivation to Macbeth could be to over-simplify or even distort. One might argue that the context in which ambition in *Macbeth* can be said to operate is very specific and that the notion encouraged by the analogy was too generalised. Macbeth belongs to a warrior society in which military ambition is held to be a virtue and it is not merely 'ambition' as such which is his undoing. Emotionally the pupils doing the improvisation might be rehearsing feelings which just might help them act out certain moments of the play with greater conviction but it seems to me very hit-or-miss, given the terms in which the exercise is set up.

The sports club setting is still within the compass of a pupil's own experience. Once one steps outside this compass, one adds another stage to the process. David Rostron, in an article in *The Use of English*, recommends role playing as an approach to scenes from *Richard II*. He instances the scene between the dying Gaunt and Richard, where Gaunt points out to the young king the error of his ways. Richard becomes a young managing director of a firm; Gaunt, still an elderly and sick uncle, becomes a long-serving director. The 'character' of the young director is closely modelled on that of the king and that of the uncle on Gaunt's. Also spelled out are the attitudes to each other. The problem for the older man is to persuade the other to acknowledge and repent of his waywardness. The pupils start from dossiers supplied on work cards, a method which makes a powerful impact difficult to achieve. The analogy itself is ingenious, but it is other aspects of the exercise about which I have reservations. Few pupils can have any direct knowledge of the world of managing directors. What indirect knowledge most of them will have access to will probably come from a television series such as *The Brothers*. The abrasive manner and language which pass for dramatic conflict in that seem to me hardly likely to prove useful in arriving at a personal understanding of Shakespeare's scene.

In discussing *Mother Courage*, I described how I asked the pupils to invent a 'missing scene' between the soldiers who, in the text, were attempting to persuade Kattrin to come down off the roof of the barn, and their irate Colonel. The problem had been that the pupils did not appear to understand the soldiers' desperation. Another method I tried in tackling this problem was to ask the pupils to act out a scene in a modern war setting, thinking that this might seem more familiar to them than the Thirty Years War. The situation was devised by the class and me in collaboration. Kattrin became a member of the French Resistance who had taken prisoner a local Gauleiter and was holding him prisoner in a building. German soldiers surrounded the place and it was vital to them that they rescued the prisoner alive. The prisoner was, of course, a new element with no precise equivalent in the Brecht, unless one fancies it was really the Colonel paraded as a living reminder of the failure the soldiers dreaded. The surrounded building had weaknesses insofar as it made practical stratagems possible to the Germans, where the Catholic soldiers in Brecht were faced with the bleak prospect of being able to stop the noise only by making a bigger noise. We therefore refined the improvisation by placing the girl and her prisoner in the centre of a circle and the soldiers around the perimeter. We made a rule that the soldiers could try whatever pleas, threats or arguments they liked but could not trespass inside the circle. If they did, they were 'dead'. This, I think, worked well in the sense that it secured much personal involvement and inspired much ingenuity. The particular context defined the kind of approach that could be made but the activity was fun enough to take their minds off the possible remoteness even of this situation. It seems odd to discuss success in these terms when the Second World War setting was chosen originally for its greater accessibility. But the exercise, in its modified form, took on some of the abstraction and structured quality of a game and seemed, thereby, to fulfil different functions. An observable benefit now was that it called into play the resources of the body. At least they could see that an actress playing Kattrin would need to respond to what she saw as well as what she heard and that the actors playing the soldiers would need to support their verbal onslaught with appealing facial expressions and with gesture.

A less ambitious use of analogy, which for this very reason can be more easily successful, occurs when a parallel is drawn not with a whole situation but with a dramatic element, a feature of the style, or an aspect of dramatic method or technique. If one wanted to illustrate the fact that the people in Genet's *The Balcony* are undergoing an experience which is not the property of freaks, in fact that we, too, adopt roles according to the circumstances we find ourselves in, it could be profitable to act out, say, a scene in a restaurant showing how a waiter behaves in the presence of his customers and contrasting it with his behaviour before his boss or his fellow workers.

To show how a scene or a play builds up to a climax; an improvisation of a scene building to an obvious, known point, such as an execution; or a scene where an important event is expected within a known time (a bomb about to explode); can provide a starting point for an investigation of structure. The Cockpit Theatre film showed work on the supernatural atmosphere of *Macbeth* which involved the pupils in constructing their own spells and ceremonials. When working on Chekhov, the pupils might be alerted to the presence of subtext by inviting them to construct a scene of their own in which there are checks which prevent them from speaking their minds. Suppose Dad comes home after a hard day's work to find that his wife has been busy with her Women's Institute affairs and has neglected to cook the evening meal, and that his mother-in-law is ensconced in his favourite chair. The mother-in-law is the kind of person one cannot bully or argue with and the husband and wife do not want to quarrel in front of her. One could refine the situation further by restricting the conversation to the subject of the weather. Any meanings for the audience must be got over by the tone of voice, pause and gesture. Suppose a class is working on *Tartuffe* and needs to appreciate how the humour might work. Tartuffe seems to show one face to Elmire, another to the audience. Suppose we construct a scene where somebody is very busy and is being pestered by a neighbour but wants him or her to go. Are there any similarities, one can ask, between the way the humour works in our scene and the way Molière's works? Let us investigate the way Chekhov breaks the news of the Baron's death to Irena in *Three Sisters* by trying out ourselves the delivery of bad news in another context.

Acting out analogical situations may not offer as much as we might hope in the way of direct or detailed insights into a text, and it may not guarantee emotional involvement in the predicaments of the original characters, but if all it does is to stimulate pupils to take a fresh look at what had gone stale or was proving intractable, supply the reassurance of the familiar and remind pupils of the many-faceted nature of dramatic activity and of the personal resources that wait to be called upon, it will repay a tactful introduction from time to time.

Games and exercises

Games and 'Warm-up' exercises are widely used in Developmental Drama, sometimes as ends in themselves to further the growth of a range of personal attributes and sometimes as preparation or toning-up before more adventurous work on improvised situations. Games themselves involve a degree of improvisation but there are agreed objectives and rules for attaining them. As Viola Spolin puts it:

Ingenuity and inventiveness appear to meet any crisis the game presents, for it is understood during playing that a player is free to reach the game's objectives in any style he chooses. As long as he abides by the rules of the game, he may swing, stand on his head, or fly through the air. In fact, any unusual or extra-ordinary way of playing is loved and applauded by his fellow players.

(P. 5)

Any teacher of drama will readily attest to the high spirits released by games. Many will also agree that the structure of the game helps to channel and control the euphoric energy, although some will, with justification, admit to being glad that they were around to guarantee that the rules were enforced.

Insofar as games fulfil the general purpose of Developmental Drama, insofar, that is, as they mobilise resources of mind, body and imagination, they do useful groundwork for the teacher tackling scripts. Insofar as students playing games combine personal freedom with an acceptance of limitations, they are gaining experience not totally different in kind from that of the actor working with a text. 'The acceptance of all imposed limitations creates the playing, out of which the game appears, or as in the theater, the scene.' (Spolin, p. 6.) The skills developed by the playing of games have been recognised by directors such as Joan Littlewood and teacher/actors such as Clive Barker as valuable to the actor in his general training. For Barker, their attraction is that they 'take the pressure off the actor', freeing him from the self-conscious preoccupation with acquiring 'technique' and allowing him to develop those very resources we have mentioned in connection with the student in the classroom.

In any particular session, a classroom teacher of scripted drama may have varying motives for choosing games. He may need to create a general atmosphere conducive to profitable work, and the advantage of games is, of course, that they can involve everybody. Thus if he deems the class just arrived looks as if it has had a surfeit of cere-bration, he may decide to offer it a game involving energetic physical movement (such as 'Tag'). On another occasion, the class may be badly in need of self-discipline and physical self-control and he may decide to play a game which mainly depends on mental alertness, for example, a word-association game, or verbal tennis.

A snag about opening a lesson on scripted drama with a game of this sort is that it can sometimes — for the student at least — seem curiously isolated. The explosion of fun appears to do nothing to improve the enjoyment of the work which follows and the game may seem to do nothing to illuminate the playtext. The teacher does not have to pander to demands for obvious relevance, although personally I feel it pays to come clean with pupils and tell them, if possible, why I do what I do. But if he can choose games which exercise skills he can relate directly to the particular text, it can provide him with a useful motivational bonus. This applies not merely to games which introduce a lesson but to games which involve a momentary stepping aside from textual work.

Personally I feel that if the teacher looks to games to provide revolutionary intellectual insights he will be disappointed. They may or may not help the actor rehearse relevant feeling, but they can help him form a vivid image of some aspect of the play. The transition from the conditions of the game to those of the play may not be as easy as we hope, but at least games can provide a valuable impetus to further investigation. This is where we, as educationalists, are entitled to invoke in our pupils the powers of reflection. The purpose and usefulness of the game itself can be discussed. If the game fails to do justice to the form and nature of the text, pupils can be invited to modify it or invent a better game of their own. One needs to decide what one can reasonably expect of a game and settle gratefully for that. My own improvisatory work on Scene Eleven of *Mother Courage* (described on pages 150–1) took on the features of a game, but the benefits I think the class derived (in the context of working on a text) were limited to an awareness of the pressures of physical confrontation to which Kattrin is subjected and an awareness on the part of students playing the soldiers of the fact that there was psychological pressure from above and that this should be taken into account.

Choosing and devising games involves a judgement as to the style and mode of the play and a decision as to which feature or aspect of the play will repay investigation by these means. The games I have so far been referring to have been competitive games. Clive Barker unashamedly confesses that his main source is the games played by children outside the classroom. Some children's games are competitive but another recurrent component is that of ritual and ceremonial. Drama, too, may involve both conflict and formality of procedure. The competition often supplies the motive and the activity exercises the skill, but perhaps the pupils' prior experience of ceremonial might be something else on which the teacher can capitalise when the nature of the play seems to require it.

A game I have used in exploring the themes and relationships in *King Lear* is a game of blindness and trust. The room is strewn with obstacles, one pupil is blindfolded and two others shout instructions as to which way he should move. One voice can be relied on to steer him clear of the obstacles, the other deliberately misleads him. He learns by bitter experience which he can trust, but half way through, the voices swop functions and once again he is confused. The usefulness of the emotional charge in identifying Lear's state of mind can be tested and the similarity of this situation to Lear's predicament with his daughters can be discussed.

The *Lear* game is probably better known in a slightly different form as a concentration game, where one half of the class pairs up with the other and one member of each pair yells instructions to his blindfolded partner at the same time as everybody else does the same. The theory is that if you can concentrate with all that to distract you, concentration on acting holds no terrors. A concentration game, though, can also be a useful introduction to practical work on Chekhov. To Stanislavsky, the involvement of the actor in his role was the prime factor enabling the spectator to become involved in the play, and this part of his system is recognised as being particularly helpful with naturalistic drama. A class is divided into pairs, and each narrates an anecdote — something that happened to him recently, perhaps — but the participants do this simultaneously. The object of the game is to see if each individual can keep his mind in the first place on his own story. Afterwards he tries to concentrate not merely on his own story but on that of his partner, to listen, that is, and not to listen. The test is whether, at the end, he can tell his partner the gist of his (the partner's) anecdote. The opening scene of *Three Sisters* shows the heroines deeply preoccupied with their own troubles and frustrations but having one ear cocked for the self-exposition of the others. The actress must emphasise the individual viewpoint and at the same time contribute to the common atmosphere. The object of playing the game is to create a vivid definition of the task the actress faces.

Clive Barker uses a game, which I have seen him conduct, to focus the minds of actors and actresses on the intrigue which is at the heart of Restoration Comedy. His aim, as with all his games, is also to divert the attention of the participants from the mere externals of technique (a temptation in working on very stylised comedy) and provide them with a framework within which they will be motivated to succeed. He describes 'The Restoration Comedy Game' as follows:

In this game we work through the touch conflict and coin games to a more finely structured game. There are two players, a man and a woman.

The woman has the money in her hand. She is an heiress, and the money represents her dowry. It is her means of attracting a 'good' husband, someone who, in appearance and behaviour, is worthy of her. She must get him to woo her, and her objective is to manoeuvre him into such a position that she can trap one of his arms under hers. This is taken as a metaphor for dragging him off from town to a country house in Northamptonshire to settle down. To do this she must take risks with her money. If she holds too tightly to the cash he will not woo her, or his job will be made difficult. If she reveals her intention by directly trying to trap his arm he will be repelled by the danger.

The prospective husband is a younger son, accustomed to wearing the right clothes, drinking and gambling at the most fashionable clubs, racing with Old Rowley on Newmarket Heath, being seen and admired on the streets and at the theatre. To do this he needs money, which he hasn't got. He must charm and woo the girl to gain her dowry. In order to use the money for his own purposes, he must avoid, at all costs, being trapped by the arm. No words are allowed, but sounds may be used. At the start there are no other rules.

The game can be played a number of ways. It is usually best, at first, simply to let the players discover what they can in the playing. Later the game can be stopped whenever either player makes a mistake; if the man, for instance, is seen grabbing for the money, he loses dignity and is no longer an eligible husband. Slowly the discipline or rule conventions of the period can be fed in. In every age there are conventions of behaviour, for example in the areas of the body one can touch. In this way a gradual and detailed pattern of social behaviour is built up.

Sometimes, the player is allowed to continue after making a mistake to see what ways he finds of recovering from it. Human beings have made social gaffes in all ages and places, and the drama is full of situations which exploit this human failing. Sometimes, the game is set up like a relay race with a succession of wooers and heiresses taking over the roles, to try to sustain some development by capitalising on what they have observed in other players, and putting their observations to the test of practice.

Playing the game goes hand in hand with study and scholarship. Objective knowledge, gained from a study of the play and its social setting, is put into direct practice and used. What usually emerges from the playing is the general pattern of Restoration movement. The actual purposes of the movements and actions are constantly disguised and transformed into elegant gestures of wooing and deportment, producing light, airy, extravagant movements in space of the whole body and the limbs. In this way the movement style emerges directly from the actors' investigation of character and situation, and ceases to be an artificial mode through which he expresses his work.

It may not be possible to relate the actions and the objectives directly to a specific situation in a Restoration Comedy, but if one gets from the game and the manner of playing it some vivid impression of the social mores which determine the style of the play, one will have progressed a little beyond the surface sparkle of the dialogue. In *The Way of the World*, Mirabel is after Millamant's money, but he acts circumspectly not because he is afraid Millamant will trap him but because he needs to win Lady Wishfort's approval of the match. Millamant wants him, but is not using her wiles against him but with him against her aunt. For students working on this relationship, the main benefit offered by the game in its present form is an experience of intrigue in action. Mr Barker himself favours both flexibility and adaptability. 'The main rules of the game can be changed according to the situation and period one wants to investigate ... The main game is then a general springboard for a more complex situation' (p. 131).

Mr Barker, as I have said, often makes use of well-known children's games. They have the advantage for children of familiarity but will need to be 'sold' to older pupils, who may feel it is time they put such things away. Mr Barker sees Macbeth's predicament when he says:

> They have tied me to a stake; I cannot fly
> But bear-like I must fight the course

as being not dissimilar to that of the victim in 'Bull in the Ring'. This person has to try to get out of a circle of hand-clasping tormentors who keep closing any gaps that he may aim for. The game can certainly create exasperation: in fact, even with adult students, I have seen it create genuine anxiety. Such a raw emotional state is not necessarily the best preparation for understanding the feelings defined by the play. The teacher needs to handle situations like this to focus the minds of the participants on the usefulness of the game in transforming the image in the play into movement and testing the usefulness of that process in helping the actor create the effect.

Another game attempting to create an image of Macbeth's state of mind, this time of his indecision, failed for me for different reasons. It was devised by a team at the Cockpit Theatre and was shown in the film I mentioned. The class were divided into three groups, Toms, Dicks and Harrys. The Toms and the Harrys were briefed together. They were to attempt to persuade the Dicks to come to them and were entitled to use any means of persuasion they liked without actually moving. The Dicks were to listen carefully to the merits of the arguments or blandishments of the Toms and Harrys. Then the class were arranged in three lines containing equal numbers of pupils, the Toms and Harrys on the outside, the Dicks in the middle. When I tried the game I found that the weakness lay in the way the rules were formulated. The scope seemed so wide that the temptations were offered and listened to with no great conviction. By the time Tom offered a million, million pounds and Harry offered a million, million, million pounds, any hope of believability was long since left behind. Given detailed personal knowledge of Dick on the part of Tom and Harry, some credible offer might have been made, but limitations would have to be built into the game. Even if the persuasions had had substance in them, though, the usefulness of the 'image' created to the study of Macbeth's indecision would be questionable. Is he really pulled two ways by similar kinds of appeal? Is he pulled towards righteousness by its voluptuous attractions or is it that he is at least partly repelled from evil by the fear of being found out? Is the game, on the whole, worth the trouble?

In discussing *The Caretaker* earlier, we noticed that movement and gesture were written in as an important vehicle for the meaning and suggested that a possible strategy for approaching such a text was for the class to select episodes of 'pure' movement, as a starting point. Even stage 'games', such as the one where Aston and Mick tease Davies by depriving him of his bag, can be slow in the rehearsal. A children's game such as 'Pig in the Middle', played in threes with the 'pig' attempting to intercept a missile thrown from one outside partner to the other, captures something of the spirit of Pinter's action and gives the players some inkling of the pace and effect they will be striving to achieve eventually. It is, as it turns out, a relatively crude substitute as far as detail goes, since the relationships of the 'outsiders' to the 'pig' in Pinter's play are not simply those of conspirators and victim. The ways in which they differ, the extent to which, for instance, Aston tries to help Davies, can be an instructive source of insight. Another non-verbal feature of *The Caretaker* which has impact for actors and audience is the setting. The jumble of odds and ends in the room are a direct expression of the acquisitiveness of Aston and a source of humour with the bewilderment they cause in Davies. In a classroom, it is unlikely that the students will be able to muster a Buddha, a gas stove or beds, for instance, and these will have to be imagined or simulated. I have used a 'place' game, borrowed from Viola Spolin, to good effect. Students are divided into groups of two or three and they are asked to imagine a setting, roles for themselves and a reason for being there. They choose half a dozen different objects or features that are prominent in that place, agree where they are on stage, and then act out a situation which involves each of them touching, handling or using the objects but must show by the actions they do and by their physical awareness of 'place' what the objects are and what the setting is like. The rest of the class are then allowed to guess all the unknowns and to comment on the performance. The students in my class did a brilliant mime of two men working on a building site. I found that afterwards the class attacked the Pinter with a lively sense of the way characters can interact with their surroundings and the importance, in the 'poor' theatre of the classroom, of clear, expressive action.

With *Waiting for Godot* actions are also important, but these are often of a grotesque and stylised kind. Beckett recommends, for instance, that the tramps become 'grotesquely rigid' at one point. While youngsters will be as uninhibited as you like, self-conscious adolescents and adult students may find it difficult to sacrifice their dignity. One way of helping them to relax is to play a game such as 'Statues'. One person is 'on' and he stands facing the wall with his back to the class. At a signal they start to creep up on him, and whenever he turns they freeze. Anyone who moves is out. The object of the game is to be first to touch the back of the person who is on. It is amazing what strange postures the 'statues' find themselves in but they have adopted them without intending to or realising they have done so. Adopting an exaggerated receptive posture when the teacher says Vladimir's line "Listen!" is not quite so difficult after that.

There is an episode in *The Second Shepherds Play* where Mak has to steal the sheep from the sleeping shepherds. A point we made earlier about this play was that, although the main impact is comic, there are potentially dangerous or tragic elements in it. The penalty for sheep-stealing was hanging. The movements of the thief must express this awareness. When I did a workshop on this play with second year pupils, I noticed that no 'Mak' had sufficient control of his movements at this point. A game known as 'Keeper of the Keys' filled the bill. In this, a player sits on a chair blindfolded and at his feet is a bunch of keys. Around him in a circle sit the rest of the class. At a signal from the teacher, one of these players moves stealthily in to take the keys without being noticed. If he is heard, the blindfolded player points in his direction and if the pointing is accurate the 'thief' sits down again. Within the framework of the game the 'thief' has a strong and real motivation to be quiet and

159

controlled. This motivation may lack the threat of death but the physical carefulness which is rehearsed in this way is at least a starting point for working on the state of mind of Mak; it can create conditions in which a relevant performance can grow.

Another class may have difficulty not merely with controlling movement but with controlling the whole mood of a scene. It may, for example, have difficulty in keeping its poker face when doing the actions and saying the words of Ionesco's *Rhinoceros*. The same may apply to comedy in a play such as *Tartuffe*, but in the 'absurdist' drama the strain may be greater in view of the patently ludicrous things the actors are asked to do or say. The poker face in *Rhinoceros* is necessary, not merely to get the laughs from an audience, but to reinforce the serious implication that people do not see or will not see the stupidity and pointlessness of what they do. Away gallops Mr Boeuf, the former clerk, who has become a rhinoceros, and he carries his wife, who has leapt down a broken staircase onto his back. "They're moving fast," says Berenger. "Ever done any riding?" says Dudard, casually to his boss, Papillon. "A bit . . . a long time ago . . . " replies Papillon. The problem for the players in a game called 'The Court of the Holy Dido' approximates closely to that of the comic actor and there are penalties for the person who fails. The court consists of a circle of players, sitting with arms folded, and is under the authority of a President. The other players are known as brothers and sisters and each is given a number. The rule is that nobody shall move a muscle or make a noise and certainly not smile. Anybody seeing another brother or sister breaking this rule can raise his hand and accuse him. The President then decides if punishment shall be administered, and if it shall he must decide what form it shall take. The alternatives are strokes on the upper deck (hand) or on the lower deck (backside) with a rolled up newspaper called the Holy Dido. The challenge for the players is to keep a straight face while the ridiculous ritual proceeds. In my experience, the game is more fairly administered if the teacher becomes the President. Otherwise personal vendettas take over or players succumb to exhibitionism and deliberately flout the rules. 'Poor Pussy' is easier to set up and easier to manage if the need is to exercise the class in controlling their reactions. A 'pussy' in the middle of a circle does comic feline antics while the observers are permitted only the solemn comment: "Poor pussy!" Clive Barker found that 'Holy Dido' has further uses as a rehearsal for comic court scenes. N.F. Simpson's *One Way Pendulum* contains just a scene which can appeal to youngsters.

A class working on Brecht plays such as *He Who Says Yes* and *He Who Says No* may find the didacticism, the blatant invitation to reflect or discuss, a difficult style to capture, especially if they have been attempting largely naturalistic 'involvement' situations. A game such as charades, or a game in which groups act out proverbs which the audience guesses, can throw attention onto the 'showing' aspect of acting and presentation and the need for clarity of 'point'. These games can usefully be played for fun at the beginning of a lesson but a game such as the one which evolved from my improvisatory work on Scene Eleven of *Mother Courage* is probably best used as the opportunity suggests itself, since it homes in on the particular problem presented by a particular situation.

Games can be used in tackling a wide range of acting and production problems in the classroom. The pupil who finds it hard to convey a feeling of where Macbeth has just been when he returns from Duncan's bedroom, in the scene we examined, might be helped by a game in which volunteers are allowed to enter a stage area conveying, purely by movement and gesture, as much information as possible about who they are, where they have come from and what the stage represents for them, while the rest of the class guess the details. Knocking on the door by someone outside can convey to an audience what sort of a mood the knocker is in, what kind of response he hopes to provoke and something about the kind of circumstances in which he imagines himself. This game provides a useful rehearsal for the creation of the same sound effect in *Macbeth*. In a scene like the trial scene from *The Merchant of Venice*, the director (part of a class or the leader of a group) may be faced with the problem of placing the actors at the beginning. The formal arrangement of the court will make some of the decisions for him but can he indicate emotional relationships and preferences by the way he disposes his actors in space? A game of 'Hunt the Thimble', where one player leaves the room and is encouraged or discouraged by the rest saying "Warm!" or "Cold!" depending on whether he approaches or withdraws from it, might suggest to the director a principle he might experiment with. Shall he isolate Shylock? Put Bassanio and Gratiano near to Antonio? Does he think the Duke is strictly impartial? If so or if not, how can he indicate this in visual terms? An elementary principle, perhaps, but the game can show to the young director that space can be expressive of warmth or coldness of feeling.

Distinguishing between a game and an exercise is somewhat academic and for some purposes pointless, but there is work a teacher might usefully do as an introduction to or a reinforcement of a practical approach to a text, which is less formalised and structured than the games we have been discussing. The exercise, like the game, can mobilise an actor's resources and in that sense it is mechanical. As Charles Marowitz puts it, exercises can deal with the actor as mechanism 'because the human being which animates the actor *is* a mechanism, just as theatre is a synthesis of many mechanisms. The danger is that the performance of those mechanisms produces a purely *mechanistic* effect — which of course has nothing to do with the intentions of art' (*The Act of Being*, p. 116). For present purposes the test of the value of an exercise is whether it makes the interplay between pupil and text more practicable and relevant.

In Michael Chekhov's book *To the Actor*, there is a chapter called *The Psychological Gesture* in which the author describes the creation of a viable physical image. An admirer of Stanislavsky, he maintains that the 'key to our will power' is to be found in action and gesture:

You can easily prove it yourself by trying to make a strong, well-shaped but simple gesture. Repeat it several times and you will see that after a while your will power grows stronger and stronger under the influence of such a gesture. Further, you will discover that the *kind* of movement you make will give your will power a certain direction or inclination; that is, it will awaken and animate in you a definite desire, want or wish. So we may say that the strength of the movement stirs our will power in general; the *kind* of movement awakens in us a definite corresponding *desire* and the *quality* of the same movement conjures up our *feelings*.

(Pp. 63–4)

He goes on to suggest that actors experiment with postures which express and crystallise their intuitions about the character. A physical description, as it were, rather than the familiar verbal ones we often require of our pupils.

Naturally, this presupposes that our pupils are able to achieve the necessary degree of concentration, that they are prepared to take the work seriously and that they have at least a nodding acquaintance with the text, either from a reading or a sampling contrived by the teacher. As described by Michael Chekhov, this sort of exercise will seem too abstract for youngsters, and it will need not merely to be sold to them but to be translated into more comprehensible terms. One might ask the pupils, working individually but all at the same time, to become a statue of a character or pose as for a publicity photograph. It could be a summation of a character who exhibits enough consistency or a character at a particular moment of the play. In order to do it, the pupil will be forced to call upon his own bodily 'knowledge' of the world and of people, and the exercise provides a focus for his own physical resources. When all have carried out their experiments, volunteers can reconstruct their statues for the class to see and the class either comments verbally on the implications for interpretation, or asks the demonstrator if he can say what he was trying to show, or asks another member of the class to adopt precisely the same pose and see how it feels to him. Does it seem a possible way of embodying that character? If not, how would *you* do it? This exercise can be done at a later stage, too, as a lead-in to a searching discussion about the character and his function in the play.

Sir Alec Guinness has said that he does not really start to understand a character until he knows how he walks. When I played Caliban, I felt embarrassed about saying the lines until I had discovered how my Caliban might move around. The quality of voice developed naturally as an appropriate way for a creature who postured like that. If the statue which 'sums up' a character now walks around, another expressive dimension is added. Often, there are direct clues in the text to build upon. In Ionesco's *Rhinoceros*, Jean turns into a rhinoceros before our very eyes, but earlier in the play he had proved himself ripe for transformation by behaving in an aggressive, self-confident and stupid manner. Some work on animal movement, the heavy swinging head, the lumbering gait, gives direct insight here into the 'feel' of the character even when he is a human being. When pupils can walk and move in character they can be turned loose in a set, where they can get some inkling of the range of movements that are likely to be possible for them should they ever dispense with the books. A physical context for the words was, in any case, envisaged when the writer wrote them. Several 'sets' can be devised by groups who can then, in turn, enter and use them.

'Clay Pigeon' is an exercise which also uses 'statues', but this time in a group and as a means of persuading a class to internalise the action implied by a section of the dialogue from a director/audience viewpoint. The number of actors required for the dialogue is placed in a ring to be 'clay statues'. In turn, pupils are invited to change the positions of these statues without verbal or facial directions to them and according to their own conception of the way the 'moment' should look and what it should, both overtly and subtextually, express. The rest of the class can then be invited to discuss the implications of particular decisions.

An element from a scene can be extracted and practised not only as a direct rehearsal but in a more oblique and abstract form as a 'warm-up'. For instance, Antony's attempted suicide in *Antony and Cleopatra* can be rehearsed individually and in a slightly changed form by letting the student borrow the line "A Roman by a Roman valiantly vanquished", saying it and seeing what kinds of stabbing and falling follow on most naturally. Which feels right, an impression of moving heroism or one of comic melodrama? Some idea of the range of possible interpretations that confront the actor playing the death of Antony may then accompany the student in his exploration of the event in the play. The structured fight in *Ernie's Incredible Illucinations*, either between Kid Saracen and Eddie Edwards or between the Kid and Auntie May, can be prepared for by rehearsing a fight in slow motion in which the pupils are invited to create their own formal sequence. This way the necessity for the fight to have an inner coherence as well as a safety factor can be stressed in advance.

Leach and Adams, in *The World of Punch and Judy* (Harrap's Theatre Workshop) suggest that pupils intending to act a *Punch* play should practise the fights by working out 'different movement, and positions, the more spectacular the better. Go from one position to the next, "frame" by "frame" ' (p. 35). Leach, writing on acting *The Bells*, suggests taking stock melodrama situations and setting up 'living tableaux', that is to say tableaux which come to life. Pupils then have to attempt to preserve the clarity of visual statement throughout the rest of the improvisation. An abstract 'machine' exercise creates a state of mind on which the actor working on the factory scene from *The Good Woman of Setzuan* can build. Pupils working on a collage might benefit by performing some of the exercises Charles Marowitz describes in *A Macbeth*. Some of these involve 'fracturing a Shakespearean scene – altering the original meaning of its text but keeping the words intact, complicating its situation with incongruous business and unrelated acting-partners' and their aim is 'to compel actors to control both disparate and multiple elements' (p. 24). They might, it seems to me, help produce a state of mind conducive to the successful creation of the collage itself.

Cecily Berry, in her excellent book *Voice and the Actor*, sees speech exercises as 'a preparation, both physical and for your whole self, which will enable you to respond instinctively to any situation' (p. 11). Though she recommends a course of training which will enable the actor to improve his breathing, his articulation, his inflexion, resonance and projection, she strongly disclaims an interest in elocution as such. 'Exercises should not make you more technical, but more free', she says, and 'You cannot consider the voice by itself, only in relation to the job you are doing.' The job we are doing is relating the individual pupil to a particular dramatic context and that is the ultimate purpose for which we are releasing his vocal potentialities. It is in the work in hand that he discovers his need to speak.

When, in Hudson's book, *Shakespeare and the Classroom*, it is suggested that a teacher could begin a lesson on a scene from Shakespeare by detaching a line and subjecting it to every possible variety of intonation and emphasis, we are dangerously close to playing at elocution. As a means of discovering what an individual actor can legitimately do, what the line in context can mean and what a particular voice is able to make of it, the exercise is valuable. How many different ways can Shylock acceptably say 'I am content' and how many different Shylocks are there to say it?

In our section on *Macbeth*, I mentioned possible methods of creating an awareness of the weight certain phraseology might carry. One approach involved translating the structure of a speech into physical movement and internalising the movement. This can also be a way of intuiting meaning. A more abstract and oblique approach to meaning through movement is described by J.R. Brown in *Theatre Language*. It also has the function of distracting attention from the self-conscious awareness of the voice, then freeing it to investigate its limits. I saw a lecturer from the Drama Department at Birmingham University, David Hirst, demonstrate the method; I have since tried it myself and my students claimed to find it useful. Russell Brown capitalises upon Rudolf Laban's analysis of human movement in terms of Weight, Space, Time and Flow; in other words a movement is strong or weak, direct or indirect, sustained or unsustained. He distinguishes what he calls 'eight basic efforts', namely:

PRESS   (strong, direct, sustained)
WRING   (strong, indirect, sustained)
SLASH   (strong, indirect, unsustained)
PUNCH   (strong, direct, unsustained)

165

GLIDE   (weak, direct, sustained)
FLOAT   (weak, indirect, sustained)
FLICK   (weak, indirect, unsustained)
DAB   (weak, direct, unsustained)

Russell Brown suggests that you take a word like 'No' and that you say it accompanied in turn by one of these 'efforts'. For example, you might be pressing 'No' into a table, punching 'No' at an invisible opponent. Certainly the 'effort' will make the word sound different each time but it can also give it a different implication. When the class are familiar with the system, the teacher can, as I myself have done, take a speech from the play and work on lines from that. I took Serjeant Musgrave's speech from the end of Act I of *Serjeant Musgrave's Dance* by John Arden. Musgrave addresses himself to God, praying that God will sustain him in his single-minded pursuit of his duty. His plea is summed up in the words: "Keep my mind clear". If this sentence is uttered by each pupil as he performs one of the efforts, he can then be asked which manner of delivery makes most sense. My own students decided that 'pressing' and 'punching' are the most appropriate kinds of delivery here. Although this example was chosen as a means of approaching Musgrave, we found it told us something about Arden's manner of writing in general and about the directness and energy needed to perform him successfully. 'Punching' can also remind actors that Brecht requires his audience to be jolted awake. With a speech such as the one near the end of *Oedipus Rex* by Sophocles, where the Messenger tells of the weighty events offstage (the hanging of Jocasta and the blinding of the king), a sense of 'pressing' may help the actor appreciate the portentousness of what he is saying.

Class-work using this method can be as elaborate or as simple as the teacher wishes. He could, for instance, have the pupils perform the line in turn, each with a different effort from the pupil before him; or he could distribute the whole of Musgrave's speech referred to above, say, around the class, letting them perform a line each with the same effort or a line each with a different effort from the person before. At the very least, this work can awaken a sense of stage language as 'audible movement', but without having to rely too much on luck, it can facilitate the discrimination between and the delivery of different styles of dialogue.

In *Young Drama* (1973), Derek Bowskill outlines an exercise designed to allow the pupils to 'explore the basis of dramatic charac-

166

ter'. The idea is that the teacher supplies the pupils with a set of lines of his own invention, of which they should preferably use all. They do have freedom, though, to allocate them as they wish and to decide for themselves the setting and the characterisation. These are Mr Bowskill's contribution:

It was all your fault things went wrong tonight
I was doing my best
But you would insist on fooling about
You were showing off and playing to the gallery
I wouldn't call them a gallery
But you wouldn't call them a handful either

Personally, I question whether the pupils doing this are engaged in anything as ambitious as exploring the basis of dramatic character. Surely neither the improviser of a role nor the creator of dramatic character is performing an act of juggling. The lines of a play are the end product of a complex process and the actor who works with this end product must strive to rediscover something of that process. Mr Bowskill's lines appear to me flat in the sense that they are the result of no personal pressure and for the improviser could restrict without offering any assurance that something meaningful can be made of them.

A passage of allocated lines would be nearer to the conventional playscript. Peter Spalding, in a BBC Theatre Workshop programme, had three actors perform the following script on the radio in two different ways:

Actor 1: Who's there?
Actor 2: It's me.
Actor 1: Must have dropped off. No wonder. Look at the time.
Actor 3: One o'clock.
Actor 1: One o'clock. You know what I said.
Actor 3: Yes. I know what you said.
Actor 1: We'll talk about it in the morning. Good night.

Listeners were asked: 'What do the people look like? What sort of room are they in? How do they stand, sit or move about? How do the two versions differ?' The writer obviously envisaged a particular setting (a room) and some limited conception of relationships. Actor 1 wakes at the beginning and he takes the lead in steering the conversation. Pupils are invited to play the scene themselves in contrasting ways and, since there is no clear indication in the words, could choose to set it outside a room. Presumably they could also play it as stage performance. The allocation of the lines gives some of the help a play does and although in context no extract from a play would be as open as this, the way different actors (or voices) inevitably change the emphasis can be starkly demonstrated.

Lines extracted for the purpose from an existing play likewise need to have a positive impact without being too restrictive. A teacher of my acquaintance took the following four lines out of Scene Eleven of *Mother Courage* and gave them to his fourth year group.

Heavens, what's she doing?
She's out of her mind!
Get her down, quick!
She'll get us in trouble.

One group used the lines as part of a scene involving a female householder who threatened to jump to her death if work was begun on demolishing the house to make way for a motorway. Pleading with her were her relatives and local officials. Admittedly the circumstances in the improvisation and the Brecht were different, but the lines had pointed the way to a situation remarkably similar in some respects and they were adopted by the pupils as the expression of fairly similar intentions.

In his *Playscripts* (Kenyon-Deand), Derek Bowskill deliberately supplies an over-abundance of lines, but there is a strong story and the words have positive style. In the story of Gilgamesh, a group point of view, such as that shared by the workmen of Uruk who are building a wall, can be expressed either by a choral chant or by individual contributions:

Never had time for breakfast
I only had a quick swig of wine
What's the hurry anyway
I've not been paid for the last job
They're always slow with wages

The style is often formal, as with the words of the god Shamash:

I've made Gilgamesh stronger than the strongest bull
More powerful than a host of warriors
And more to be feared than a savage lion

The experience this particular work makes possible is analogous in kind to that which John Arden attempts in *Ars Longa, Vita Brevis*, where the headmaster's speech, for instance, offers a plethora of platitudes from which an actor can select or which he can adapt at will:

Mr Chairman, Governors, Ladies and Gentlemen, on this our annual speechday and prize-giving at St Uncumbers, it falls to me as Headmaster to present my usual report upon the work of the school during the past year, and to offer up to you in public some predictions prophecies suggestions intentions plans plots devices designs confederacies conspiracies collations collections confidences and pious hopes for the succeeding twelve months time from today when I hope as many prizes will be awarded to as many deserving pupils.

Exercises such as I have been describing can lay a useful foundation for theatre work in that at the very least they encourage the open-minded acceptance of given material. Some can be used as warm-ups, preceding or accompanying work on an actual text, some obviously require a fair amount of time for themselves. I think the teacher must ask himself, though, whether any of them will prove more helpful than a passage taken from the said text itself.

There are other areas of work offering their own educational satisfactions but which are also likely to result in 'spin-off' benefits for the teacher of scripted drama. The dramatisation of stories is a contentious issue among developmentalists. Dorothy Heathcote strongly eschews them. Acting out stories can indeed be a deadly and uncommitted activity, but it seems rash to assume that archetypal patterns of experience endorsed by the generations of man will be scornfully rejected by any self-respecting improviser, that living through the solutions the story proposes can do nothing to prompt a reappraisal of one's natural response. There are ways of tackling stories that encourage the pupils to test out the validity of the narrative, for instance, by exploring the implications of taking it in a different direction. A good story, like a good play, can allow a wide range of interpretation.

A story I have used with countless classes of children usually of first or second year age in the secondary school is the story of the Cyclops from *The Odyssey*. I usually simplify it to make it manageable and then either begin by telling it in my own words or lead the class through it. Briefly, Odysseus and his men, homeward bound from Troy, land on a strange shore and discover a cave. In it are the remains of a meal and various utensils but everything is of giant size. Suddenly, the earth starts to quake and a loud bleating is heard. Somebody spots the one-eyed giant approaching, driving his sheep, and the men scuttle to hide. The sheep are driven in and penned and a huge stone is pushed to block the cave entrance. The Cyclops notices two sailors, grabs them and eats them. Odysseus steps forward, attempts and fails to reason with him and ends by offering the Cyclops wine to wash down his grisly meal. The wine puts the drinker to sleep and Odysseus calls his men forth to decide what to do. Eventually they sharpen a handy stake, harden it in the fire and drive it into the eye of their sleeping gaoler. He wakes, roars and attempts to catch them, settling at last for rolling the stone back and sitting with his legs across the doorway, daring his tormentors to try to escape. Odysseus calls another council and the solution proposed is to cling to the underside of the sheep as they pass out so that the giant will feel only woolly backs. Once outside, the men get into the ship and row away while a fusillade of rocks hits the sea around them.

I first have the whole class being sailors and exploring the dark, frightening and revolting cave. I create the thumps of the giant's feet and leave the sailors to articulate their reactions. The most natural response, given the circumstances, is, as in the story, to hide in the recesses of the cave. One child now becomes the Cyclops. I have a mask which I issue and which emphasises the fixed and elemental aspect of the Cyclops's personality. Sometimes half the class are sheep, but, after being penned, they emerge and join the sailors again. The next part can be done in pairs, with a Cyclops and Odysseus thrashing it out and the drink being resorted to only when defeat by argument has been conceded. Assuming the Cyclops is asleep and can be temporarily ignored, the class divides into groups, each with an Odysseus, and they discuss the problem of escape. At this point all kinds of solutions can be aired, including non-violent ones. The last one to be tried is the one proposed in the story. One in each group becomes the sleeping Cyclops and the rest do a group mime of gouging out his eye. The episode stops with the scream. Members of the group are now given numbers. Number one is the Cyclops first and he is allowed to chase the others (with his eyes closed) around a demarcated area as in blind man's buff. When I shout 'Number Two!' the second person becomes the Cyclops. And so on through the group. We now jump to the moment when the Cyclops in the story is sitting guarding the exit. He is purely imagined at this stage and the class, in its groups, discuss this new development and pro- pose new solutions. As a class, we try out some of these with a volunteer Cyclops taking up his position. Lastly, again we try Homer's solution, discussing its merits and implications. Here, the people who weren't sheep at the beginning can now be given the honour. Once the workshop is complete, I let the class put the whole 'play' together in two large groups, this time with people playing fixed roles. What was possibly a fragmented experience now acquires continuity. Finally, each company can perform their version, if they wish, to the other half.

As well as being (I would maintain) a relatively open and flexible way of using 'shaped' material, work such as this has much to recommend it as a foundation for work where even the spoken words are prescribed. It examines the terms on which an outsider's (the writer's) ideas can be accepted. It brings pupils up against the problem of style. If the Cyclops is seen simply as a quintessential baddie, Odysseus is easier to accept as a hero. If, as happens, some feel sorry for the one-eyed loner, Odysseus has to be justified in terms of necessity with no real alternatives open to him but to fight with violence and cunning. The story offers opportunities for both physical and verbal expression and communication. The flexibility of organisation allows each pupil to have a go at several roles, and to empathise with all the characters. The workshop shows how the immediate concerns of presentation can be shelved in the interests of involvement and exploration; and the performance demonstrates that form, pace and tempo also have their contribution to make to the meaning of the experience.

The presentation of drama based on a story can provide opportunities for the class to develop relevant theatrical criteria. A story I have used successfully with fourth year pupils is Alan Sillitoe's *The Match*, in which a mechanic called Lennox goes to a football match with his next door neighbour, Fred. Lennox has a number of worries and frustrations in his private life. He has crossed swords with his boss at the garage, been insulted by a junior and his sight is deteriorating. The neighbour has an attractive wife, while Lennox's own sex life is in the middle-age doldrums. This particular Saturday afternoon, Lennox's home team, Notts. County, loses and he goes home in a foul temper. At home, he throws his tea on the floor, kicks the cat, abuses the children and drives his wife finally to the end of her tether, so that she walks out on him. The 'given circumstances' from which to build the role of Lennox are obvious and accessible. What is left open is the role of the wife and individual actresses can flesh this out according to their own creative intuitions. The children can also be given a life of their own and I have known groups successfully add an interfering neighbour or in-law. Versions of the final encounter can thus be widely varied and what is highlighted is the way the playing of a role can affect the meaning of even a 'structured' experience. If the wife emerges as a harridan, the playing of the role of Lennox could be affected and furthermore the whole balance of the audience's sympathy shifted. It becomes plain that the actor and actress, and any others taking part in the scene, are to be numbered among the premises on which the experience is based. What is of prime

171

importance is the question of the credibility and coherence of the event, a theatrical event, in effect.

A story such as *The Pardoner's Tale* by Chaucer, while allowing groups of children to explore the workings of greed, can also, when it comes to presentation, bring them up against problems of focus. Three men, fleeing from the plague, ask an old man whom they meet to show them the whereabouts of Death, so that they can kill him. The old man directs them to a pile of gold and after deciding on equal shares, they despatch one of their number to a tavern for some drink. While he is away, the other two plan his murder but he simultaneously plans theirs by buying poison at an apothecary's and doctoring the drinks. 'Developmentally' the incidents can take place at the same time but theatrically the actors have to think whether simultaneous staging is appropriate or whether they wish to focus on the events sequentially.

Any work on the performance of poetry gives the pupils valuable practice in the control of tone and rhythm and assurances of the importance of individual words. As actors in poetic drama, they will need to be able to give the lines due weight if the audience is to catch their full meaning. Poems which are literally dramatic, consisting of perhaps a mixture of narrative and dialogue, can offer a particularly useful discipline when it comes to making the transition to theatre, especially if they can be used in their entirety.

An old favourite with first years is *The Daniel Jazz* by Vachel Lindsay. It narrates the story of Daniel being consigned to the lions' den by King Darius, the lions refusing to eat him, a plea on behalf of his womenfolk for his rescue and God sending Gabriel to chain the lions down. Judicious cutting would remove the list of arrivals whom Daniel, as butler, lets in to the place and the rest can be done by assigning the parts of Daniel, Darius, the sweetheart, the mother, God and Gabriel and the lions, and using the other members of the class (if it is to be a class effort) as narrators. Parts of the acting area will need to be designated different locations: for instance, the cage for the lions and Heaven. If God and Gabriel are put on a table then we have spatial symbolism of the kind appearing in Medieval Mystery plays. Other characters (Daniel, Darius, the sweetheart and the mother) will also need to be seen as in different places but they can define their location by their actions, thus introducing a fluidity in the transformation of space which Shakespeare would have recognised. The narrators (if there are enough of them) can establish the periphery of the acting area. A solution will have to be found to the problem of how to get Daniel into the lions' den, when the poem does not tell of it happening, and a decision will have to be made as to whether to retain the lyrical description of the sweetheart when nothing is happening onstage. The actor playing Darius might feel uneasy about having his annoyance with Daniel's praying appear quite suddenly and will have to decide whether it will be in keeping to allow it to build up visibly. Can the young directors, they might be asked, find a way of fitting ritualistic actions to the line which the poem, living up to the 'Jazz' in its title, repeats at the end?

> And the Lord said to Gabriel:
> "Go, chain the lions down,
> Go, chain the lions down,
> Go, chain the lions down."

The alternative might be a God showing mounting irritation with an inattentive or deaf angel!

What pupils will be doing, in effect, is acting and producing a dramatic script, since they will be acting out the words without departing from them and will be putting them in the context of a theatrical performance. They will also be gaining experience of the way words can help an actor. Far from being more difficult by being in rhymed verse, these words encourage the actor to master them so that he can be the vehicle of the desired effect, which, in lines such as the following, is a comic one.

> He said: "Your Daniel is a dead little pigeon.
> He's a good hard worker, but he talks religion."

The narrators might experiment with everybody saying "Lord, save my soul" with Daniel, as against leaving him to say it himself. Does this establish a community of empathy between him and the narrators? Have we the beginnings here of a dramatic chorus? Acting out poetry is, of course, nothing new and the use of dramatic techniques to bring out poetic meaning is impressively described by Christopher Parry. *The Daniel Jazz* may be fairly trivial — albeit not negligibly so — and the approach I have described might seem, if poetic appreciation is our business, taking a sledgehammer to a nut. But in the context of an interrelation between poetry and drama, I feel such work lays useful foundations.

Polishing an improvisation in the sense of repeating and refining it has the effect of 'fixing' certain elements of it. Writing it down fixes the whole thing, at least temporarily. The transcript can be con-

173

sidered and discussed, but if this is the motive for producing the transcript it is a cold and clinical exercise. If the motive for fixing an improvisation is that there is a felt need to hold a form that has been achieved or promised, then such writing can have an educational function. This may presuppose a deliberate search for form, and the activity is analogous to playmaking. Another way of fixing an improvisation is to record it on tape (sound or video). This serves better as a reminder of the original, since it gives a fuller sense of the personal qualities of the participants. It allows them to become their own audience and share with their recorded selves the unfolding of the experience in time. But even a tape recording, of course, can be translated into a script and this kind of script is more likely to contain a greater amount of detail.

Making a written or taped record of an improvisation is only one way of producing a script, but it has the advantage of basing itself on an experience that involves movement and position in space, a particular locale and an awareness of who exactly is present, practicalities which an inexperienced playwright might be inclined to forget. Fixing a performance may threaten spontaneous creativity but it does encourage the performers to give attention to effectiveness of construction and phraseology. Writing it down may make the writers self-conscious and detached but it can have the advantage of persuading them to take a larger view of the construct. Pupils who, in writing, build a dramatic action from scratch will in effect have to improvise in their heads. If they are capable of doing this, they will even more effectively have been forced to appreciate the many-sidedness of a situation and will mentally have had to play or consider all the roles. They may also be learning from the inside something of the process which produced the scripts that they will meet should they move into the kind of theatre work we have been describing.

A script that is a record of an improvised performance can be used as a basis for a re-creation of it by the originators. It can also, if it has sufficiently dynamic qualities of form, characterisation and dialogue, be used by a different group as a basis for a version of their own. Thus what was perhaps formerly an 'audience' can help to validate the original discoveries in a very direct and practical way. For our present purposes it is a small step to the introduction of the notion of interpretation. It should be said, though, that writing a script which can be used by other people is a sophisticated activity and teachers who blithely invite their pupils to 'write a play' sometimes don't realise what a task they have set.

If pupils are working on a script which presupposes an audience, then some knowledge of the conventions of presentation is needed. Pupils improvising onto tape, not merely so that they have a record of what they are doing but so as to make a statement to be shared, will need at least an elementary knowledge of the conventions of radio. From the pupil's point of view, the most vivid way of learning these is by trial and error. An uncomprehending audience will soon make it clear that a more effective exposition is required before it can understand what is going on. Experimentation with a microphone can teach pupils how the relationship of the actors to it can affect the audience's sense of whom it is 'with', in other words where the focus is. After the sea-sickness induced by a rhythmical zooming in and out of a television camera operated by a pupil, an audience can soon register its feelings about the use of close-ups. One should perhaps stress (again), however, that whatever the medium and whether or not we are working on an improvisation from a script, what matters educationally is the creative involvement of the pupils and not the technical polish. The desirable end-product is the experience itself and not the finished script or tape. There are grounds for forgiving the radio actor who turns his back on his interlocutor and marches away if this helps him to feel the part even though to the audience he has leapt for the horizon.

The possibilities of an art-form can also be learned from other practitioners, in this case established dramatists. Far from inevitably cramping the pupil's style, the work of a successful playwright can liberate his imagination. In 'imitation' of Ionesco's *Rhinoceros*, three third year girls wrote me a scene in a maternity hospital where mothers were giving birth not to human babies but to baby rhinoceroses. They were obviously influenced by Ionesco's manner of comically having his characters fail to recognise the true horror of a situation, but it did not stop their own wit from flashing:

> (*The ward is in an uproar as the visiting bell goes. In walk the husbands, Mr Jenkins and Mr Peterson. They walk over to their wives who are both in tears.*)
>
> Mr Jenkins: Oh, isn't she lovely! She's the image of you.

Three boys, writing about being trapped in a pit, were influenced in their choice of mode by a memory of an encounter with Pinter several lessons previously.

175

Pause

ML: That noise . . . again.
DM: Don't believe you.
LD: I've got this plan. To see . . .
DM: See what?
LD: What's up there.
DM: There's nothing up there.
ML: I heard a noise, twice.
DM: There's nothing up there.
LD: I've got this plan.
DM: There's absolutely . . .
LD: I've got this plan.
DM: Nothing.
LD: A good plan.
DM: Up there.

In performance, this dialogue helped them define three distinct states of mind.

I have suggested that creating a dramatic script for presentation can give valuable insights into the way published plays have come about. This is true whether it is the result of an encounter with published scripts or grows out of the need to hold and share a free improvisation. We have been talking about the script that is a guide to a complete performance and that consists of words and actions invented by the pupils. The script does not, though, have to be complete to be useful. Perhaps the writer(s) may supply only a scenario, with perhaps the odd speech. Pupils may be adapting a story and may incorporate some of the original words. The documentary play may contain speeches by well-known figures, historical documents, slides, transcripts of interviews or even the interviews themselves on tape. Material from whatever source needs to be arranged in some sort of order and this brings the pupils up against the relationship of form to meaning. They may also find themselves struggling to establish a valid point of view. I worked with some students on a documentary play on the subject of The Silver Jubilee (their choice). The various sketches and episodes the groups produced struck us all initially as vapid and sentimental, the idea that everybody celebrated with warm royalist sentiments in their hearts seemed false and we set out to redress the balance. We added scenes like the one where an interviewer passed a line of stationary figures representing the occupants of a row of houses. As she knocked on an invisible door, the appropriate figure came to life and became a householder, expressing an opinion about the expenditure of money on the Jubilee. The opinions were widely diverse, and the mood of the piece acquired a humorous flavour, the presentation more balance. What emerged at the end was some sort of concensus to the effect that, despite official ballyhoo, a celebration in itself was no bad thing and might be a human necessity. Apart from the developmental benefits of this kind of collaboration, pupils engaged in an exercise such as this are learning relevant things about the dramatic uses to which 'factual' material can be put, a valuable preparation for an encounter with *Oh What A Lovely War* and with chroniclers like Shakespeare and Robert Bolt.

In producing a documentary play, a whole class can be involved in the same project while concentrating in small groups on researching or evolving a part of it. A class radio play can be put together in a similar way if, for instance, it is episodic in structure. The life story of a chosen character (such as Eustace Ardluck, a man blighted by ill fortune) falls easily into phases. It may be that to avoid confusion the class will prefer the same actors to perform the roles throughout, a move in the direction of theatre that will require the production of scripts for each episode. If they are not so fussy, each group can perform its section directly onto tape (still not precluding, of course, the script). This method of organisation is particularly useful when there is only one tape recorder. Should there be several and should there be different recording rooms available, it is possible to have groups simultaneously recording their own plays but it is also more difficult to monitor while it is happening. When groups are creating plays, a single scribe can take down agreed lines. Within the same (large) room it is possible for groups to be improvising and writing down and for individuals who prefer it and who are capable of the feat of theatrical imagination (older pupils, in my experience) to be drafting their own scripts or scenarios. I have even had a class writing a play together; but progress was so slow, the difficulty of achieving the inner commitment in such an atmosphere and the temptation to settle for facile solutions so great, that I don't honestly feel I can recommend the procedure.

Changing the text

Actors and directors in rehearsal temporarily expand or add to the text of a play on occasions but the aim is usually to bring about a more meaningful engagement with the text as written. There have been writers and directors, though, who have, for artistic or ideological reasons, made alterations which changed the nature of the

177

experience itself. Is this self-evidently an act of vandalism? Not necessarily, if we are to believe R.G. Collingwood:

Let all artists who understand one another, therefore, plagiarise each other's work like men. Let each borrow his friend's best ideas, and try to improve on his friend's ideas, at least let him borrow them, it will do him good to try fitting them into works of his own, and it will be an advertisement for the creditor. An absurd suggestion? Well, I am only proposing that modern artists should treat each other as Greek dramatists or Renaissance painters did . . .

(*The Principles of Art*, O.U.P., 1938)

Brecht's *Coriolanus*, like Dryden's *All for Love*, is, in effect, a new play. A writer such as Nahum Tate, though, produced an adaptation of *King Lear* which leaves some of Shakespeare intact but smoothes out what doesn't fit Tate's and his contemporaries' prejudices or sense of artistic decorum. In our own day the all-powerful director has sometimes used his power in a similar way, usually in pursuit of contemporary 'relevance'. Thus, Peter Brook might excise a speech from *Lear* because it introduces a ray of hope and destroys the Beckett-like atmosphere of unrelieved nihilism he hopes to establish. John Barton might decide to give *Richard II* more of a political emphasis, so he imports speeches from later plays such as *Henry IV* to build up Bolingbroke's importance and deflect attention from the purely personal tragedy of Richard. Barton even writes in his own speeches for *Dr Faustus*. The most drastic of the modifiers is Charles Marowitz who throws the whole form of the play overboard and re-arranges the material in a collage. Such a collage is intended more clearly to bring out Marowitz's conception of *Macbeth* as a play pervaded and determined by black magic.

What use can a teacher make of practices such as these? He can, of course, encourage his students to have a go themselves and this can be a rewarding exercise in self-expression. I believe it can also enhance the appreciation of the original work and provide a particularly 'concrete' critical method. If this is the aim, it is, I feel, best done with older or more sophisticated students. Where an altered text such as Tate's *Lear* or Bowen's version of *The Bacchae* (*The Disorderly Women*) exists, the most simple approach is straight production work on that. Even on only part of it, production work can throw features of the original text starkly into relief.

Tate's version, with its omission of the Fool, its preservation alive of the King and its happy marriage of Cordelia and Edgar, displaced the Shakespeare for 150 years and was preferred by Dr Johnson as better satisfying the laws of natural justice. Work on Act V alone reveals Tate's urge for symmetry and explicitness in structure and grouping. It should preferably be tackled without hostile preconception, in an attempt to understand it in its own terms. Even so, the obvious manipulation of the climax in the prison, the sudden, timely rescue by Edgar, will make pupils aware of what happens to a great play when you allow your wish-fulfilment free rein. In the case of *Lear* it may be that Tate's wishes articulate some of the pupils' own and the exercise results in a personal reappraisal rather than a self-congratulating dismissal of the Tate. To this end the teacher would be advised not to attempt an external reproduction of the manner and gestures of Restoration heroic action, documented as these are by Betterton. He will probably find that the style of the speeches and the structure force the actors to strike formal attitudes in any case, and if they do he can then invite the pupils to try a section of the unadulterated Shakespeare to compare what that does for the actor.

Texts of the various Marowitz experiments are on the market. Practical work on *A Macbeth* by pupils who have been working on the Shakespeare challenges and disturbs responses in danger of becoming customary and frees the performer to experiment with a different subtext. The play begins with a bold and expressive image, an effigy of Macbeth.

> *In front of it, back to the audience, stands Lady Macbeth. On a signal, the three Witches enter and surround the effigy. Each adds bits to it until it clearly resembles Macbeth. After a pause, Lady Macbeth begins to intone an incantation.*

Lady Macbeth: I'll drain him dry as hay
> Sleep shall neither night nor day
> Hang upon his penthouse lid.
> He shall live a man forbid.
> Weary seven-nights nine-times-nine
> Shall he dwindle, peak and pine.
> (*One of the Witches hands Lady Macbeth a smoking poker. With it, she slowly obliterates the wax eyes of the effigy. The lights fade.*)

A startling out-of-sequence modulation now occurs:

> (*Lights up. Enter Duncan, Banquo, Malcolm and Macduff. The stage is filled with a pleasant, summery glow. Birds are chirping in background.*)

Later, thematic link-ups are vividly postulated:

Lady Macbeth: Are you a man?
Macbeth (*firmly*): Ay, and a bold one.
Lady Macbeth: Ay, in the catalogue you go for men
> As hounds and greyhounds, mongrels, spaniels, curs,

SCRIPTED DRAMA

Shoughs, water-rugs and demi-wolves are clept
All by the name of dogs.

It might be argued that the Marowitz too offers an experience
which exists in its own right, but the words are Shakespeare's and
surely some of the excitement (and irritation) legitimately derives
from encountering the familiar in an unfamiliar setting. Comparisons,
in other words, are natural, and such comparisons might encourage
lateral thinking about the source material as well.

Where there is no convenient 'alternative' text for a class to work
on, the class may have to rely on reported accounts of a director's
experiments. This puts a responsibility on the teacher to keep himself informed about current and past productions and to spend a lot
of his time, himself, in theatres. He will often find it useful to search
the theatre magazines and books on theatre and collect reviews and
programme notes. He may, for instance, have seen Peter James's
production of *As You Like It* at the Crucible Theatre, Sheffield, in
1977 and he may have the programme note in which the director
says: 'We do not hop backwards and forwards between "court" and
"forest", but rather play all the "court" scenes together, and then
move once and for all to the "forest".' The pupils can follow through
the implications of this by performing an early section of the play
which allows them to jump a forest scene. The first of these, Act II,
Scene i, occurs after the banishment of Rosalind, giving a glimpse of
the forest life to which she will flee, and it is followed by a short
'court' scene in which Duke Frederick discovers that Celia has gone
with her and he decides that Orlando might yield a clue to their
whereabouts. It is some time before the search for Orlando is taken
up. By rearranging (temporarily) the text, the pupils will be encouraged to question whether the satisfaction of following a story-line
such as this directly through is what the play offers an audience. The
actors playing the banished Duke and his 'co-mates and brothers in
exile' will be asking what difference it might make to their manner of
playing if their first scene is sandwiched between 'court' scenes as
against finding itself the first of a long sequence of 'forest' scenes.
This leads naturally to an enquiry into the structure and meaning of
the dramatic experience itself.

If pushing a well-known director's predilections to the limit strikes
the teacher as a somewhat academic exercise, he may prefer to let his
class exploit their own convictions. A group of pupils or an individual
may themselves be given the freedom to chop and change the text in

180

ways which will reinforce their sense of its meaning, whether it involves cutting or subtly modifying those parts which are intractable or re-organising the material as Marowitz does. The aim is to persuade the pupils to make a personal or group statement about their experience of the play, but this can also be a valuable critical exercise, based firmly on the evidence of performance itself and not on abstract and possibly jargonised verbal comment. Discussion will doubtless still arise as pupils feel the need to extend their reactions to the new construct and understand the implications of the changes that have been made, but it will reinforce rather than replace theatrical experience.

If the class or group is able to originate practical ideas for itself, the teacher can leave its members to it and rejoice, but if they need help, he will have to try and sense the impression they have formed and (hopefully) formulated and offer suggestions as to the kind of experiments they could conduct to test it. Suppose the pupils are working on Chekhov's *The Cherry Orchard* and feel that the political content should be emphasised. Some directors would feel that the way to bring out that dimension is to distance the actors and audience from the personal emotion and to apply the recommendations and copy the example of Brecht. 'Brechtian' productions of *Measure for Measure* and of *Hedda Gabler* have been tried on the professional stage. A class which was familiar with Brecht might try a Brechtian version of, say, the episode in Act III where Lopakhin reveals that he is the new owner of the property. The words as written, of course, would require a less naturalistic style of playing and actions, such as the weeping of Liubov while Lopakhin delivers his speech of triumph, would require a less naturalistic style of playing, and actions, such as invent words of their own they might add expository narrative designed to mute the suspense or they might decide to write a song.

Students feeling with John Barton that *Richard II* is largely political in emphasis might test their intuition by adding the odd battle, for example, at Flint Castle; battles being a luxury which Shakespeare, for reasons of his own, denies himself in the text. What happens to the focus when the audience has actions of this kind to absorb its attention as against Shakespeare's army merely moving silently across the stage? A class which was convinced (like Marowitz) that the supernatural is the most important element in the atmosphere and the motivation of the characters in *Macbeth* could experiment (less dramatically than Marowitz) by allowing the witches to be present at moments in the play where Shakespeare omits them. For instance, what does the dagger episode look like if a witch carries the air-drawn weapon? Is *Hedda Gabler* a play about the mind of a heroine? What happens if you do as Ingmar Bergman did and allow her to eavesdrop when she is not officially onstage? Suppose you play the first scene, between Aune Julle and Tesman, with Hedda watching and listening. What does this do to the motivation of actions when she officially enters, such as her mistaking of Aunt Julle's hat for that of Berthe, the maid? Is this particular action any longer a matter of impulse for her?

Altering the text, then, may result from an attempt to test out an impression, to validate a viewpoint, to see whether the text can bear a particular emphasis; but it can also be conducted in a spirit of dis-interested inquiry, an extension of the kind of experimentation actors and directors carry out on the lines in the natural course of discovering their potential. The pupil might be curious to know what would happen if Uncle Vanya had really killed Serebriakov when he chased him with his pistol at the end of Act III. Let him rewrite or re-create the episode with that particular outcome. What does it do to the tone? More valuably, how does the pupil now gauge the tone of the original? In *Arms and the Man*, the middle-aged servant, Nicola, refuses to be ruffled. Petkoff accuses him of being muddle-headed when he brings out Captain Bluntschli's bag, while the audience knows that he is acting under orders from Catherine, Petkoff's wife. It is just that he knows if he keeps quiet Catherine will tip him. If he had not been so bland and compliant, what would have happened to the comedy of the scene? Try it out and see. In *The Widowing of Mrs Holroyd* by D.H. Lawrence, the wife of the miner who is killed in a pit disaster confounds the audience's expectations by discovering that her deepest feelings are still for him rather than for her lover with whom she is now technically free to go away. What would happen to the experience of the play if the scene where the news is received were re-written to make her glad he was dead and allow the characters to fulfil the expected outcome?

We have said that directors often have artistic or ideological reasons for altering the text of a play, but sometimes their reasons may be the less exalted one that it makes for convenience. Peter James accounts for his treatment of *As You Like It* by saying he has edited 'in order that you leave the theatre before midnight' and also 'to avoid continual scene changes'. The teacher might galvanise his class into action by pretending that for practical reasons, because, say, the last bus goes at ten o'clock or there is a shortage of actors, or the actors we have got are poor at comedy or remembering and delivering long speeches, there will have to be cuts in the text, transposition of parts, changes to certain lines or a reallocation of them.

Practical limitations have forced performing companies to make even more radical reductions to the text of a play. A professional company in Yorkshire (The Pocket Theatre) boasted an acting team of only two men and a woman and with these gave a performance for schools of *Othello*. Obviously justice cannot be done to the complexity of the play and the company deliberately concentrated on the theme of jealousy. Another decision they made was for each player to take only one part throughout. They were concerned to follow the plot as it originally developed but an extract from the beginning of their script (with the line numbers from the original text) shows the kinds of transposition they felt free to make. The words or stage directions underlined are invented by the producer.

```
           (From Act I, Scene ii)
Iago:           I pray sir                                        10
           Are you fast married? For be sure of this,
           That the magnifico is much belov'd,
           And hath in his effect a voice potential
           As double as the duke's; he will divorce you,
           Or put upon you what restraint, and grievance,        15
           That law (with all his might to enforce it on)
           Will give him cable.
Othello:        Let him do his spite;                            17
           My services, which I have done the signiory,
           Shall out-tongue his complaints;
                Yet, for know, Iago,                             24
           But that I love the gentle Desdemona,                 25
           I would not my unhoused free condition
           Put into circumscription and confine
           For the sea's worth. But look what lights come yonder.
Iago:      These are the raised father and his friends,
           You were best go in.
Othello:        Not I, I must be found:                          30
           My parts, my title, and my perfect soul,
           Shall manifest me rightly:
                Exit
           (From Act I, Scene i)
Iago:      I follow him to serve my turn upon him:               42
           We cannot be all masters, nor all masters
           Cannot be truly follow'd. You shall mark
           Many a duteous and knee-crooking knave,               45
           That, doting on his own obsequious bondage,
```

Wears out his time much like his master's ass,
For nought but provender, and when he's old, cashier'd,
Whip me such honest knaves: others there are,
Who, trimm'd in forms, and visages of duty,   50
Keep yet their hearts attending on themselves,
And throwing but shows of service on their lords,
Do well thrive by 'em, and when they have lin'd their coats,
Do themselves homage, those fellows have some soul,
And such a one do I profess myself, . . .   55
(From Act I, Scene i)
I am not what I am.
(From Act I, Scene iii)
Othello: Most potent, grave and reverend signiors   76
My very noble and approv'd good masters:
That I have ta'en away this old man's daughter,
It is most true: true, I have married her,
The very head and front of my offending   80
Hath this extent, no more.

In this context, speeches delivered to confidants in the original become soliloquies (Iago's speech: "I follow him to serve my turn upon him" is actually spoken to Roderigo) and other speeches actually intended to be addressed to a number of other characters leave the audience to people the stage with their own imaginations (present during Othello's "Most potent, grave and reverend signiors . . . " there should be the Duke, Senators, Officers, Brabantio, Roderigo and attendants as well as Iago and Desdemona).

Limitations as to number of actors can be artificially imposed by the teacher, artificially in the sense that he looks at the play text and gauges in advance the minimum number of players required to explore in performance a particular aspect of the play. He can also choose or decide with the class the convention within which they will operate; for example whether girls can play men's parts or whether individual performers can double up. Working on *Othello* in threes or with threes in mind, pupils will be obliged to consider such issues as the importance of the influence of Iago and whether the contribution of Emilia really requires that *she* say all the lines attributed to her. If the class is small (a Sixth Form, perhaps) limitations as to number will be natural and the teacher may find some merit in challenging the students to devise a performance of a play with the resources they have got. Playing time might also be deliberately restricted, as happens with Open University versions of some of the texts their drama students study. If you have to do *Waiting for Godot* in fifty minutes, what is the best strategy? Even if you choose to do Act II as near complete as possible, what can you miss out? Will keeping in all the references to Godot but omitting some of the games affect the feel of the roles or the impact on an audience?

Peter Whittle, in an article in *The Use of English* (Summer 1976), describes how he reduced a performance of *King Lear* to half an hour. He also used only twelve performers, only three of whom were male. To avoid confusion for the audience of Sixth Formers from another school, he used costume and masks to disguise the doubling-up and the playing of men by girls. He was further helped in this by his decision to do the whole thing as a dumb show. Although he sacrificed something of the range and complexity of the play and all of the words, what was starkly highlighted were the imagery and symbolism. The mask convention itself emphasised the divergence between appearance and reality which the play explores and actions such as blindfolding fulfilled the purpose of showing the importance of key metaphors. Words, lost in the performance, were granted to cast and audience afterwards as they discussed the appropriateness and expressiveness of what was done. Everybody had read the play, so the discussion was broadly based.

The dumb show does not have to be prepared for public performance with costume and mask to disguise reality. I have seen a successful dumb show version of *Lear* lasting only a few minutes, done by half a dozen students for their own benefit alone. They were asked to select six significant moments from the play, set up tableaux and then link these up with unspoken action. As well as encouraging them to think in theatrical images, the exercise led, at preparation and comment stage, to a vociferous assessment of the relative merits of different themes, and to an awareness of repetitive patterns, such as the rejection of one human being by another.

The setting up by students of a collage in the Marowitz manner is potentially confusing if done at too early a stage but can be a useful means of revitalising work on a text that has become too familiar, a means, as it were, of 'alienating' students from their own habitual responses. The dramatic method of a playwright such as Shakespeare lends itself better to this kind of treatment than that of a more linear craftsman. Roger Lewis (in *The Use of English*, Autumn 1973) describes a project he did with Main Subject English students in a College of Education. They were working on *Hamlet* and in terms of intellectual study had done the play to death. What was needed was an approach which allowed their affective responses full scope. Mr

Lewis handed over responsibility to the students as a group and in effect invited them to make a personal statement about the play in terms which involved the many resources of the theatre and of the actor. As there were only ten of them, a full length production of the play was impossible and so they decided to re-write it. 'For the most part, the actual words of the text were used but these were juxtaposed in an unusual way, isolated in new contexts, to persuade the audience to listen to them as for the first time.' The kind of sequence that resulted is exemplified by this extract:

Claudius then had a 'jollying along' speech, followed by a kind of cocktail party, to make himself known. In contrast, Hamlet and Horatio entered, talked about the ghost and Hamlet (played at this point as an aspiring actor 'produced' by his friend) practised what he was to say to his father on his next appearance. The ghost told of his murder and while this was unfolding Claudius (embracing Ophelia on the other side of the stage) went through one of his long speeches; his was the voice which finally came out on top, as that of the ghost faded away with the dawn. Then as the stage became at times Hamlet's *mind*, the scene ended with Claudius kissing Ophelia (Hamlet now saw *all* women as corrupt).

An important feature of the exercise was the critical discussion which was precipitated at various stages. Two students each week were responsible for writing a scene and they had to justify their objectives and procedures to the others. The experiment was also designed to be validated by an audience and they, too, were involved in the discussion. At this juncture, presumably, members of the group who were individually at odds with group decisions would be liberated to identify and define their own responses. A Sixth Form, say, would not have to aim at a complete version of the play, although a large Sixth Form that was in two classes might well engage in the kind of project that Mr Lewis executed. Even if they did a section or an aspect of the play, though, they would need to be clear on the range of alternatives, the kinds of 'statement' that are possible; and here a brief introduction to a text such as those of Marowitz or a description of an experiment such as Mr Lewis's would be invaluable.

I was not privileged to see for myself Mr Lewis's class in action but I did observe the work of a friend and sometime colleague of mine, Mrs Velda Harris, who produced what was in effect a collage 'using movement and rhythmic speech techniques'. The exercise was the afternoon part of a day workshop for Sixth Formers on *Antony and Cleopatra*, the students coming from a variety of schools and in many cases not knowing each other. The conference members were divided into groups and those that felt they had something to 'show' at the end of the day were invited to do so, although the emphasis was on exploration rather than presentation. Given the time available, Mrs Harris's dominant role in devising and directing the performance was inevitable. She did admit, however, that the onus should ideally be placed on the students themselves. Even in a group, of course, students must sometimes sacrifice their individual intuitions in favour of group decisions but this happens, to a lesser degree, I grant, in a straight production. Mrs Harris describes her project in this way:

Account of a workshop session on 'Antony and Cleopatra' using movement and rhythmic speech techniques as an approach to the text.

Initial conception

I decided to concentrate movement activities on the contrast and conflict in the play between Rome and Egypt. The range of movements associated with Rome would be direct, strong, aggressive, militaristic, dominant; those associated with Egypt would be indirect, slow, weaving, sensuous, sinewy. Words could be used to reinforce and give greater definition to the movement sequences: words like 'power', 'control', 'obey', 'conform' to accompany the Rome sequence; words like 'amorous', 'love-sick', 'passion', 'mirth', 'Lethe' associated with Egypt.

These contrasting speech and movement sequences could be incorporated into a dramatic presentation or dance drama using Antony as the central figure, showing him turn by conscience and duty on the one hand, and love and sensual pleasure on the other, and leading through a nightmare climax to his eventual destruction. This dramatic framework could be given shape by the inclusion of passages from the play text.

Rehearsal

(i) **Rome.** I asked the group to respond with strong, abrupt movements to a sharp percussion sound (a wood block). We experimented with the use of different body parts moving in response to the sound; we varied support positions, related the abrupt movements in pairs, and explored different ways of progressing around the acting space, retaining the same quality of movement. We then talked about Rome; what it stood for, its significance in the play, and decided on a word sequence to accompany the rhythmic movement. We combined the movement and speech, building up patterns of movement for the whole group using the acting space.

(ii) **Egypt.** We talked about the sounds associated with Egypt: sounds of waves, winds, sighs, laughter, and produced a variety of vocal sounds that would particularly evoke the arrival of Cleopatra in her barge. The group offered a variety of words and phrases from the text, which we built into an overall sound texture of Egypt. We added to this mime activities suggesting the temptations of Egypt, slow movements of eating, drinking, beckoning, swaying, and more abstract movements suggesting a trance-like state.

I then gave each member of the group an outline 'script', arranged the stage area, and allocated parts. We rehearsed the parts of the drama in order, using the lighting and sound effects available to prompt the action where necessary, and to supplement the effects of voice and movement.

Performance

The stage in darkness. A low rostrum centre. The chorus spaced in a semi-circle behind and around the rostrum, their backs to the audience.

A loud gong off stage. The chorus turns abruptly. Lights flood on. The chorus shouts *ROME*.

The chorus moves freely around the acting space, their movements abrupt, aggressive, mechanical. They chant,

ROME — POWER — ROME — CONTROL — ROME — OBEY — ROME — CONFORM — ROME!

1st Voice: Once there was an Emperor Antony

Antony is thrown forward on to the central rostrum. The lights dim on the chorus. A strong spot appears on Antony. The chorus echoes in a decrescendo, ANTONY, ANTONY

Then Antony shouts, raising his arms slowly.

His legs bestrid the ocean, his reared arm
Crested the world!

The chorus mirrors Antony's movement, raising their arms as in reverence. The respectful salute slowly dissolves into pointing, accusatory gestures, sneering looks, as they begin to mutter,

DOTAGE! FOOL! FETTERS! FOOL! FOOL!

The word 'Fool' gradually dissolves into the sound of the wind blowing over the Egyptian plain, the sound textures of Egypt. The body shapes of the chorus relax, lose their rigidity and melt into the relaxed swaying shapes associated with Egypt. The swaying of some suggests the rocking of a boat; others use drawing movements as if pulling a barge towards them.

Meanwhile Antony, looking out into the audience at the imagined barge approaching him, says,

The barge she sat in, like a burnish'd throne
Burn'd on the water: the poop was beaten gold;
Purple the sails, and so perfumed that
The winds were love-sick with them: the oars were silver,
Which to the tune of flutes kept stroke, and made
The water which they beat to follow faster,
As amorous of their strokes.

The chorus then, using their rehearsed movements and words, offer Antony different temptations. He steps down from his rostrum and moves among them. The movements are sensual and slow, voices soft and lulling.

The chorus gradually moves into two concentric circles surrounding Antony. The inner circle takes hands and begins a slow rhythmic dance moving in one direction, chanting, slowly at first, then faster and faster.

Come thou Monarch of the vine,
Plumpy Bacchus with pink eyne!
In thy fats our cares be drown'd,
With thy grapes our hairs be crowned ...
Cup us till the world go round,
Cup us till the world go round!

The outer circle now begins to move in the opposite direction, repeating the militaristic movement of the first choral sequence, and reiterating the chant,

ROME — POWER — ROME — CONTROL — ROME — OBEY — ROME
— CONFORM — ROME!

Antony reacts with movements suggesting anguish and confusion. In his nightmare state fragments of his past experience are recalled. He cries,

> Duty, honour, obedience.
> Where's my serpent of Old Nile?
> Give me to drink mandragora.
> Fie wrangling queen.
> These strong Egyptian fetters I must break.
> Kingdoms are clay.

The antiphonal choral chant is continued until Antony cries,

> Let Rome in Tiber melt.
> Melt Egypt into Nile.

At this the outer circle echo,

> LET ROME IN TIBER MELT!

The inner circle reply,

> MELT EGYPT INTO NILE!

The chorus very gradually sinks away repeating,

> MELT. Melt. Melt.

When all is still Antony, illuminated by a central spot, says,

> I am dying, Egypt, dying.

He very gradually sinks away to nothing, as

> *Voice 2*: The crown of the earth doth melt,
> O, wither'd is the garland of the war,
> The soldier's pole is fall'n: young boys, and girls
> Are level now with men: the odds is gone
> And there is nothing left remarkable
> Beneath the visiting moon!

The spot begins to fade on the motionless body of Antony.

> *Voice 3*: Think you there was or might be such a man
> As this I dreamt of?

It was, in my eyes, a highly successful collaborative venture offering a group experience of the play to the actors and offering to the
audience the excitement of discovering familiar material in a new
context. In terms of words, the actors had been able to make some
original response and the movements permitted individual variations
according to their interpretation of the contrasting values. Over-
simplification is a recognised convention of the exercise and this, in
itself, can stimulate discussion as to the complexity that the montage
ignores. But, positively, the words are given body in a literal sense
and the importance of the stage-image is made evident through an
exploitation of the imagery in the words.

Another colleague, Dr Bernard Harrison, constructed a collage
based on *Much Ado* which his group of Sixth Formers acted and discussed. He writes:

The collage that was devised sought to bring out the 'dance of courtship' that the play celebrates, and naturally it was devised around Claudio — Hero, and Benedick — Beatrice, with Don Pedro and Margaret as 'approving' chorus and Don John as a 'sinister' chorus. The Balthasar song became a central feature of what quickly began to look more like a masque, or scene from a Mozart Opera, than a play; and dance and stage movements were carefully arranged, to convey the element of formal dance — which would echo the highly formalized language patterns and exchanges between the personae enacting their game of courtship. Collated and printed out, the 'collage' took about twenty minutes to perform, ending with the 'dark' movement of the play when Claudio and Don Pedro are convinced by Don John that 'they' have indeed been deceived by Hero and declaim operatically:

> *Don Pedro*: O day untowardly turned!
> *Claudio*: O mischief strangely thwarting!
> *Don John*: O plague right well prevented!

Dr Harrison was satisfied that the 'formalities of courtship' element came into prominence and that attention was focused on 'Shakespeare's treatment of human patterns of encounter and relating' rather than on 'characterisation' of which, perhaps, in this play it is common to make too much. Although he admits that ideally the students would have devised their own collage, they were free to choose whether they regarded his as fair comment on the experience of the play.

In his books, *The Group Approach to Shakespeare*, David Adland experiments with the notion of a montage of recurrent ideas and images intended to be performed purely by voices. His volume on *The Merchant of Venice* contains *A Montage for Three Voices* which 'draws together a number of references throughout the play to "flesh", "blood" and the idea of feeding on the prodigal Christian, Antonio. While the main source of these references is Shylock, there are also significant speeches by Bassanio, Jessica, Morocco, Antonio, Portia and Salerio' (p. 121). None of the three voices, then, 'represents' a character exclusively and one character's speech may be divided among the three. Speeches do not have to appear in the correct chronological order and single words (such as "blood", "flesh", "prodigal", "feed") may take the form of an incantation. The aim of this particular montage is to reveal 'the inhuman nature of Shylock's revenge and the intense ferocity with which he is prepared to carry it out' (p. 122). There are a number of dangers from a teaching point of view. Unless the rules of the game are made crystal clear, the images and ideas, detached from context, may, in raw juxtaposition, create an impression which the play as a whole does not support. Another objection is that the montage in the book is Adland's own and that ideally the pupils themselves should be making

190

the selection of ideas and the selection of examples and that they should be placing them in an order which seems significant to them. Adland's montage, though, does show the educative potential of unusual juxtapositions:

a: The words expressly are
c: A gaping wound

but it is more meaningful if the students discover these for themselves. The similarity of the ideas expressed by different characters is, indeed, something of which an actor should be aware and it is a unifying force, sometimes the source of profound irony, from the point of view of spectators.

Professor Peter Thomson, of the University of Exeter, puts his students into groups to produce what he calls an 'acted essay'. What he is doing is 'asking people to enact an encounter with the text rather than talking through it'. The technique may involve selection from the original words to highlight felt significances. In a letter to me, he writes:

I've just been working, along with a highly gifted Drama teacher, on a Genet project. Tiny, you might say, if your measure of success was the amount of ground covered. We looked for four sessions at Scene One of *The Screens*, and then the students in pairs looked at different sections (each about 1½ pages only) of the play in order to enact their discoveries. The analogy seemed to me with sudden vividness to be exactly with what, as an English student, I have been accustomed to call practical criticism: i.e. something closer to appreciation. But the tools for a Drama student are not the intelligence and the pen so much as the intuition and the body. It is important, in our course, that we should be encouraging the students to rely on their intuitions — something which other courses discourage in one way or another. A performed essay, if it's going to be something more than a mere translation of an idea, will rest on the clarity of the intuitions.

I asked him if the students at any point used words to explain their intentions. He replied:

The Genet 'Practical Criticisms' were of a very special kind. The actors did use words, but only Genet's. The instructions were to divide a small scene into a series of sections, and to use only one sentence from each section as an accompaniment to an appropriate gesture or gestures. What fascinated me particularly was that Genet emerged from the exercise as a much better disciplined writer than I had supposed. The phrases gathered a surprising cluster of imagic equivalents. The scene chosen (the students were divided into pairs) for the first and most remarkable of the classes was the opening scene of *The Screens*. That is a play that seems to me impervious to an orthodox dramatic reading.

All right for advanced drama students, the hard-pressed schoolteacher may reply, but the literary essay itself is a technique which has to be learned through practice. At least the 'acted essay' eloquently asserts by its very nature the necessity for a new and bolder kind of thinking when it comes to tackling drama problems.

Adapting a play for another medium may involve changing the text. Well managed, the result can be a creative statement based on the interaction of adaptors and text rather than simply an ingenious hunt for 'equivalents', verbal or aural equivalents of visual effects, visual of verbal etc. Incorporating a narration of the stage directions in a radio production of *The Devil's Disciple*, for example, is not to provide an equivalent to the instant impact of a stage set but to involve the adaptor in a selection of aural effects that will provide an appropriate lead-in to the scene as a radio experience. The test of all the text-changing exercises, however, in the context of my argument in this book, is whether they help to define and make more accessible experiences the original text allows. A free adaptation may be a valuable expressive act, but in our terms it should reflect or progress to a meaningful engagement with what the dramatist wrote.

6
Strategies

In my examination of teaching method, I have so far attempted to distinguish and illustrate a variety of classroom activities. Sometimes it has been possible to demonstrate a range of these with reference to a single scene and I have preferred to do this because it also makes for ease of reference for the reader. A strategy might be defined as a procedure for dealing with a part of a play or a whole play as a structural entity and it can include a mixture of those activities we have hitherto separated into broad categories for the sake of convenience.

Pre-planning a sequence of educational experiences may seem a fruitless and artificial exercise on the face of it. As we observed in talking about activities, what a teacher does with any particular class may frequently be the result of inspired opportunism as it is better that the material be made to fit the class than the class the material. But teachers doing extended work on a text often feel safer if they have some idea of at least which aspects of the play it might be profitable to explore, if only so that their pupils enjoy the fullest possible encounter with it.

Again, as with the choice of activity, the strategy a teacher adopts will depend on a number of variable factors. A public examination may force him to categorise and label and to ensure that his pupils know the text extremely well. With another class he may be able to concentrate on simple enjoyment with no academic strings attached. With a third, he may be required to home in on thematic content as a contribution to a programme of integrated studies. The kind of play, the complexity, the style and mode, the date, the length, will also influence his overall approach. So will the facilities available: the amount of space, the equipment. The nature of his class and their mood on any given occasion will have to be taken into account and indeed the personality of the teacher, his strengths and limitations, will determine what procedure he adopts. Finally, he will be influenced by the amount of time he has at his disposal, which may vary from a lesson a week for a year to one double lesson in all.

Whatever the ostensible purpose of his strategy, the underlying aim, to me, should always be the same, that of exercising all a pupil's ways of knowing. This means awakening in him a sense of the play as a piece for performance. As far as the play is concerned, we are attempting eventually to discover what it is 'about', not in the sense of unravelling the plot or digging out a 'message', but of elucidating what Bentley (in *The Life of the Drama*) calls its 'wisdom' or 'vision'. This is 'more than is commonly meant by thought, or idea, or theme, or statement, and as such is not a part of the play but a precipitate of the play as a whole' (pp. 145–6). I am talking of the 'import' of a play, seen as the significant development to which all the elements of the experience add up. If we are to encourage a theatrical orientation, possibly the most useful question to ask is 'How does this play work?' What kinds of theatrical effects does it urge the stage artist to create? In what terms can its meaning be apprehended by an audience and on what grounds can a judgement as to its quality be formulated? In attempting to understand how a play works, we are led quite naturally to a consideration of all the factors that help to clarify our sense of its distinctive style. These include the age in which it was written, the nature of the person who wrote it, the theatre he wrote it for and its intended audience. But insofar as a play is not a fixed and static object but a dynamic event, there are other factors which make a contribution to its essence and we have also to consider the contribution of the here-and-now setting, real or speculative, physical and human, of the people working on it and spectating.

With junior pupils, we may feel little compulsion to isolate 'elements', but with senior pupils some teachers may feel bound to undertake a systematic treatment of them, elements such as theme or idea, character, plot, structure, dialogue, imagery and symbolism. A thorough job would also take account of specifically theatrical elements such as setting, focus and tempo. It is important, though, to remember that identifying elements and fitting a play into a category is not a satisfactory end in itself. Asking how a play works persuades the student to concentrate on the function of these things. Insofar as he acts, produces and spectates, or imagines himself doing these things, he will test the usefulness of the concepts in helping him execute or conceive a performance. Successful performance will involve an awareness of both detail and totality, of the synthesis to which analysis should lead.

'Background' work on the social, political, philosophical and

194

literary context of the play falls into place, also, as an aid to the making of artistic and theatrical decisions and to an understanding of an event as it is. The temptation to indulge in historical or biographical research for its own sake is thereby minimised. Similarly, pupils might find it more profitable to compare their own improvised versions based on source material with the dramatist's written version, or to consider the usefulness of such material in helping a director to decide on the style of presentation, than simply to enumerate changes the dramatist makes.

Another possible procedure in the teacher's strategy is to relate a play to more recent thought. Thus Freud may be invoked to help us understand the psychology of Oedipus or Berne may be invoked (*Games People Play*) to give support to Albee in his rendering of human behaviour in *Who's Afraid of Virginia Woolf?* Again, the test is whether the actor plays the part better for an acquaintance with Freud's ideas or whether a director can use Berne's games to help the actors better to understand the spirit and purpose of Albee's games. Sometimes a teacher may wish to include comparisons with other plays by the same playwright or other playwrights. An enactment of the 'jealousy' of Othello as an approach to the acting of that of Leontes can be a valuable exercise in clarification. Sometimes comparison with a different art form can be helpful. A look at *Animal Farm* may illuminate an aspect of the style of *Volpone* and make a director see some advantage in stressing the bird-animal-insect metaphor as well as the psychology of the characters. Scholarly work on the changing of meanings through time has an obvious importance, but the performance-orientated pupil will also become aware that the meaning a play can have for us is what matters in the end. It may be that even a dated Shakespearean joke can raise a legitimate laugh if the actor can crack it with sufficient aplomb. Fourth Form pupils of mine were easily able to invest 'colt' with enough meaning to evoke the obligatory groan in the following exchange: (Falstaff is horseless and harassed)

Falstaff: What a plague mean ye to colt me thus?
Prince: Thou liest: thou are not colted, thou are uncolted.

Finally, a teacher of pupils doing advanced work will probably want to refer to comments by the writer himself and by critics and reviewers. If his strategy has the orientation we have described, it is hoped the pupils will find it easier to ask whether the comment by the writer squares with his own experience or conception of the

195

performance. Peter Nichols says that in *Forget Me Not Lane* he was getting his own back on his father, but does the part of the father as written seem grotesquely unplayable or has it a positive stage vitality? Does the critic seem to be aware of the difference performance can make? When the pupil was an 'audience' at a class rendering of *Oedipus Rex*, did he notice inconsistencies in Oedipus's behaviour? Did he, as an actor, feel it necessary to play the king as stupid?

We have been talking of the range of areas the full-scale treatment of a substantial play may cover. Bearing in mind that circumstances alter cases, where might a teacher begin? I think his choice of introduction is very important. In it he needs to alert the minds of the pupils to the possibilities of the play whilst taking care not to anticipate their response to it.

Talking of a class reading, Michael Marland recommends a verbal introduction by the teacher which 'has to be brief but well judged to establish rapidly in the pupils' minds the atmosphere, setting, and characters, and to hint at some of the issues to which the group should be alive' (*The Use of English*, Winter 1966, p. 109). His aim is to ensure that the reading is a 'fully educational experience', and I would accept the justification with the reservation that the teacher should confine himself to things about the play which are virtually incontrovertible. Initial help of this kind can give a group confidence to plunge into a play in an unfamiliar idiom. A teacher may be tempted to approach a period dramatist such as Shakespeare by establishing the 'background' first. A study of Elizabethan stage conventions may help us to understand the advantages of a particular method of staging but in practical terms the space in the classroom is what has to be adapted to. If the play is allowed to make the initial impact, the background then has a reason for being interesting.

Some teachers prefer to supply a quick summary of a whole play with a dynamic recital of the juiciest speeches. Insofar as this tempts the pupils to want to have a go themselves it fulfils a worthy aim. But there is a risk with virtuoso displays that a particular interpretation will receive the unalterable stamp of Sir's authority. The risk is even greater if the teacher reads a whole scene aloud himself before starting to work on it with the class, especially if — as I have seen — he merely follows it with literary discussion. To avoid the danger, his reading would, in fact, have to be unbearably neutral.

Better, in my opinion, if it can be managed, to begin with a quick reading by the more able readers in the class. If a complete reading is difficult (say, of a Restoration play) a selection of episodes with linking narrative by the teacher is possible, but a play like *Billy Liar* presents no such problems. At least by this approach the play can be seen from the start to belong to the pupils and tentative exploration will already have started. The quick summary by the teacher kills curiosity about what happens next, but the 'scan' reading by the class satisfies it. Furthermore, it allows some early sense of the pace at which the audience will receive the play in performance, makes it possible to be aware of the significance of the part in the whole scheme and frees the class to concentrate on aspects of the drama other than simple plot. One does not have to be working on Brecht for this to be a benefit.

There may be objections to the quick read-through as an opening gambit on the grounds that this also falls badly short of the experience the dramatist offers and that the moment-by-moment build-up through practical exploration is the only truly open-ended and pupil-orientated approach, whether it be done by a class or in groups — and I have some sympathy with this view. I find in practice that unless the pace of this kind of work can be relatively quick it can try the pupils' patience. An actor starting rehearsals has usually at least read the play and his decisions can be facilitated by his sense of the way he knows the play develops. They will certainly be influenced by the director's perspective view. An idea of the overall picture does not have to stunt the capacity to discover, as the overall picture will be susceptible to change.

Suppose a teacher is able to arrange for the class to see a stage performance before opening the book. Again the risks are fairly obvious. An intelligent production can inspire the pupils to want to re-live the event for themselves and can make the non-verbal aspects of the play vividly present during future readings. But a poor performance may make it difficult for the teacher to re-sell the play and both good and bad performances may cramp the pupil's style. I feel that it is vital for the teacher to 'case' the production in advance, for he may find the director has taken outrageous liberties with the text and what he is exposing the pupil to is not even an interpretation of the original. The danger even with a relatively faithful rendering is that it acquires in the pupil's mind the prestige of a definitive performance. I wouldn't say this is inevitable and would trust a good teacher to capitalise on the benefits and counteract the fossilisation. After all, experienced teachers will testify that the opposite procedure has equal dangers; that is to say that pupils whose opinions have hardened in classroom work refuse to accept any performance of their favourite piece that does not square exactly with their established preconceptions.

A factor which somewhat minimises the danger of a performance being accepted as definitive is the realisation which can dawn that actors and audience interact, that shared excitement is infectious, for instance; that the performance, in other words, is not entirely 'fixed'. The same is not true of a sound or videotape recording or a film, which have a unique air of inevitability about them. Sometimes, these versions try to capture a theatrical presentation without the advantages of the theatrical atmosphere. If they remain true to their medium, they will adapt and the emphasis will shift. The Open University's version of *The Wild Duck*, for example, comes out more solemn than a stage performance might, insofar as running gags, such as Hjalmar's eating in Act IV, tend to lose continuity in the montage of selected camera shots. These versions can have a great value in highlighting certain features of a performance, as a good recording does the words, but a wise teacher will probably save them until later. Preferably, the introductory work should face the pupils as early as possible with the distinctive nature of the stage play. I deplore the practice of using gramophone records as a short cut to save the pupils wrestling with the words for themselves. Of course, if the class is working on a radio or TV script, an experience of acting and directing television material may not be possible to reproduce in the classroom. But, especially with scripts written with particular actors in mind, such as *Steptoe and Son*, it will only too forcibly be brought home how prior exposure to a performance can determine once and for all the way a text can be read.

A complete, theatrical performance is sometimes actually brought to the schools by a Theatre in Education team. If the play is a 'set' text, then the teacher will probably have some overall strategy for dealing with it and may have some choice over how and where he interpolates the performance. Often, though, the play is one which the pupils will not have met and on which they will not subsequently be working. It may, in fact, be a play which the company have themselves devised. The successful integration of such a performance with the ongoing drama work in the school will depend very much on the amount and quality of the liaison that the company manage to establish with the teachers. The pupils may at no stage have scripts of their own (despite the fact that some T.I.E. scripts have been published) and practical work of the kind we are concerned with will, in consequence, be difficult. Follow-up work may consist solely of a discussion with the actors of issues raised, as happened in the area where I live with a performance of Athol Fugard's *Hello and Goodbye*. At least, though, the pupils have an artefact to which to respond and a structured experience within which to discover meanings.

John O'Toole, in his excellent book, *Theatre in Education*, distinguishes three kinds of presentation, where the audience's function is either Extrinsic, Peripheral or Integral. The first kind I have just described. In the second, a complete script is acted out but members of the audience, probably rehearsed in advance, take part in selected scenes. I wrote such a play for the Nottingham Playhouse Company called *Maoris, Missionaries and Muskets*, a story of the colonisation of New Zealand. At agreed points, children rose from their seats and became Maoris doing a 'haka' or members of a church congregation. There was little or no room for the pupils to 'interpret' for themselves: they were confined to minor roles and they achieved an audience-perspective only on parts of the play in which they weren't participating. Another programme I helped to devise, this time for the Sheffield Crucible Vanguard Company, highlighted the uneasiness of the compromise more dramatically. At one point, some primary school children mimed the working of a scythe-making factory. After it, an actor asked them how they'd like to do that for the rest of their lives. He prodded and provoked them until they were on the point of riotous protest. Such commitment might have been channelled into fruitful discussion but the structure of the play frustrated such a development and it ground on its way regardless, fulfilling at least one useful purpose, however, that of cooling the rising tempers. *Snap Out Of It*, a programme on mental illness devised by the Leeds Playhouse team, seems to have been much more successful, making the active involvement of the audience integral to the central experience of the play.

In some respects, *Snap Out Of It* qualified to be considered under O'Toole's third category, programmes where the children are allowed to take a hand in shaping the action itself, becoming playwrights with the actors. These actors, in role, freely interact with them, stimulating them into discovering and solving problems. Educationally this has attractions which the 'peripheral' experience lacks and arguably it is the T.I.E. team's unique and proper field. However, the

199

actual theatrical element may, in O'Toole's words, be 'relegated to a servicing function' and the whole process is perhaps too open-ended to fall within the scope of this book. Theatre in Education interests us here insofar as it offers or contributes to a strategy for dealing with a script.

Some teachers, especially of younger pupils, like to begin their classroom strategy with an improvisation of the action of a play or scene before touching the text. The trouble with this as a first encounter with a play is that it is shaped entirely by the teacher's account and if he tries to be faithful to as many of the features of the style as he can, his presentation may be so complicated that he might as well have let the pupils meet the original words in the first place. The indirect introduction which involves the use of analogical situations, although it has the worthy aim of moving from the familiar to the unfamiliar again, can suffer, too, from reliance on the teacher's pre-existing conclusions about the structure and meaning of the experience. There are, of course, games and exercises that can be valuable as 'warm-ups' to any drama session and even those employing skills that bear directly on a particular script can have the general function of preparing the mind and body for the kind of work peculiar to drama. If the particular relevance escapes, then, unacknowledged, time will not have been wasted.

Having decided on his opening move, what ways are there in which the teacher can proceed? He can work his way through the play, section by homogeneous section, either as a reading-cum-sedentary workshop or using active techniques, inter-weaving discussion (and writing?) throughout and helping his students at the end to link up their impressions and attempt some general statement about the nature of the experience. The significance of background information will have been assessed and established as opportunity arose. Rehearsed readings, sedentary or not, will have given the class a useful setting for critical discussion. The teacher may decide that, in spite of the wealth of possible modes of presentation a play can afford, the pupils are ultimately going to work on an agreed style of production. This has the advantage of forcing pupils to follow through the implications of decisions made without conveniently forgetting them when the next section makes the going sticky. It is a method which Patrick Berthoud proposed to adopt in his Open University unit on *Oedipus Rex*:

We have to find a means of approach which will preserve and nourish the best of

200

our subjective response without succumbing to the limitations of our own isolated individuality ... When we discuss the play in greater detail we should do so in terms of specific performance, whether in its original setting or in any other, provided we retain always the distinctions proper to productions in different times and places. We have to avoid an amorphous and messy heap of impressions which could not be produced as a whole play at any time or place.

(Pp. 57–8)

It is possible, of course, to work towards an actual class performance of a play as a strategy for dealing with it. This, naturally, sets the play in its true context and creates a theatrical event in all its completeness. If there aren't enough students in the class, as happens with some Sixth Forms, it may be possible to drum up recruits from outside. Unless such an exercise is interlarded with experimental workshops and discussion, though, the individual may, in the exigencies of meeting deadlines, come in for something of a raw deal, be landed with a small part or backstage job and be given no say in how the production is to shape up.

Hodgson and Richards recommend improvising a whole play. They hasten to allay the fear of teachers who would protest that they haven't the time by saying that the firm grasp on the text that the exercise leads to means that time is ultimately saved. Here, too, a production on a stage is a natural conclusion, and the benefits and the snags of this still apply. Improvisatory work which tests the limits of the experience the text helps to define can be a valuable way of personalising the text and of discovering the relevance to the pupils and to their own lives. David Self found that having his Sixth Form invent games around relationships gave their subsequent work on *Who's Afraid of Virginia Woolf?* a grounding in authenticity. Certainly with youngsters the first wise move after an initial reading can be to get them up and about, interacting face to face and free of the books.

The teacher does not, of course, have to start at the beginning of a play. If he is approaching it through its 'elements' he may decide to work, say, on *King Lear*, by first experimenting with the scenes involving the Fool. Another play may tempt him to proceed via the language. The important thing is to allow the individual play and the needs of the pupils to determine the priorities he accords to the elements and the order in which he tackles them. With some classes, he does not have to do the whole play at all. If he deems the students will enjoy only the Bottom scenes of *A Midsummer Night's Dream* or the Falstaff escapades in *Henry IV Part One* or selected scenes from a

201

Brecht play then he merely supplies as full a picture of the surrounding context as he thinks necessary. But even when doing a full play, he may decide that the best way to grip and hold interest is to jump to a particularly lively or accessible scene or set of scenes. The style of a play, as John Russell Brown points out, can be adequately sampled from any slice, wherever it comes from: 'Treat the play like a cake and cut one slice or, better, several small slices from different parts. Then take each sample in turn and separate each crumb, examine it carefully and discover of what it is composed and then ask how these minute elements fit together and react on each other.' (*Effective Theatre*, p. 23.)

Having sorted out the situation which obtains in Wycherley's *Country Wife*, for instance, the teacher may decide to begin with the famous china scene, the experience and memory of whose comedy can sustain the student through some of the more turgid topical persiflage. With an episodic play like *Ernie's Incredible Illucinations*, it doesn't much matter where you begin, and if the class needs livening up and liberating from the script, the middle scene in the boxing booth might best set the process rolling. In general, though, it is best to restore the scenes to their original order eventually. A radio or TV play can be recorded higgledy-piggledy and the tape spliced so that the play returns to its pristine shape, but the pupils then have to make do with living through their experience as an audience and they don't get a chance as actors and directors to make the adjustments and alterations that an evolving performance or a sense of an evolving performance dictates. On the other hand, once a class is very sure of a text, deliberately making a montage or a collage version and performing it can freshen up what was stale and restore the dynamism to an appreciation of the dramatist's form. At this stage, too, students might engage in adapting for another medium. The TV version of the death of Antony I saw done by Sixth Formers (see page 86) threw new light on the *staging* of the scene.

Discussion, we have said, will occur at all points, whether it is institutionalised or not. For set discussion, starting points will often suggest themselves without our stir. I feel Michael Marland is right when he says it is 'best based on specific quotations or detailed moments. (*The Use of English*, op. cit., p. 109.) These quotations may be lines or even whole episodes. The Lieutenant in *Mother Courage*, Scene Eleven, asks (of Kattrin) "Is nothing sacred to her?" If we, too, ask that question, we are into the matter not merely of Kattrin's values but the Lieutenant's and, broadening the argument, of the scene's. Instead of asking 'Is *The Wild Duck* a Play of Ideas?' we would find it more profitable to conduct a reading or performance of the episode between Gregers Werle and Dr Relling and ask if their opposing statements about the need for a life-lie are a good guide to somebody (a director) seeking a satisfactory interpretation of the play. A provocative statement, especially about the play as performance, can open up fruitful dialectic. The following review of *The Winter's Tale* (in *The Guardian*) does not need the reader to have seen the performance in order to provoke a response:

The Winter's Tale has defeated more experienced directors than Penelope Cherns. At least she is in good company if she has failed to get on top of the text in this production at the Chester Gateway.

It is a monster of a play from which to make any sort of sense. Almost everybody in it, from the short lived Princeling Mamillius to Leontes himself seems to be a pompous old bore. Only Autolycus has any lines worth uttering and few of them would make it into a decent dictionary of quotations. And the things they get up to, from consulting oracles to being eaten by bears must take up a good term of explaining to fifth formers.

Nobody could accuse this director of not trying to throw some light on Shakespeare's fuddled dream of cyclical change with the passage of time. If anything, she tries too hard. What coherence there is — and its precious little — is lost in inventive embellishments.

The playing, which was shaky in the shallows, was simply too theatrical at the top end. Peter Machin's high pitched Leontes jumped straight in with pyrotechnic passion at the suspicion that his wife was having a bit on the side. So that by the time his entire family had been wiped out by the gods he had nowhere to go.

Writing can never occur as 'naturally' as talk, especially if our general strategy is based on a goodly portion of practical work. Set essays can discipline thought and are most relevant when they assume that there are more ways of investigating dramatic experience than by simply reading the words. Some kinds of writing, as I have tried to show, can be directly useful to the stage artist and to the spectator, facilitating classroom workshops and reflecting on theatrical events, wherever they occur. The placing of such exercises is usually self-evident. Relevance to theatrical practice can be a useful condition to apply to other, more established forays with the pen. The teacher of the examination form, who launches his pupils on the summary of a plot, might ask himself whether this would help a director. It is certainly valuable for a director to know who is on stage, who enters and who leaves and when they do so; but 'plot' co-exists with so many other elements and the exercise may force the reader to give the wrong kind of attention to the text. Summarising *The Way of the*

World is a strenuous intellectual exercise, but whether one needs to have all the details clear, especially at the beginning, is open to doubt. It is the atmosphere of plotting that needs to be brought out and the student might be better employed sorting out the relationships and general intentions of the characters. Niceties can be left until practical necessity forces them to be clarified. Writing more conventionally describable as 'creative' can also be tied in with practical work in progress. Many of the activities involving improvisation could involve writing, if the children concerned are up to it. Writing additional stage dialogue between characters in imaginary situations or in 'missing' scenes can be fed into acting or can afford valuable critical insights.

There follow, now, some examples of possible strategies for two scenes and two plays. They are chosen principally to illustrate how a variety of activities might be deployed. Naturally, I would not expect them to be neatly applicable to any class of an appropriate age or stage of development, but they are at least based on my own encounters with particular groups of students.

Example 1 A scene from 'The Travails of Sancho Panza' by James Saunders

(1)

> *The 1st Bandit appears. He comes on stealthily, makes sure the two are asleep, and beckons. The 2nd Bandit enters. The 2nd Bandit examines Rozinante. He looks inquiringly at the 1st Bandit and points to Rozinante. The 1st Bandit shakes his head and points to Sancho's ass. The 2nd Bandit nods. 1st Bandit points to an overhanging bough above Sancho's head. The 2nd Bandit goes off, while the 1st Bandit unbuckles Dapple's saddle-girths. The 2nd Bandit comes back with a length of rope, to one end of which are attached a number of hooks. He throws the other end of the rope over the bough. The 1st Bandit hooks on the saddle. Both Bandits haul on the other end, and Sancho is raised an inch from his ass. They tie the rope to a low branch or root. The 1st Bandit takes out a carrot which he holds in front of the ass. The ass advances and follows him offstage. The 2nd Bandit takes the panniers attached to the saddle, and also makes off.*
>
> *A pause. Sancho wakes up. He snorts, groans, feels his bruises.*

Sancho: Now it's raining ... And I ache all over ... Well, now, Sancho, enough bellyaching. Copy your valiant master for a change. Look on the bright side, if you can find one. Let's see — rain's good for the crops ... As for your aching bones, at least you've still got a mouthful of teeth. What's more, you've got your dear Dapple. Life's not so bad ...

He pats the ass's neck, or tries to. He feels around frantically, then looks down, to see himself suspended in mid-air. He gives a terrible cry of anguish, and topples out of the saddle on to the ground, where he continues to cry out, waking Don Quixote who jumps to his feet waving his sword.

(2) *Don Quixote*: What is it! Are you bewitched?

Sancho: Worse! Robbed! They've stolen my ass from under me!

Don Quixote: A very powerful charm, to spirit an ass from under your weight.

Sancho: Charm nothing! Look! (*He waves at the rope and saddle.*)

Don Quixote: Most ingenious. 'Twould be worth the loss of an ass to have seen that operation.

Sancho: Oh would it! I'm glad of that! I'll bear that in mind!

Don Quixote: Come, Sancho, what's an ass after all?

Sancho: Nothing to you, I daresay. But to me, I'll tell you what she was. She was born in my own home; she played with my children; she carried my burdens; she earned my living; she was my child, my friend — my bit of property. (*He cries.*)

Don Quixote: Come now, Sancho. Listen: At home I have five ass-foals. I'll give you two of them.

> (*Sancho looks up, sobbing.*)

Three.

> (*Sancho stops sobbing, sniffs, gets up, wipes his nose.*)

Sancho: Three ass-foals?

> (*Don Quixote nods.*)

You'll write it down to make it official?

Don Quixote: If you wish.

Sancho: Well, then . . .

> (*He clears his throat and wipes his eyes. Then he calls offstage to his absent ass.*)

Short tears, Dapple. That's the way it is. Don't think too bad of me. Three asses for one ass. I can't afford sentiment . . . Just don't let them beat you . . .

> (*He turns to Don Quixote.*)

Enough of that. Now let's forget it. Sancho's got a bargain for once. I think. Let's move on, Master, for suddenly I hate this place.

> (*He begins to untie the rope and saddle. Don Quixote looks offstage, where there is the sound of hooves and a man singing.*)

(3) *Don Quixote*: Wait, Sancho! Here comes someone to reverse our fortunes.

> (*Sancho looks.*)

Sancho: A travelling barber? To reverse our fortunes? Master, if all I needed was a beard trim —

Don Quixote: That is no barber.

Sancho: Oh, *Master* . . . (*He shakes his head.*) The *giants* . . . The *castle* . . . The *wizards* . . .

Don Quixote: I don't follow your drift. What have they to do with yonder Knight?

Sancho: Nothing, nothing . . . (*He looks at the sky.*) It's not a travelling barber, who's put his basin on his head to keep off the rain . . . It's a *Knight* . . . with a *helmet* . . .

Don Quixote: *The* helmet. If I mistake not, the helmet worn by yon Knight on his dappled steed is no other than that fabled golden helm of Mambrino, the most coveted in the world.

205

(Sancho nods, past disagreeing.)
Draw aside now, and see how I shall take it from him.
Sancho: That I'll do. As for what comes out of it, I'm past meddling.
(Sancho withdraws behind the tree, Don Quixote mounts Rozinante, takes up his lance and goes offstage, the opposite side from the approaching barber. The Barber enters, in good spirits in spite of the rain. He sees Sancho behind the tree and stops singing.)
Barber: Good day to you, friend.
Sancho: Oh, is it? Mark what I say then: Let it be what it will, it's none of my business.
Barber: What?
(Don Quixote appears.)
Don Quixote: Defend yourself, vile caitiff creature, or render up of your own will that which by all right is mine!
(So saying, he puts spurs to Rozinante and charges. The Barber yelps, slides off his ass and runs, leaving both ass and basin.)
A wise man. Pick up the helmet, Sancho.
(Sancho comes from behind the tree, picks up the basin and looks at it.)
Sancho: It's a good basin. *(He raps it with his knuckles.)* Solid brass. Worth a real of anyone's money.
He hands it to Don Quixote with a sour expression. Don Quixote puts it on, turning it to find the vizor.
Don Quixote: But no vizor.
Sancho: They don't often put 'em on barbers' basins.
Don Quixote: Truly it is like a basin.
Sancho: It is. I've never seen a basin so like a basin.
Don Quixote: This is what I think has happened. This enchanted helmet —
(Sancho strikes his head.)
— has fallen into the hands of some smith ignorant of its magic, who melted the vizor half down for its gold, and fashioned *this* half into a barber's basin. But it matters not, the magic is still in it.
Don Quixote examines it again. Sancho turns away in disgust; on the turn, his eye lights on the ass. He does a double-take. He looks in the direction taken by the Barber, looks at the ass, at Don Quixote, at the Barber, at himself, at the ass. He strokes his chin.
Sancho: Master . . .
Don Quixote (*looking at the helmet*): The steed, of course, you may keep as spoils of battle.
(Sancho's face breaks into a smile.)
Sancho: And not a soul in sight to pummel me for it!
(He advances cautiously on the ass, afraid it might disappear, then catches its bridle. He laughs with glee.)
(4) *Sancho*: *Four* asses now. Three paper ones and one flesh. Oh, I'm a rogue! Tell me, your honour, did you ever hear of any rogue of a merchant who multiplied his stock by four in as many minutes! Oh, he's a — *(He looks.)* She's a good ass. A well-kept ass. Let's have a look under her saddle . . . *(He takes it off.)* Look not a rib showing. This ass has lived on the fat of the land. Good-natured too; aren't you, my beauty, my

206

darling? This ass has a loving disposition, I can tell you that. Women are a mystery to me, but asses I can read like a book. This is an ass in a million. I pity that barber, he must have doted on her. She how well he kept her. Fed her with titbits from his own dinner, petted her and combed her and told her his troubles; and sang songs to her as they travelled, to while away the journey. And now she's gone. And he's sitting behind a rock somewhere, I daresay, in the rain, without a soul for company, minus his basin, minus his ass, the only friend he had in the world . . .

(He is now blubbering freely. He looks at the ass, then yells at it.)

Traitor! Wretch! Temptress! Is there no pity left in the world, that you'd leave your master after all he's done for you, and just when he needs you most, having just had his ass stolen by some vile, heartless, stinking knave! Go, go back to your master, you brazen bitch, you slut! Go back, you bag of bones! Go back! Go back!

(He beats her off the stage, and cries.)

(5) *Don Quixote:* I'm beginning to wonder if you've taken leave of your wits. Are you to weep at every ass you see? You'd do well to model yourself on Knights errant such as me. Do I weep at misfortune? No. Do I worry over my possessions? No. Hungry or thirsty, weary or wounded, I make no complaint. My satisfaction is not of the body but of the spirit: my most cherished possession the thought that throughout the land the poor and the oppressed are thinking of me with gratitude for the wrongs I have righted and the loads I have lifted from their backs. Fie on you, Sancho; copy me though you be only a squire.

The Shepherd Lad enters.

And see — as if sent from Heaven to prove my point. Do you remember me, boy?

Lad: I do not!

Don Quixote: Where are you off to now lad?

Lad: Running away, what d'you think?

Don Quixote: What! After I made your master pay you! Ungrateful wretch, would you undo all the good I did?

Lad: If only I could. *(He turns to Sancho)* He paid me alright! When he got home he gave me the biggest beating I've had in my life, and I've had some. He beat me for myself, then he beat me for him. That's how he paid me, and he's promised me the same wage again next week. So I'm off. And you might tell that master of yours in future to keep his help for them as is strong enough for it, and for the rest, to mind his own business.

The Lad leaves. Don Quixote watches him go, full of consternation.

Don Quixote: There must be some mistake . . . I don't understand . . .

Sancho: Don't you? Then let me explain.

He stands looking at Don Quixote's crestfallen figure, trying to avoid pitying him.

The devil take it! The devil take it all! The devil take all Knights and all castles, and the devil take wandering about this lousy world on kicks and empty bellies, and the devil take doing good and the devil take chivalry! And the devil take you for separating me from my wife and

SCRIPTED DRAMA

my home and my ass for the sake of an Isle when I don't even know
what an Isle is, and the devil take me for being a fool enough to be
taken in by it all!
> He stops. Don Quixote falls to his knees, utterly dejected.
> Sancho looks at him for a moment and shakes his head.

Take no notice of me Master. (*He goes up to him.*)
Take no notice . . .

Strategy

This play, which was performed at the National Theatre in 1969—70,
is based on Cervantes' *Don Quixote*. The Don, imagining himself to
be a medieval knight, sets off through early 17th century Spain to
right the wrongs of the world in a chivalric but simple-minded way.
As his 'squire' he takes with him his servant, Sancho Panza. In spite
of his reluctance and embarrassment, Sancho humours his master,
while keeping a weather eye open for his own advantage.

The play is described as 'for the young': in the classroom, this
would probably mean second or third years of the secondary school.
It is episodic in structure and has the advantage, for practical class-
work, of being divisible into fairly self-contained sections. For the
sake of this exercise, however, it must be assumed that the session
below is part of a sequence of lessons on the play as a whole and that
it would undoubtedly mean more to a class already familiar with the
characters and the style of event.

The play brings the wish-fulfilling dream into comic clash with
everyday reality, gently nudging those working on it into a reappraisal
of an impulse, in many ways laudable, that youngsters often feel.
The aim with this scene is to allow the class the opportunity to
explore its comic potential, the adjustments made to each other by
the dreamer and the realist, and the reactions of an audience to their
attitudes to life.

The ways in which the approaches described are used will vary
according to whether the class consists of pupils all of whom can
read with a degree of fluency or whether the class is of mixed ability,
with some who can hardly read at all. With a mixed ability class, a
quick introductory read-through by the best readers can help to give
coherence to the work which follows it.

All children can do these preparatory warm-up exercises:
(a) Sit in a large circle (or circles). One pupil takes a chunk of
aerial substance and shapes it into an object of his choice. He passes
this object on to his neighbour, who squashes it back to its original

208

shape and creates a new object for himself. Nothing is said until everybody has had a turn. The pupils then confirm that they guessed right (if they did) what object they received. This exercise requires a concentrated effort of imagination and an expressive use of the body and involves, incidentally, the sort of transformation of one thing into another (here, nothing into something) that Quixote carries out 'for real' every day of his life.

(b) The class plays 'Keeper of the Keys', as described on page 159. While practising control of movement, the pupils are also, without yet perhaps realising it, rehearsing the activities of the bandits.

(c) Sitting on the floor, each pupil has an imaginary rope looped under his arms which passes over a pulley above and into the hands of the teacher. When the teacher pulls, each pupil feels himself being lifted onto tiptoe. When the teacher lets go, on a signal, they all collapse in heaps. Here they are all being Sanchos, as well as giving their bodies into the control of their imaginations.

The scene can be tackled in five sections (marked on the extract supplied) and the titles of the sections can be written on a blackboard for regular reference. (1) The theft (2) Sancho gets another ass (3) The attack on the barber (4) Talking to the ass (5) The Don's disappointment.

(1) The theft

In groups of four, mime the theft of the ass. By a stroke of luck, the scene begins with pure physical action. Once the sequence described in the stage directions has been absorbed, (it can be read out by the teacher or by a reader in a group) the performers are free of the script. Go as far as the point where Sancho hits the floor and the Don leaps up. Ignore Sancho's first speech. If you have tambourines or something of the kind, one of the bandits can create 'rain' noise. Change roles.

(2) Sancho gets another ass

If all are reasonable readers, rehearse this duologue in pairs. There is not much overt action and the scripts are that degree less restricting, but those pupils less adept at reading could improvise the exchange. In both cases explore Sancho's rapid change of mood. Discuss with the pupils what they have discovered about the way this should be played.

209

(3) The attack on the barber

This episode would be appropriate for *all* to improvise, since there is a lot of overt action and it is this which is the source of the comic quality. Some preliminary class exercises will help mobilise their imaginations: for example, all pupils rehearse walking in armour and charging on a horse. They should then try these actions as Don Quixote. They will need to bear in mind how the charge will look from the point of view of the barber and from the point of view of the audience.

From the script, discover the order of events (as a class or in groups, depending on the general reading ability).

In threes, act out the events; improvise the appropriate dialogue.

(4) Talking to the ass

The key feature of this section is Sancho's address to the ass and through working on this, the actor can explore Sancho's emotionally volatile nature.

If all are fair readers, divide the class into pairs. In each pair both are Sanchos and between them is an invisible ass. One Sancho starts to read the speech and as soon as a change of tone is sensed, the other Sancho takes over. If a class has a wide range of ability, the teacher could read out the speech in a neutral way while all combine to identify the implicit changes of attitude. Then the fluent readers proceed in pairs as above, the less able readers improvising in pairs, at least initially. A performance of either of these versions by selected pairs will be entertaining and valuable.

Rehearse the whole episode, with or without scripts, in pairs, one pupil now being Sancho, one Don Quixote.

(5) Don Quixote's disappointment

The Lad who now arrives was rescued from his tyrannical master by the Don earlier in the play but has in the meantime had to return to reality and a beating. On the stage, the Lad's narrative and the contrasts of mood defining character and relationship in this section would be quite clear from gesture and movement only. In the classroom, this gives all pupils a chance to empathise physically with the characters and make a direct, individual approach to their feelings. In groups of three they explore the episode in mime.

If it is feasible, the pupils can next rehearse the episode with the words added, although the mime itself will bear repeating with a change of roles.

The whole script

Casts of four, with Bandits doubling as Barbers and Boys, are now in a position to rehearse the whole scene, either with or without scripts. If there is to be more than one 'presentation', an element of theatre can be surreptitiously introduced by changing the position of the audience. Eventually the performers can be asked to comment on the difference in orientation required. Another way of treating the performance is to divide the class into fours, threes and twos. The fours rehearse Section 1; the threes Sections 3 and 5; the two Sections 2 and 4. Then a complete version can be tacked together in the style of a medieval 'mystery' performance. The success of this enterprise, though, does depend on the thoroughness with which the teacher has switched the roles around during the earlier work.

It is likely that an improvised version will have more apparent life in it than a performance at this stage with a script. How far a teacher wishes to polish the scripted performance is a matter for his judgement, but he shouldn't be down-hearted with crude results. What he has to ask himself, as we have stressed before, is whether the present reading is better than the earlier one; whether, in fact, the actors have started to make the action more securely their own. If he doesn't go for polish, he will find it educationally valuable now to mix in the less able with the more able readers. Poor readers will have a familiar dramatic context and (with luck) a supportive social context to give them confidence.

This whole schedule is very full and would occupy at the very least a double period. Work of this kind, however, on only a part of the scene would be sufficient to give the class a feel of how the rest could go.

Example 2 An extract from 'The Merchant of Venice', Scene One, Act Four (lines 1−396 of the New Shakespeare edition)

Strategy

I have referred several times to this scene in the course of the book and it seems appropriate to include a possible strategy for it in this section, putting some of the activities suggested in a coherent educational setting. I have conducted a workshop on the scene with Fifth Formers studying the play at 'O' level and was given a whole afternoon for this. The following plan draws on that experience and incorporates improvements, and could spread over two such afternoons, if the teacher so wished it.

The Merchant of Venice is a romantic comedy and although the trial scene is fraught with danger, the expectations built up in the preceding three acts will undoubtedly affect the audience's attitude to events. The scene has long, difficult speeches but strong melodramatic action, suspense and conflicts. My strategy would aim at helping the pupils to discover how to play the roles, sense the rhythm of the action and the atmosphere, and decide on an acceptable distribution of sympathies. I would attempt to include as many of the following approaches as possible.

(1) Read the scene through in class for the overall shape, clarifying the main line of the story, broadly establishing the emotional and intellectual positions of the characters and identifying conflicts.

(2) Divide the scene into working sections. (Elicit suggestions from the class.) I found three main sections were useful for my purposes, one ending after Antonio says "Most heartily I do beseech the court to give the judgement", a point at which Portia gives up the attempt to dissuade Shylock from his course of action, one ending where Shylock, defeated, says "Why then the devil give him good of it" and heads for the exit, and a last section where he is awarded his legal punishment. The first of my sections could be divided into two at the entrance of Portia, but it actually continues the work of persuasion that the others had already been engaged in.

(3) In the first part of the scene pupils can work in pairs on polishing a skeletal dialogue between the Duke and Antonio.

Duke: What, is Antonio here?
Antonio: Ready, so please your grace.
Duke: I am sorry for thee.
Antonio: I do oppose
      My patience to his fury.

(4) Volunteers can enter the room as Shylock, with the rest discussing the varying effects.

(5) In sixes, five pupils try to persuade a Shylock to budge from his stubborn intention. They may use any arguments they wish.

(6) The parts of Antonio, Bassanio, Gratiano, the Duke and Portia are assigned to the other five in each group and then all the Antonios,

212

all the Bassanios and so on are called together in groups of the same name and invited to clarify that character's position and his objectives, if he has any. Help with this briefing may be offered by the teacher. Now the characters return to their original groups and are told that they are in a tavern, say, and an attempt is being made to persuade Shylock to settle out of court. They may improvise their arguments but confine themselves to their character's viewpoint.

(7) Discuss a possible setting for the court, deciding where the Duke and the magnificoes will sit, where Antonio and where Shylock will be located, where the knife and scales will be kept, where the entrances could be. A selected cast can now act the part of the scene from Shylock's entrance to the announcement of Portia's arrival, possibly using a 'cut' version, where, in long speeches, the actors deliver only the gist or only selected lines, improvising where necessary in such a way as to reproduce the tone and intention of the originals. A prior reading of these speeches by the teacher himself can provide a basis for the choices the performer can make. The rest of the class sit where it is agreed the audience should sit, but they can also imagine they are present in the court. Decisions can be invited from them on the grouping of characters and how space can be made to express the legal impartiality of the court and the personal preferences of the characters.

(8) The best known feature of the next part of this section is Portia's eloquent plea for mercy, and I feel all the pupils should have the chance to do some work on this. A way of sensing the structure is to divide the class into groups of four, each containing a Duke, an Antonio, a Shylock and a Portia. The speech contains many references to different locations, real or metaphorical, and to different people, sometimes as themselves and sometimes as political or social representatives. A physical orientation or a gesture at the appropriate moments helps forcefully to demonstrate the argument of the speech, which is, after all, intended to be a forceful argument. Mercy "blesseth him that gives" (Shylock) "and him that takes" (Antonio). "It becomes the throned monarch" (the Duke, for instance?) "better than his crown". It is "above this sceptred sway" and is "an attribute of God himself" (above the Duke — corny, perhaps, but effective). "Therefore Jew" (guess who). "None of us should see salvation" (an all-embracing gesture). "This strict court of Venice" (Duke, again) "must needs give sentence 'gainst the merchant there" (back to Antonio). Having tried this speech this way, the pupil can try it with-

out all but the most explicitly indicated gestures and orientations. He will have experienced something of the pressure and urgency behind the speech and handled some of its ideas, perhaps, in the earlier improvisations. If time allows, a performance of it by a volunteer, with the other members of his group in position in the agreed 'court' and the rest of the class as spectators, gives the speech its proper public setting and allows Portia to play to her audience.

When the rhetorical power of the speech is appreciated in the context of an exploration of the sequence as a whole, the climactic and pivotal importance of Shylock's defiant retort becomes fully apparent.

> My deeds upon my head, I crave the law,
> The penalty and forfeit of my bond.

(9) The next section begins where Portia says:

> Why then thus it is
> You must prepare your bosom for his knife.

The climax comes where Shylock is prepared to strike with his knife and the dialogue is littered with clues to action. I should investigate the dangerous element in the action at this stage by omitting the by-play between Portia and Nerissa on the one hand and Bassanio and Gratiano on the other, which reassures the audience that a complete catastrophe is unlikely. I should also speed up the process by simplifying Antonio's long farewell, keeping only the first two lines of it. In fives (Portia, Shylock, Bassanio, Gratiano and Antonio), groups of pupils can mime the specified actions, filling in also the implied ones as they see them, and afterwards fit the words to these actions. A performance by volunteers, first with, then without, the sequence we omitted, highlights the effect on the tone when it is added later.

(10) A vivid and exciting way of investigating the structure and atmosphere, I found, was to choose the most lively performers from the previous exercise and cast the rest in the role of two sets of courtroom spectators. One was labelled Jews, the other, Christians. They were allowed briefly to clarify their general attitudes to the proceedings, then the actors performed the whole section with the Jews or Christians vociferously supporting their respective sides and cheering when their side was winning. The Jews are led to believe their champion will come out on top, but the cheering switches to the other side and the scene changes direction when Portia stops Shylock with:

> Tarry a little, there is something else.

A spin-off from this exercise for me was the theatrical atmosphere that was created. It drew out of the actors a more rhetorical and bravura manner of playing, and that gave some kind of insight into the relationship between actors and audience that could have existed in Shakespeare's theatre and the noise level with which actors might at times have had to cope. Part at least of the audience was drawn into emotional empathy with one or other of the 'sides'. (Shylock's aside: "These be the Christian husbands", for instance, evoked a fierce agreement matching in tone Shylock's own sardonic delivery.) One might argue that a real audience will be sympathetic largely to the Christians even when Shylock is winning, but it is by no means that clear cut. What the exercise does provide is a vivid image of the shifting balance of power.

(11) For the teacher who thinks improvisation would be timely, an opportunity occurs in this section to devise a parallel situation as a means of investigating the relationship between Shylock and Portia. I suggest the parallel should not be too detailed; perhaps the notion of somebody being given enough rope to see if he hangs himself, providing an opportunity to examine the motives of the rope-dispenser and the psychology of the victim.

(12) Our last section begins where Shylock tries to leave but is held back by Portia with:

> Tarry Jew,
> The law hath yet another hold on you.

By this stage it rings a useful change to let groups of the requisite number (Duke, Portia, Antonio, Shylock, Gratiano, Bassanio) work the episode out for themselves. If the teacher thinks they need help, they might be asked to consider whether their characters still have recognisable objectives and, if they have, to bear them in mind even when they are not speaking. This especially applies to Shylock, as he has only three short speeches, and to Bassanio, who has none. Pupils might be asked to try out what lines Shylock does have in many different ways and in different physical postures. In the following exchange, for example:

Portia: Art thou contented Jew? What dost thou say?
Shylock: I am content

they can try saying Shylock's speech resentfully, sarcastically, humbly. They can discover what it does to tone and meaning and relationships when they go 'down' when Portia orders them to, or when they stand defiantly erect. Which posture helps the most? If the teacher would prefer the pupils to explore the scene themselves

215

in the first place, he might focus on these issues at performance stage. Further questions can then arise. What does the actor playing Shylock want the audience to think and feel about the character? What impression in fact was given? How did a particular way of playing Shylock or a particular person playing him affect the way the others played their roles? What contribution did the different characters make to the overall effect? Does Gratiano want the audience to go on laughing with him in this episode and, if he does, what effect might this have on their attitude to Shylock? What individual adjustments did actors find they had to make to accommodate the personality of fellow actors? Intervention by the teacher at an early stage could show his historical scholarship fulfilling a useful and meaningful function if he reminded the performers that when Antonio forces Shylock to become a Christian, Elizabethan audiences would see this as doing Shylock a favour. An atheistic pupil might be tempted to be luke-warm about Antonio's generosity. Finally, both actors and audience will be affected by the rhythm of the scene as sensed by the group and by the pace and tempo of the playing. How long a pause, if any, would they prefer between the two speeches quoted above?

(13) After working intensively on the scene in these ways, the pupils should have a fair idea of the grounds on which the characters stand. If the teacher wishes to make their grasp more sure and their insights more conscious, he might now introduce the 'talk-back' exercise I described earlier, setting up a TV talk-back show with himself as inquisitor and having the pupils as the different characters being quizzed. There can be several Shylocks, Portias, etc. The teacher keeps the discussion on the rails as far as relevance is concerned. It is possible, actually, to have this exercise earlier as an aid to the kind of exploratory work I have recommended.

(14) The scene must eventually be reassembled and run through in its entirety, either in groups, or again with a volunteer cast.

Example 3 'Ernie's Incredible Illucinations' by Alan Ayckbourn

Ernie's Incredible Illucinations is a play which was commissioned for use in the classroom and on the school stage by Alan Durband on behalf of Hutchinson. It is a short play which can be read comfortably in a lesson and, in my experience, is a sure success with twelve- to fourteen-year-olds of whatever ability. It is a mixture of satirical comedy, fantasy and knockabout farce and the language ranges from the witty to the deliberately dispensable. It makes gentle fun of stuffy institutions and unimaginative experts, allows scope for wish-fulfilment while at the same time satirising heroic postures. Ayckbourn also observes and incorporates the sort of games young children (especially boys) naturally play. The zany events appeal to those who would like a glimpse of the world turned upside down and there is a touch of Pinter and Ionesco in the humour.

The story is as follows: Young Ernie is taken by Mum and Dad to the Doctor on account of his 'illucinations'. The difference between these and ordinary daydreams is that what Ernie imagines actually starts to happen. The Doctor asks for an account and the play enacts three examples. The first example occurs at home. Dad and Mum conduct a boring conversation and Ernie reads an exciting book about the French Resistance. Bidden by his imagination, some German soldiers march up to the door and demand admittance and the production of an illegal radio transmitter. Dad thinks it is the men come to reclaim the telly and he starts to carry it upstairs. At that moment the door bursts open, persuaded by the shoulders of two charging soldiers, and the three characters end up on the floor in a heap. Ernie machine-guns the whole troop and Dad and Mum dispose of the bodies. In the second episode, Auntie May takes Ernie to the fair and succumbs to the enticements of the barker advertising the boxing. Kid Saracen is the resident champion and he challenges all comers. He defeats Eddie Edward and Auntie May is so incensed that she herself volunteers to take him on. Ernie imagines she is the 'new heavyweight champion of the world' and she duly fulfils this promise, flattening the champ. In the final episode, Dad takes Ernie to the library. Prominent here are a Lady with glasses and a tramp. The Lady complains that the light is kaput. Ernie and Dad enter and, through the intervention of Ernie, the Tramp makes an excuse to pass Dad a mysterious parcel, after which the tramp is followed out by a mysterious stranger. An attendant returns with a ladder to replace the bulb and when he climbs it Ernie transforms him into Captain Williams, a mountaineer. The Captain hurts himself and is unable to get down. To the rescue comes Dad, only to be covered with embarrassment when reality reasserts itself. In comes the second librarian with the news that the Tramp has been found knifed. Back in the waiting room, the Doctor dismisses the phenomena as examples of group hallucination and to prove him wrong Ernie wills into existence a brass band composed of all the patients.

This play is fun to read to oneself, more fun to read in class and most fun to perform. For performance, it falls neatly into manageable sections and the three examples can be worked on in any order. A reading of the first scene in the Doctor's waiting room, and the first episode, give a feeling of the style, and practical work could begin at once — I suggest on the home scene rather than on the exposition.

The home scene

Work on this scene could take a single or a double lesson. It offers opportunities for small-group workshops and large-scale presentations. A natural excuse for immediately involving all the class in exciting action occurs with the marching of the German soldiers. 'Officers' can be disengaged in turn and given the chance of issuing orders. This exercise also has the advantage of establishing the importance of the physical dimension of the comedy.

Next, in threes, the pupils can be allocated an area and invited to create a room and place in it a number of real or imagined objects. There will have to be two chairs and the television set but pupils can also locate a window, the door and a fireplace and add a table. In each group, Ernie and his parents can improvise the boring conversation, using the props as they need them. After this, they can move on to the script of this section.

Groups of six could cope with the arrival of the Germans, which means amalgamating existing threes, some to keep the roles they have been developing, some to be the officer and two soldiers. The officer's function is to knock on the invisible door (thereby fixing it in space) and demand it be opened. For this he can make use of the easily-remembered lines of the original script as he feels the need and in any order.

Open zis door. Open zis door!
Open zis door immediately or I shall order my men to break it down.
We know you're in there, English spy! Come out with your hands up. Zis is your last chance.

When the last chance is given, the officer signals to the other two, who break away from what is now merely an imaginary column and charge the 'door'. Meanwhile, Dad gets up, picks up the television and starts for the stairs. Mum opens the door as the charging soldiers reach it and Dad is knocked over. This sequence can be done in mime or with improvised words. Pupils should be encouraged to experiment with the manner and timing of the actions, the objective being to discover how best to create the comic effect. A slow-motion version, it might be suggested, can be both funny and safe. After the first run-through, the original threes can reverse their roles, allowing continuity with the earlier domestic episode to those who became Germans.

If the teacher judges the class to be ready, he can invite the groups now to merge the actions with the given lines, as far as the point where the heap of bodies is on the floor.

The officer marches into the room and the ensuing dialogue can be improvised or performed up to the point of the shooting. At this juncture, there are not enough soldiers for Ernie to shoot or for the class to get the visual picture that the play intends. Momentarily the class can all become soldiers with the exception of volunteer Ernie to mow them all down with a "Da-da-da-da-da-da!" The last section, where Mum and Dad and Ernie discuss what to do and where the doctor intrudes, can be conveniently done on behalf of the class by volunteers.

The whole scene can be put together now by two casts who will eventually perform to each other.

The fairground scene

This scene, again, could take a double lesson. The setting, the fairground, requires a lot of things to be going on at the same time and a class improvisation of fairground activities is an entirely relevant opening. Eventually, the focus of the play settles on the barkers. Two barkers are given speeches addressed to the crowd in general and half the class can be scattered around the room and invited to improvise similar speeches each offering a fantastic attraction. The other half can listen to the barker of their choice, depending on the power of his voice and appeal of his blandishments. At a signal, the noise can be silenced and a third barker allowed to address an Ernie and an Auntie May. The dialogue is very simple and soon a fourth barker succeeds in attracting the two characters and any others into the boxing booth.

The acting area can now be used to rehearse slow-motion boxing matches in pairs. The slow-motion requirement helps to ensure safety but also allows all members of the class to participate in the principal activity of the scene. It also gives the pupils a chance to plan a meaningful sequence of actions which can be shown to the rest. At this stage, pairs can also rehearse the fight between Auntie May and the Kid – in fact girls will probably prefer this. Now the room can become the boxing ring of the play. There are parts for a referee, a time keeper and Kid Saracen, but seconds can be added and there can be a sequence of challengers, not simply the one, Eddie Edwards, who is specified. If desired, the whole personnel can be changed over with each bout and the pairs of boxers can incorporate their rehearsed fights into the scene. Crowd comment can be freely improvised. Sooner or later, the script demands that we focus on Auntie as she decides to take up the challenge herself. In the present context, volunteer readers can cope with this while the rest content themselves with improvising crowd responses.

In the last part of the episode, Auntie May defeats the Kid while Ernie functions as a commentator. We discussed this section earlier and could follow the procedure there described, letting the pupils form smaller groups containing Auntie, Ernie, the Kid, the Referee and two or three other commentators (see pages 132–3). The dialogue is simple yet useful and is easily learned in rehearsal. The commentators can be from various radio stations and it can be the fight which determines the words, not, as in the script, the words which steer the actions. What matters here is the involvement of the commentators. The section can be shown by a group to the class, who then become the crowd for them, both audience and supporting cast. Finally, the whole fairground scene can now be acted with a selected cast as a class effort. Ernie's asides to the audience to the effect that he is mentally transforming the possibilities can be replaced by an aural signal such as a gong.

The library scene

This scene, too, opens with a public setting and a library atmosphere can be established on a class basis. Group improvisations are possible with the ladder/mountain climbing sequence, but the crowd involvement is not as inevitable as in the boxing scene. Furthermore, there is a change in mode here which can be confusing. In the two previous scenes what Ernie imagines becomes literally present, while here we never actually leave the library and an audience would always be aware that 'Captain Williams' was standing on a ladder and not a mountain. For variety, a teacher could legitimately organise merely a lively reading of the whole scene, with sound effects of the mountain wind being added. In the reader's imagination the transformation of the library is accepted more readily and the scene has the force of the others.

The waiting room

With a sound of the brass band on disc or tape, the final episode becomes very possible as a class event. If all start at the Doctor's key speech where his words take on the rhythm of a march, the episode can be done simultaneously in groups using the same musical accompaniment.

The opportunities for invention open to pupils realising a play such as this are considerable. In fairly obvious ways, it can also be used as a basis for creative work of the pupils' own. Further episodes can be devised, for example, showing the operation of Ernie's imagination. If the pupils are trying to capture the spirit of the original, perhaps with a view to fitting their episode into a performance of the play, then this can be a valuable exercise in appreciation as well. Actors working on the play and classroom audiences watching it will be engaging in critical activity on their own account in any case, accepting this as diverting, rejecting that as boring, corny, or impossible to act. But even with a lightweight drama such as this, and with young performers, the teacher might unobtrusively encourage the budding critical awareness with a well-placed invitation to comment. Does it make any difference whether you stick to Ayckbourn's words or not? Does it matter in which order you do the scenes? Does the episode in the library present the same problems for a producer as the other episodes? Does it 'fit'? Should you, when you play the dream episodes, try to carry away the audience with excitement? Do you feel different when you play those episodes from when you play the real-life sections?

Example 4 'The Wild Duck' by Henrik Ibsen

The most appropriate age range for *The Wild Duck* would probably be sixteen to eighteen. There are nine important characters and other parts are also available. It is a play which reads well but, like any other play, it opens out in performance. It lends itself to practical work in pairs and small groups, and no scene involves all of the main characters. My own strategy for this play with, say, a class of twelve to fifteen Sixth Formers would include a wide variety of approaches, but any opinions the pupils were encouraged to form would be firmly based on the text in action.

For preference, I should choose McFarlane's vigorous translation (Oxford). One way to begin is with a class read-through of the play. At this stage, the pupils can be alerted en route to various issues that will need clarifying eventually, but if the teacher chooses this course it would be wise for him to leave these issues fairly open for the moment. He might announce the read-through as a preliminary introduction for prospective actors and directors, so that the answers to some of the questions will seem to be undiscoverable until a flesh and blood cast explores the play's potential. The major issue likely to arise is what the play is 'about', that is to say, what import the totality of the action can have for an audience. The 'message' that seems to be spelt out for us is the desirability of leaving a person his life-lie to ease his passage to the grave. The duologue in Act V between Gregers Werle and Dr Relling explicitly argues the case for and against. This can be re-read and left in the pupil's mind with the query: 'Is this the key to the play?' The class will need to investigate how the characters are built up and what contribution they make to the whole design. They may be asked to observe how the play evolves, what combinations of characters Ibsen uses. Some impressions can be articulated of the kind of play it is, the settings as described in the stage directions, the lighting changes, the closeness (or otherwise) of the dialogue to speech, the way words can mean one thing on the surface but a great deal more underneath.

At first reading, the symbolic use of the wild duck will be apparent, although a judgement on its theatrical success will have to be suspended. Something, too, of the mood of the play will be gathered; but final decisions as to whether the end is tragic or comic, fatalistic or optimistic, will better follow an encounter with the play as a timed event. Sooner or later it could be useful to consider Ibsen, the man, in his historical setting and *The Wild Duck* in the context of his dramatic output, reading, say, *An Enemy of the People* and *Ghosts* beforehand; and at some time it might be salutary to remind the pupils that they are dealing with McFarlane's words and not Ibsen's and that this variable should temper any over-confident assertions.

Teachers may prefer not to raise these issues at all here and allow them to emerge from the practical work. The appropriate open-ended approach would then be to act the whole play. Even in this, it will help the teacher, though, if he has his own mental check-list of features worth investigating. The teacher choosing this line of investigation and basing his strategy on it does, I suppose, court the danger of doing his pupils' thinking for them, but it is by no means inevitable and it is in this belief that I want to consider this kind of strategy as applied to *The Wild Duck*.

One way of beginning is to discuss the setting as described in the text, since the setting determines the shape of the space the actors will be working in. There are two sets, one for Act I and one for the rest of the play, and I should concentrate on the second of these since it is on Acts II to IV that I should do the bulk of the practical work. Pupils can work in small groups with bric-à-brac creating a model and then the alternative versions can be realised using classroom furniture and classroom space. Any pictures of actual productions can be introduced as illustrating solutions by other designers to the problems the pupils have just tackled. If one of the sets can be agreed upon and chosen, some of the subsequent work, especially that involving highlighting and comparison of other features, will be greatly facilitated. There will be the proviso, however, that modifications may have to be made as the usefulness of the set is tested.

Games and exercises designed to create trust and to liberate expressive powers can, of course, be introduced at any stage and with each meeting. Those which create a sense of place (not merely onstage but off it), of time of day, of identity and of the importance of gesture can prove particularly useful at this stage. The building up of dossiers is appropriate to the Ibsen characters, as a sense of their past and as yet undeclared experiences might be seen as a feature of the dramatic model.

In a play which goes to such lengths to elaborate character, an investigation of the major personages and of their contribution to the effect meets it on its own terms. Since the quality of the domestic life of the Ekdals has to be assessed before one can comment on the beneficial or detrimental effect of Gregers' interference, it makes sense to home in on the four members of the household first — Hjalmar, Gina, Hedvig and Old Ekdal. Groups of four (or five, if a producer is felt to be useful) can work on the scene in Act II where the old man and Hjalmar return from the party late in the evening. Possibly the teacher may wish to develop an early sense of the functioning of the subtext and for this purpose may decide temporarily to dispense with the text. There are signposts in this scene to guide an improvisation: for instance, Hjalmar enters, takes his coat off, is questioned by Gina and Hedvig about the party, reacts to the entry of Old Ekdal, talks of his recitation, changes jackets, is asked by Hedvig about the present he promised, disappoints her, asks for his flute and plays it. More personal improvisations could be employed in an attempt to understand the feelings of Hjalmar and Hedvig along the lines of 'letting someone down' or private experience can be invoked merely by reference. There could be presentation of one of the Ekdal improvisations with discussion of its closeness to the original or presentations of versions of the scene as written with comment by the audience on style, subtext, rhythm and tone. With its prior acquaintance with Act I, the audience will now be in a position to appreciate the ironic contrast between the true events at the party and Hjalmar's account of them. It may be found that this absolves the actors from heavy 'pointing' of the comedy but they could experiment with different degrees of emphasis. The generosity and love of the two women can be explored.

A similar range of approaches can be made by the same groups, if desired, to the other 'domestic' scene in Act III, the scene which includes the ritualistic opening of the loft and allows us to consider the attractions of this strange place for the men and for Hedvig. The class will all need to be reminded that 'daylight' is stipulated for this scene and that this will be an element to take account of. The stage directions describe various activities, such as hammering and shooting, which the audience hears offstage. Ingmar Bergman turned the set inside out and had the loft in full view. Some groups can be invited to shift their audience and explore this method of staging, and then the effects of the different versions can be compared. How important is it that the loft preserves an atmosphere of mystery from an audience viewpoint?

Gregers has been in the play since Act I and is by Act III already established in the Ekdal household. Detailed investigation of his character can help the pupils make up their minds how far he is merely a mouthpiece for a viewpoint that Ibsen is attacking and how far he is himself a bitter, twisted victim of circumstances. Pupils can begin by a textual search for relevant information about his past that might be useful to an actor. Work on Gregers brings the pupil up against a basic feature of Ibsen's dramatic structure, the use of duologues, although the function of these in the existing play will need to be considered at a later time in the context of an evolving performance. It does mean not just that pair work is possible but that, without too much expenditure of time, roles can be reversed to allow all the pupils a chance to live this part. If the Gregers duologues are taken in order, the setting for Act I will need looking at in more detail, although for Gregers and his father, Old Werle, a mere awareness of the direction from which the noises of the party would come may suffice for present purposes. There are further exchanges between Gregers and Hedvig in Acts III and IV, Gregers and Hjalmar in Act III, Gregers and Relling in Act V. The teacher may prefer to have a number of these duologues going on at the same time, have them performed and compare by discussion the impact of Gregers's different appearances on other characters and on the audience. The advantage of the duologue is that it is watchable without the participants worrying too much about orientation. An opportunity occurs also for experiment with another teaching method, that of asking the actors to improvise a missing scene. Continuity of performance might be helped by filling in the episode between Acts III and IV, where Gregers takes Hjalmar for a walk and enlightens him about his marriage. The acceptability of this extension can be subject to audience consideration. Although the play is in translation, pupils can investigate the state of Gregers's mind by the 'Laban' approach described on pages 165–6. What becomes evident, for instance, when one 'twists' the following speech? Hjalmar has asked Gregers what he intends doing with himself:

Gregers: Ah, if only you knew *that*, my dear Hjalmar . . . it wouldn't be so bad. But when you are burdened with a name like 'Gregers' . . . ! 'Gregers'! And followed by 'Werle'! Have you ever heard anything so hideous?

In the Gregers duologues, the symbolic status of the wild duck is raised and pupils performing them are faced with the problem of delivering the relevant lines with conviction. Do they find that words are being put (by Ibsen) into Gregers's mouth or can the utterance be delivered by a consistently developing character?

In terms of plot, Act IV shows us the effects of Gregers's missionary interference when the letter arrives containing a deed of gift for Hedvig from Old Werle. The meat of the Act is a four-hander involving Hjalmar, Gina, Gregers and Hedvig and it immediately precedes one of the duologues (Hedvig/Gregers) on which pupils have already been working. The scene can be produced in groups and the different emphases examined. After the presentations, the audience can articulate its reflections on the attraction and repulsion of sympathy occasioned not merely by Hjalmar and Gregers but by Gina, whose child is being attacked, and by Hedvig.

The end of the play involves seven characters and may need to be a class exploration. Preferably, though, at least two groups should tackle it simultaneously, starting, say, with the Hjalmar/Gregers duologue which we have hitherto avoided and which leads up to the climactic shot offstage. The mood is so complex that two different casts can be encouraged to experiment with manner and with pace and tempo. Should a note of ritual be introduced and, if so, how seriously should this be taken? Pupils can even try two different sets to complicate matters further. Pace and tempo are so important that it would be desirable that the words be learned, at least of a section of the dialogue. The Hodgson and Richards technique of learning the words by improvising closer and closer to the text can be valuable here, especially as the cast have the benefit of considerable practical acquaintance with the characters and a sense of the way the play works.

As well as contrasting different possibilities with the same set of words, pupils can here be introduced to the effects of different translations, having, by now, a base to work from. The purpose is to see what different ways of playing the translations seem to urge. One translation might more obviously 'send up' Hjalmar in his posturing: McFarlane's, by giving the word "Rubbish!" to Relling when he replies to Molvik's conventional Christian consolation, makes him much more forcefully dismissive than the rendering by Una Ellis-Fermor, who gives him "Nonsense". Once again, the test is the audience's reaction and the bearings it manages to find.

The play has to be put together again now and further modifications to interpretation will occur. Ideally, a practical exploration of the whole play is desirable, probably Act by Act, but if there is time only for re-reading, theatrical activity should ensure that it does not degenerate into mere words. If a sound recording or a videotape of the play or part of it is available, this is the stage at which to introduce it. The Open University has an excellent performance of part of Act IV and all of Act V. Pupils viewing this have the benefit of seeing professionals offer their solutions to problems they themselves have tackled; of watching the elements interlock and of seeing what it does to the stage play to have the camera do the focusing instead of the actors and stage technicians; and, in this particular example, of weighing up the effects of the omnipresence onstage of the

226

loft and all it means, an effect notably absent from their TV production.

Discussion and written work may now focus attention on the types of performance the different dramatic and theatrical qualities of the text can give rise to. Pupils may at last be able to decide whether they think the ideas *in* the play are the idea *of* the play (see Bentley, op. cit., p. 131) and whether it is about honesty versus the life-lie or about love, innocence, fate. The teacher may decide to continue in a practical vein, by making plans now for a putative production. A working decision about the set has already been made and may already have been revised or even substituted for. Individual or small-group projects are now possibly more feasible. General consideration can be given to the style of production desirable. Should it be set in Ibsen's time or in a more modern period? Here, facts about Ibsen's life and times are relevant. What sort of society is reflected in the play and how vital is it that society with its prejudices and pressures should be re-created on the stage? Work on the lighting changes will reveal the relationship of visual effect to meaning. The selection of tableaux for publicity photos involves fundamental decisions as to interpretation, as can a declaration of intent in a programme note.

7
Choosing the material

Sometimes a teacher may have little room for manoeuvre as far as choice of material goes. Examination boards may force him to use texts he is out of sympathy with or which he would himself deem inappropriate. Where such texts appear on some English Literature 'A' level syllabuses, he may avoid them only at the expense of leaving the drama under-represented. Yet he is surely right, wherever circumstances permit, to exercise his critical judgement prior to making his selection. The question of what constitutes a good stage, radio or television play is a matter for lengthy debate. The answer will probably contain some reference to the truth to life of its representation, the organic nature of its form, the unity of its action, the consistency of its style, the objectivity of its tone. It will also take account of its power, vitality and entertainment value as a theatrical, auditory or televisual artefact.

While a play measuring up to these demands might satisfy the teacher as a person, is it fair to apply such a yardstick on behalf of immature youngsters? Courtney thinks it is not: 'The teacher's main problem is not to judge plays on an adult standard. Children's standards are different: the most paltry one-act play may seem significant to them. It is best to start from their standards and slowly lead them to better dramas' (*Teaching Drama*, p. 82). I admit that the degree of rigour with which selection is made may be scaled to fit particular circumstances (egos may need to be boosted, a desire for escape or reassurance pandered to), but the teacher is a member of the classroom community as surely as the pupils are and the play must work for him as well as for them. Indeed, unless he is convinced that it has imaginative potential, he cannot with confidence recommend it.

An assurance of the inherent dramatic power of a piece, then, is for the teacher the minimum requirement. His selection will also be affected, though, by the developmental needs and the interests of his pupils. It is impossible to draw up a chart to show these needs arising in neat progression according to age, however convenient that might be. Individual differences are wide, even within the same school class.

228

But working on a play is a communal activity and the teacher is forced to try and satisfy a number of people at the same time. Willy nilly, he will find himself looking for common denominators and it is inevitable that some customers will be better pleased than others.

Plays with setting and situations which seem close to the reality of the pupils' lives unfortunately do not always produce the shock of recognition for which we might be hoping. We should perhaps ask if a play such as Giles Cooper's radio play, *Unman Wittering and Zigo*, enjoys its wide appeal merely because it is 'about' a school or because it is a rattling good thriller, or 'about' authority, about the kinds of order that society achieves. Modern plays which seem to offer a literal representation of the known world may disappoint on closer acquaintance or may disturb without offering a healthy perspective on experience. Identification may be achieved but at a cost.

Even those teachers most sold on matching material to a developmental model would be well advised to remember that it is the success of the play as metaphor which counts in the end. This said, though, even the sceptical, or those who believe that a good play has appeal at different levels for all ages, will probably admit that the understanding of certain experiences is made more difficult if pupils are unable to relate them to analogous experience they already know. The compulsions and frustrations of sexual love, for instance, may be outside the ken of younger children, as may the fears and deprivations of old age. A nihilistic view of the world (Beckett's?) may simply not, as far as they are concerned, match the evidence. Some preoccupations, on the other hand, the awareness of death for example, do persist in different forms at whatever age.

Most teachers who agree that developmental needs are a factor to be reckoned with in the choice of play material will probably prefer to work from an intuitive knowledge of children built up through experience. The beginner, whose sense of what adolescents are like is derived from coloured memories of his own development or observation of teenage relatives, may find it helpful to examine the descriptions of expert researchers. He may then construct a provisional model from these. The descriptions I have seen have a lot in common and the variations are largely in emphasis. Some see the major indication of the start of adolescence as a new awareness of the distinction between subjective fantasy and objective reality. With this goes a greater power to generalise or a greater interest in generalisations. Others stress the search for self or, as Erikson does, the search for identity. Identity, as Lowe observes, becomes disrupted in early adolescence, re-integrated in mid-adolescence and, hopefully, becomes more stable in late adolescence. The search for identity is forced on the youngster by biological changes (particularly sexual changes) within himself and by 'the social expectations and opportunities he meets'. 'Western urban societies', according to Trefor Vaughan, 'set three main tasks to be accomplished, or at least seriously entered upon, before the age of twenty: the achievement of sexual status as man or woman; selection and preparation for a career; the acceptance or development of a sense of civic responsibility.' (*Observer Magazine*, 19 Nov. 1978, p. 39.) The difficulty is that from the teenager's point of view this society offers no clear leads, and the discovery of a desirable role is a daunting task. To add to the confusion, the teenager has to cope not merely with the rational demands of society but the emotional needs within himself. Some observers, like Witkin, see adolescence as a period of heightened emotionality and of extremes. 'Adolescence is a period of stirring emotionalism, of deep shifts of affect, the discovery of passion and the embrace of commitment, of undying love of absolutes and total involvement.' (*The Intelligence of Feeling*, p. 59.) Even Sixth Formers often see the world in terms of black and white.

The adolescent, then, is faced with the need to make his choice from the range of possible models of the world that are forced on his attention. If he is to find out what stamps him as an individual, he needs to try out a number of possible roles to see which, if any, fit. 'Since his search for identity is urgent, he needs models that are stark and clearly defined . . . In a sense, what the adolescent requires is not merely people, but heroes and heroines.' (Lowe, *The Growth of Personality*, p. 160.) In the process, certain established idols may come crashing down and there is the danger that an easy cynicism may prove attractive. Richard Jones sums up the issues of prime concern to adolescents as 'dependence and independence, conformity and rebellion, membership and individuality' and adds that 'in imagination, themes of justice, reform and utopias become compelling' (*Fantasy and Feeling in Education*, p. 125).

With twelve- or thirteen-year-olds, plays as different as *The Second Shepherds Play* and *Mr. Punch* may owe something of their appeal to the irreverence of the hero-figure, who threatens order with anarchy yet does not upset the basic moral certainties. On a more trivial level, *Ernie's Incredible Illucinations* offers the thrill of outraging adult

230

rationality, as do heroes of the comic papers, but it is all good fun. *The Second Shepherds Play* makes use of families feelings of greed and fear of discovery, and the forgiveness bestowed on Mak is a mode of the comic harmony; but some of the 'certainties' on which other medieval mystery plays rely, such as the certainty that God does right by Abraham in *Abraham and Isaac*, might be more difficult to stomach for older children. It may be deep, unacknowledged tensions with parents that make MacLeish's adaptations of *Oedipus Rex* and *Antigone* capable of appealing at a surprisingly early age. Greek heroes, such as Jason in Alan Cullen's *The Golden Fleece*, though, may simply offer a direct identification, this time with a figure who is an admired representative of an established order.

Third and fourth year pupils may be interested in plays which seem to help them cope with their developing sexuality; plays dealing with the relations between the sexes. *The Private Ear* by Peter Shaffer tackles the delicate problem of the first date, and a relevant radio play might be Alan Plater's *The Mating Season*. The hopes of a young girl and the promise of a burgeoning relationship are dashed on the rocks of reality in *The Glass Menagerie* by Tennessee Williams. *Romeo and Juliet* might, at this stage, provide a beneficial blend of romance and mutability.

Relations between parents and children are examined in some of these plays and this, too, is a conscious teenage preoccupation. This may partly account for the attractions of a play such as *Billy Liar*, by Waterhouse and Hall. *Billy Liar* does, though, in my experience, succeed in producing a surprising balance of sympathies in youngsters, giving father as fair a crack of the whip as the son, which suggests that it has qualities of dramatic objectivity that make no small contribution. A play such as *Roots* does the same for mother and daughter. Beatie Bryant, who oozes with self-confidence for much of the play, is shocked to discover that she is guilty of the same faults that she accuses her mother of. It is the mother, too, who points them out:

When you tell me I don't understand you mean you don't understand, isn't it?
When you tell me I don't make no effort you mean you don't make no effort.

Caryl Churchill's radio play, *The Ants*, confines itself to the child's-eye view, but the adult world is captured in the powerful metaphor of the ant hill which Tim justifiably (and symbolically) destroys. In Ronald Eyre's television play, *The Victim*, the 'children' are a middle-aged couple and the parent is the grandfather who feels himself to be an intruder.

The day-to-day reality of these pieces may be an adventitious attraction. An 'absurdist' drama such as Albee's *The Sandbox* can, in my experience, be equally successful. The play deals with the 'problem' of grandmother but makes her exaggeratedly aggressive, sends up the cosy hypocrisy of Mommy and Daddy in curdling satirical dialogue and involves action and setting which are surreal rather than real. Perhaps a liking for the inconsequential and zany indicates a persisting need for fantasy.

In the fourth and fifth years one might argue a need for plays which help pupils adjust to and understand society, plays on social, political or religious themes where the issues are clearly defined. Mentally these pupils may hover between conforming and opting out, and the figure of the rebel or outsider can focus feeling and argument in a compelling way. Figures such as Jimmy Porter, Pip Thomson, Galileo, John Proctor, Bamforth, Dr Stockmann, Berenger (in *Rhinoceros*) and Antigone can be symbols of great power. The plays which contain them will be valuable, though, insofar as they present not merely the need for reform and rebellion but the responsibilities of it, plays which put the situation in a healthy perspective.

At this age, a character like Falstaff can be particularly popular and, although the fun associated with his adventures is possibly the prime reason for this, he does encourage the critical questioning of values such as honour and courage. Reputation (or what people think about them) is a source of recurrent anxiety for teenagers and they need to make decisions about what ideals deserve their loyalty. The justice or injustice of the treatment of Shylock can arouse passions, and Galsworthy's *Justice* more stridently assures the audience that the rejection of moral and social axioms can be emotionally and morally right. Plays which are sentimental and melodramatic may nevertheless fulfil a genuine emotional need. But there may be a complementary role for plays which are tough and optimistic in outlook, plays which encourage the belief that change is not only necessary but possible or even that Utopia is achievable. Brecht and Arden can provide such a bracing experience. Brecht's Lehrstücke *He Who Says Yes* and *He Who Says No* vigorously demonstrate how changing circumstances change the scope for choice. *Live Like Pigs* puts the case for human tolerance but refuses to romanticise the victims.

For many Fourth and Fifth Formers, an imminent experience is that of working for a living or, sadly, of failing to be allowed to do so. The teacher may feel that some plays offer insights into the world of work. Wesker deals directly with working relationships in *The Kitchen* and with job satisfaction in *I'm Talking About Jerusalem*; *R.U.R.*, by Capek, shows in an exciting way the menace of mechanisation; *Strife*, by Galsworthy, contains an industrial dispute. Even the Galsworthy, though, might, in the end, turn out to be more interesting as a study of the consequences of pride and inflexibility. *Skyvers*, by Barrie Reckord, depicts the potential leavers themselves and cocks a critical eye at the education system and its relevance, something which the brighter pupils will have been increasingly doing for themselves. Much of what is said in *Gotcha*, by Barrie Keeffe, is what some of our pupils would probably like to have said had they been in the same position as the boy who has temporarily got his headmaster at his mercy; but this play illustrates the limitations of seeking purely thematic relevance, being too embarrassingly outspoken for use in most classrooms.

One of the most persistent themes among compilers of anthology material for this age group is that of war. Since war is now capable of ending the existence of the race, it is perhaps felt that it might be educationally good for the citizens of tomorrow to alert them to its dangers. The danger for the teacher, though, is that he uses dramatic literature to further anti-war propaganda which is strictly his own and, if the child feels he is being got at, the campaign may backfire anyway. Certainly, Fourth and Fifth Formers, especially boys, are of an age where they are capable of violence on an adult scale and the ways in which adults deploy this power may for this reason have some fascination. Violence does not have to occur onstage as in *Serjeant Musgrave's Dance*, but the effects of it are shown in many plays accessible to this age group, plays such as *The Shadow of a Gunman* or *Mother Courage* or *Journey's End*. It may not be the violence of war that connects in the long run but the quality of human relations that the institutions of war can create, the attitudes it makes men adopt towards each other, as in *The Long and the Short and the Tall* or *Chips with Everything* or *Me McKenna* (Don Shaw).

Many of the plays mentioned as appropriate lower down the school will yield deeper meanings at Sixth Form level. But where *Julius Caesar* may prove interesting not simply as a story of murder and retribution but as an insight into the farce of politics, *King Lear* is likely to appeal more specifically to older pupils, that is to say, to pupils capable of contemplating and understanding Lear's quest for a meaning to life and his prior disintegration. *Richard II* is a play which depends for its interest on a presentation of the spectacle of a man losing all his familiar certainties, and it might be felt that this too is a sight for the eye of someone mature enough to consider the vanity of human wishes.

The nihilism of a Jacobean writer, such as Webster, or a modern writer, such as Beckett, might be something with which a Sixth Form is not yet ready to cope. Malcolm Povey, in *The Use of English* (Spring 1976), sees Beckett as potentially harmful:

I think teachers should also recognise that a play like Beckett's, with its message that the 'essential never changes', will, if students take it seriously, produce a resistance to social change. For teachers to believe that 'Nothing can be done' can only lead to an increasingly alienated society, and plays like *Godot*, in their over-simplification, help to confirm those suffering from adolescent depression in their highly selective viewpoints and narrow ways of life.

Admittedly, it is not so much the inclusion of themes that Mr Povey objects to as the invitation to do dirt on life; but he seems pessimistic that even the critical awareness that the good Sixth Form teacher could foster will be sufficient to counteract the play's insidious attractions. I don't say I go along with this, but it is a case where an individual teacher might, from his knowledge of a particular set of pupils, decide to make developmental needs one of his criteria of selection. He may on these grounds avoid the untimely introduction of works by Genet and Strindberg, too.

A play such as *Who's Afraid of Virginia Woolf?*, on the other hand, may be felt to be developmentally right for this age group, critically illuminating, for the pupil, the posing and social games-playing such as he himself is becoming (sometimes patronisingly) aware of. The capacity on the part of the reader/performer/audience to attempt a fundamental criticism of social behaviour may help the plays of Ben Jonson to burst the language barrier for late adolescents. Plays which deal with areas of experience which our society finds it embarrassing to discuss in a manner that is outspoken and shocking can be more easily handled in a class mature enough not to snigger on principle. A play such as Peter Nichols's *Forget Me Not Lane* has caused me anxious moments in certain classrooms.

To select plays which relate in some way to what the teacher estimates to be the burning personal concerns of the child seems to me to be a perfectly legitimate means of securing his involvement.

But to expect the plays to solve his problems for him is to make the wrong kinds of demand on the material. If they offer him only the reassurance that he is not alone in his predicament, they supply what is one of the basic consolations of art for people of all ages. In any case, adolescents, in my experience, are particularly prone to wonder if they are freaks.

On the whole, I am chary of recommending too energetic a pursuit of 'relevance' to personal need. It can make the teacher conservative and unadventurous, and he will miss the play that 'clicks' unexpectedly and unaccountably. He will also underestimate the extent to which a good play can enable the pupil to transcend his personal vision and enlarge his imaginative sympathies. In a constructive way, a good play takes him out of himself and involves him, in collaboration with the dramatist, in the building of a new world. The play is an experience in its own right, exhilarating and worthwhile because it is what it is. What determines its accessibility may not be so much the extent to which it mirrors what is already known but the capacity of the pupil to understand how it works. The governing factor may be less the experience of life than the experience of drama.

If the teacher wishes the class to experience a play as theatre and not simply as a story, he will need to know if there are expectations he can build upon or expectations he will have to change. We have discussed possible ways in which work in improvised drama can provide a natural preparation, but literary and theatrical experiences outside the classroom will also have to be taken into account. The pupil's ability to understand the nature of dramatic convention will be increased by his prior familiarity with it in his play or as a member of an audience. His own childhood games will have exercised him in ritual and ceremonial, in formalised language and in the symbolic use of space. He may have seen performances in which characters talk directly to the audience and invite their collusion, and in which animals are given human characteristics. He may have seen stage plays with a school party or on the school stage. He will almost certainly have watched a great deal of television, ranging from zany comedy such as Monty Python to the terse 'naturalism' of 'adult' crime series. Television or the cinema will have shown him silent comedy films, cartoons, 'psychological' dramas and musicals. I am not suggesting that the teacher should seek merely to reproduce the virtues and failings of the child's own cultural experiences in his choice of dramatic scripts. There are times when he will have boldly

to establish a new convention himself, and in any case a good dramatist will not be content just to ride on a wave of what custom makes
acceptable but will modify convention to suit his individual ends.
But the child's existing and developing experience of theatre can be
an important factor for the teacher when it comes to securing his
agreement to participate and his readiness to give the dramatist a
hearing. On the very simplest level, for instance, I have found it useful to be able to remind pupils who gib at the fact that the characters
of Shakespeare speak in verse that they (the pupils) have already
accepted the fact that the characters in *Joseph and the Amazing
Technicolor Dreamcoat* burst into song.

I hope I won't be taken as suggesting that a flip comparison solves
all one's problems when it comes to deciding when to introduce
Shakespeare. With all the good will in the world, some pupils are not
going to be able to cope easily with an unfamiliar idiom, disentangle
an unfamiliar syntax or understand an obsolete vocabulary. The
variety and quality of his pupils' reading experiences will affect the
teacher's choice, but he may decide that there are structural conventions or conventions of dramatic mode which he can invoke to
make the behaviour of the dialogue more comprehensible and this
may sway him in favour of sticking his neck out.

Plays are read at primary school. *Playspace* (Methuen) contains
plays especially written for the under elevens which base their form
on familiar, ritualistic playground games, plays such as *The Cutting
of Marchan Wood*, by Richard M. Hughes, or *The Boy Without a
Head*, by Edward Lucie-Smith. But personally I think a sequence of
dramatic experiences leading to the introduction of scripts in, say,
the second year of a secondary school would be more desirable.
Certainly, one does not have to start at any age with the 'naturalistic'
and move on to the 'stylised'. It is worth remembering that naturalism
itself is a style and that it is not the same as life. One is looking perhaps, at this stage, for a clear narrative line, for robust and overt
action, for obvious conflicts and for traditional structural qualities
such as climax, suspense and dramatic irony and for direct and telling
(rather than 'clever') dialogue. Much folk drama which imitates a
folk idiom is useful to begin with. The plays of Hans Sachs (*The
Wandering Scholar from Paradise*) have a robustness which, when
they were first performed, allowed them to override the kind of
inattentiveness a classroom audience might be heir to. I have mentioned *The Second Shepherds Play* and suggested how use might also

be made of the children's experience of silent films and of their experience, in their play, of the expressive use of space. John Arden, whose plays have the expository quality of a ballad, offers opportunities in *Death of a Cowboy* for the teacher to make use of his pupils' experience of Westerns and of their games based on Westerns, while compelling a re-examination of the notion of heroism. Mumming plays may be comprehensible only in their general outline but this and the very outrageousness of the logic can tempt the pupil to learn the lines by heart:

Black Prince: I am Black Prince of Paradise, born of high renown,
This night I've come to fight King George
And take his courage down.
King George: Mind what thou sayest.
Black Prince: What I say I mean.
I'll fill thy body full of holes and make thy buttons fly.
King George: How canst thou fill my body full of holes and make my buttons fly,
When my head and sword are made of steel
And my fingers and toes are double-jointed?

I learned this play from my father by oral tradition and have never forgotten it. What made me want to learn it was the enthusiasm, the promise of fun in store, which he communicated. As Robert Leach points out in *The World of the Folk Play*, these pieces have the appeal of a game and, in *Folk Playtexts*, he makes available the very version (*The Comberbach Soul-Cakers Play*) that I have quoted from. I'm not suggesting, by the way, that the right way to approach the play is for the teacher to con the words and tempt the pupils to do the same, although there could be less effective methods. At least when the pupils possess the words, the drama itself can start to become their property.

Plays of Aristophanes in MacLeish's translation have the accessibility of folk drama to youngsters. On another level of quality, the Victorian melodramas (like *The Bells*) have a simplicity of attitude and a directness of approach which are easily comprehensible. Many of their conventions will be familiar through pantomime but the intended solemnity of tone may prove elusive. It may not be the situation so much as the rhodomontade required of the actor that produces self-consciousness. Persistence, though, in learning this new theatrical language can lay a useful foundation for work on more ambitious plays requiring a certain bravura in performance, such as Shakespeare's. The success in performance of radio plays (whose 'content' seems appropriate to this age group), such as *The Nosebag* by Louis MacNeice, will depend on the ability of the class to 'think radio', to deny themselves physical action in favour of an arrangement of vocal and aural effects.

A consideration which may be relevant in certain classrooms is the ease with which the children can approximate in improvisation to the words and situations of the original script. I have discussed already *Ernie's Incredible Illucinations* from this point of view. The situations in plays such as *Punch and Judy* can be improvised, as the main appeal is in the violent action. Here the teacher has the child's experience of silent films and of the grotesque cartoons like *Tom and Jerry* on which to build.

Ernie is one of a number of scripts on the market written especially for pupils of this age range and level of sophistication; plays, for instance, in the Macmillan *Dramascript* series, the Methuen *Young Drama* series or Hutchinson's *Playbill* and *Prompt*. Such plays can also be deliberately constructed to take into account the teacher's difficulties in the classroom. I feel, though, that unless they offer something that the child improviser could not provide unaided, they are better left alone. David Bowskill's *Burn Up* has the verbal excitement of the chant and mass involvement. I tried, in *A Day in the Mind of Tich Oldfield*, to keep the naturalistic dialogue as selective and sharp as I could and I tried to cash in on the children's familiarity with the conventions of the television quiz. But I can confirm from experience that I was most happy with the script when it meant something for me and was not simply an exercise in contriving something to fit a formula. Some available plays focus on social problems or strive for mass involvement to such an extent that they give the individual performer too little scope to personalise the experience — including even more successful plays such as John Pick's *Carrigan Street*. Occasionally one is frivolous and ham-handed in its satire, like *Hijack*. Some resort to too much verbalising and miss the opportunity to provide exciting action. Sympathies are superficially allocated (e.g. protesters are good, officials bad) and the language is flat. One feature of the plays written for classroom use is their shortness, and this can be a positive advantage in itself as it means that the child has a chance of grasping the total structure relatively quickly and has a better chance of doing practical work on a larger proportion of the play.

The *Young Drama* series contains the scripts of T.I.E. performances, such as *Snap Out of It*, *Rare Earth*, *Sweetie Pie* and *John Ford's*

Cuban Missile Crisis. While the original events quite probably did have the impact that is claimed for them, it is difficult to see how one could reproduce the effect in the classroom. Brian Wilks, in his notes on *Snap Out of It*, admits that 'its theme is a serious and even disturbing one, its form and demands on its actors quite exacting' and 'considerable skill is needed in the playing of the first part of the show' (p. 48). It is not that the disturbing nature of the impact is something from which to shy off, but that the play probably needs the surprise that is sprung at the end, when the audience participates, and the agency of outside performers tuned to handle them sensitively. *Rare Earth* aims to 'disturb' 9—11 year olds with the horrors of pollution. Again, the early introduction to a social problem is not in question, since most of the young audience will be able to absorb this particular experience on the metaphorical level of encroaching monsters in any case. I would query the classroom viability of this script, too, with this age group and should imagine best use could be made of it by a team of actors wanting to present the play in the way it was originally intended.

The fourth and fifth years may be filled with work on an 'O' level or C.S.E. syllabus, but if there is a choice for the teacher he will do well to bear in mind what experience of theatre he has managed to offer in the earlier years and the kinds of work currently being done by him or (if he is an English teacher) by the Drama specialist. He will probably find there is still a lingering preference for plays with more obvious physical action. But more discursive scenes, where the interest is in the issues raised, may be tackled. Characters with more subtle psychology will appeal and so will plays with subtextual meaning, where the reality is often behind the appearances. At this age, pupils will take an interest in technical subtlety and in how effects are brought about. Some teachers may feel that the growing self-consciousness of the pupils is an argument in favour of plays which are apparently realistic. It may indeed be that pupils feel more at ease if they are able to hide behind representations of everyday reality or intellectualise the content into a formulated social 'problem', but the appeal of a naturalistic play may turn out to be its verbal effects. Apart from the sanctioned use of 'bloody', surely one of the pleasures for the young performer of playing the part of Geoffrey, in *Billy Liar*, is the clever selectivity that heightens Geoffrey's attitudes. Even *Z Cars* scripts operate in a stylised way. I have found that overt verbal wit, such as Shaw's, can also

239

arouse the admiration and a desire in the pupil to be the one to use the lines.

Shaw was canny enough to build on his audience's familiarity with pantomime and melodrama and for pupils, too, with this background, he can lead from the known to the unknown. *The Devil's Disciple*, *Androcles and the Lion* and *Pygmalion* all offer the thrills of an accepted convention but hold up attitudes associated with it to witty scrutiny, without taking discussion to extremes of boring abstraction. The strong formal outline of the folk drama is preserved in parable plays of Brecht such as *The Good Woman of Setzuan*, a play which also has the advantage for young performers of a firm developing plot. In this, as in plays such as *The Exception and the Rule*, the punchy directness of the language survives translation. Plays of Shakespeare which can match the lurid excitement of melodrama, such as *Macbeth* and *The Merchant of Venice*, while at the same time offering a strong psychological interest will be easier of access at this stage than those relying more on symbolism. Possibly the class will be engaged in quite subtle role building in their improvised drama. They may also be involved in attempting to tackle social problems in this area of work.

In terms of dramatic experience, a greater variety of forms can and should be tackled now. Works by Pinter, N.F. Simpson and David Campton often frustrate habitual expectations by offering inconsequential action and dialogue and unmotivated character. There will be some new ground to be trod here but, as I observed in connection with *The Sandbox* by Albee, the pupils' experience of zany television comedy shows like *Monty Python* and *The Goodies* can make a useful point of reference and at least guarantee a hearing. Where a form (such as melodrama) has become established with the pupils, a self-conscious gloss on the form itself in the shape of burlesque (*Passion, Poison and Petrifaction* by Shaw) can be profitable. One appeal of the TV scripts which Longmans publish is the challenge to translate the TV conventions into terms which make them viable in the classroom. A 'new' form such as radio drama can be tackled in its own terms using a tape recorder. It is very easy, however, for a class to get so absorbed in technical problems that it forms no opinion as to the worth or otherwise of the entreprise in which it is engaged, and the teacher still needs to make a prior judgement on the likelihood that the play will prove aesthetically rewarding.

Ideally, Sixth Forms should be acquainted already with a sufficient variety of forms to make almost any adventure into the new in this respect feasible. Where they are not, a teacher may find he can create an atmosphere of tolerance by helping the students to understand the nature of dramatic convention itself and by emphasising that the only logic which matters is dramatic logic. They should be able to accept that narrative is only one of the instruments a dramatist has at his disposal and that he may discard it if he has other fish to fry. Their attention should be focused on action as the direction in which the whole play moves rather than as a set of physically obvious events. Shakespeare plays like *Richard II* are thus more appropriate for pupils able to accept the lack of battles; and Greek tragedies, the bulk of whose narrative action takes place before the play began or whose violence takes place offstage, are more capable of being understood for the themes they do, in fact, develop, whereas younger pupils might need to improvise the whole story. Once the nature of inner action is understood, discursive dramas like *Major Barbara* become more acceptable. Perhaps this play is really 'about' thought versus deed rather than about its declared subject matter. Previously, pupils may have encountered representative figures or situations (e.g. in mystery plays or plays with a message) but the Sixth Form should be capable of coping with less direct and obvious forms of symbolism, as, for instance, in the storms in *King Lear* and *The Tempest* or in the setting of Chekhov's major plays. Theatre itself, in *Waiting for Godot* or *Six Characters*, becomes a metaphor and it is an accumulation of theatrical experience that makes this comprehensible.

In Chekhov's plays, the interest is spread over the group rather than the individual. Sixth Formers who have developed a more self-conscious grasp of the function of character should be able to place less reliance upon a strong central hero or anti-hero to identify with. Practical work should have shown the varying amounts of information a dramatist furnishes for the actor to work upon and the different kinds of interest in the characters he expects his audience to take. If practical work has shown the importance of theatrical effect, the student might be less inclined to demand consistent development not only in characters in Shakespeare (such as Enobarbus or Polixenes) but in plays by Pinter and Ionesco, where disintegration may be one of the effects deliberately aimed at.

Embarrassment may still make practical work on some of the more obviously stylised plays difficult to set up. Artificiality of gesture and posture may inhibit the playing of both Restoration

SCRIPTED DRAMA

Comedy and *Waiting for Godot. Godot* illustrates the fact that it is
useful for the pupils to have had experience of styles which include
the Commedia dell'arte in their classroom work and of the cross talk
act by television comedians. Restoration Comedy still presents
difficulties of language. If, by the Sixth Form, the students have
been able to acquire a sense of the way stage language works, they
will be better placed to tackle not only Restoration Comedy but the
satires of Ben Jonson. They will be able to see that language functions
as a manifestation of a situation and that a focus on the situation can
make the language easier to wield. This may apply also to language in
plays by writers such as Howard Brenton, Howard Barker or Barrie
Keeffe which offend our social taboos. Concentration on the end for
which it was invented may help where the maturity of the pupils
may not be taken completely for granted.

We have been considering what factors might influence the choice
of a teacher in looking at available material. We have mentioned his
own conclusions about the quality of the play as a piece of dramatic
writing, in other words, whether the play works for him; the use he
makes of pronouncements about, and his own observations of, the
psychological needs and developmental processes of adolescents,
their emotional and intellectual grasp; and the nature of the pupils'
previous educational experience in the field of drama and their
encounters with theatre, radio and television.

The weight given to any one of these three criteria in a specific
instance will depend upon the individual teacher and the nature of
the class. Sometimes he may decide to compromise and introduce a
text of lower quality than he would have preferred because it fulfils
a particular need at a particular moment, although he should, I
believe, be prepared to draw a line. A text of whose quality he is convinced at least has its inbuilt checks and balances and may, for that
reason, be developmentally more healthy anyway. Sometimes the
class may be dramatically very sophisticated but the teacher may
decide to forgo a text they could, in technical terms, tackle, because
as yet they are not mature enough to handle the experience. Again,
as I said before, the teacher will need to be certain that he is
not underestimating the power of the drama to be itself an instrument of growth. Finally, he may deem a play thematically relevant
but beyond the range of his pupils' dramatic sophistication.

This brings up the question of practicability and another factor

242

which may govern the teacher's choice of text is the skill with which he can devise methods and approaches to make a particular text acceptable in a particular classroom. But methods and approaches are what the book has been about.

Appendix
Plays, books and articles

Play texts

There follows a list of plays I think worthy of consideration by the teacher. I have roughly allocated them according to the age range to which they are likely to appeal, but, of course, any teacher knows how provisional such a classification has to be and if he decides the plays are in the wrong category or can be much more widely useful, that is his undoubted privilege. I have limited myself to plays I have used myself, seen used or had reliably recommended. In the interests of economy I have sometimes avoided the texts which examination boards ensure are in the forefront of the teacher's mind in any case. Some of the plays are extracted from anthologies but in case the teacher wishes to follow up these collections I have listed them also.

Second and third years

Arden, J.	Death of a Cowboy
	Ars Longa, Vita Brevis
Aristophanes	The Archarnians
	Peace
Ayckbourn, A.	Ernie's Incredible Illucinations (*Playbill One*)
Bolt, R.	The Thwarting of Baron Bolligrew
Bowskill, D.	Burn Up (*Playbill One*)
Campton, D.	Do It Yourself
Chekhov, A.	The Bear
	The Proposal
Cullen, A.	The Golden Fleece
England, A.W.	A Day in the Mind of Tich Oldfield
Lewis, L.	The Bells
MacNeice, L.	The Nosebag
Obey, A.	Noah
Sachs, H.	The Wandering Scholar from Paradise
Saunders, J.	The Travails of Sancho Panza
Shaw, D.	Me McKenna (*Playbill Three*)
Shaw, G.B.	Passion, Poison and Petrifaction

Fourth and fifth years

Albee, E.	The Sandbox
	Zoo Story
Anouilh, J.	Antigone
Arden, J.	Serjeant Musgrave's Dance

PLAYS, BOOKS AND ARTICLES

Barrie, J.	The Admirable Crichton
Brecht, B.	The Caucasian Chalk Circle
	The Exception and the Rule
	The Good Woman of Setzuan
	He Who Says Yes
	He Who Says No
	Mother Courage and her Children
Bolt, R.	A Man for All Seasons
Campton, D.	Little Brother, Little Sister
	Mutatis Mutandis
	Soldier from the Wars Returning
Capek, K.	R.U.R.
Churchill, C.	The Ants
Cooper, G.	Unman Wittering and Zigo
Frisch, M.	The Fire Raisers
Galsworthy, J.	Strife
	Justice
Hall, W.	The Long and the Short and the Tall
Halliwell, D.	Little Malcolm and his Struggle against the Eunuchs
Hopkins, J.	Talking to a Stranger
Ibsen, H.	An Enemy of the People
Ionesco, E.	Rhinoceros
Kaiser, G.	The Raft of the Medusa
Lawrence, D.H.	The Widowing of Mrs Holroyd
Leach, R.	The Wellesbourne Tree
Livings, H.	Nil Carborundum
Miller, A.	The Crucible
Molière	A Doctor in Spite of Himself
	Tartuffe
Mortimer, J.	Voyage Around my Father
Nichols, P.	A Day in the Death of Joe Egg
O'Casey, S.	The Shadow of a Gunman
Patrick, J.	The Teahouse of the August Moon
Pinter, H.	The Caretaker
	The Birthday Party
	The Dumb Waiter
	Revue Sketches
Plater, A.	The Mating Season
Potter, D.	Son of Man
Rattigan, T.	The Winslow Boy
Reckord, B.	Skyvers
Saunders, J.	Barnstaple
Shaffer, P.	The Private Ear
	The Royal Hunt of the Sun
Shaw, G.B.	Arms and the Man
	Androcles and the Lion
	The Devil's Disciple

	O'Flaherty V.C.
Sherriff, R.C.	Journey's End
	The Long Sunset
Synge, J.M.	Playboy of the Western World
Terson, P.	Zigger Zagger
Turner, D.	Semi-Detached
Waterhouse and Hall	Billy Liar
Wesker, A.	The Wesker Trilogy
	Chips with Everything
	The Kitchen
Whiting, J.	A Penny for a Song
Wilder, T.	Our Town
Yeats, W.B.	At the Hawk's Well

Sixth Forms

A list for Sixth Forms could include almost any 'adult' drama and, with the coming of 'A' level Theatre Arts the range is very wide indeed. Since the bulk of the drama done in Sixth Forms tends to be prescribed, and in the interests of economy, I merely append some suggestions for teachers able to choose plays for general interest, by no means implying that examination texts which have been omitted would not also fulfil the same function.

Albee, E.	Who's Afraid of Virginia Woolf?
Arden, J.	The Happy Haven
	The Workhouse Donkey
Barker, H.	Claw
	The Love of a Good Man
Beckett, S.	Come and Go
	End Game
Bond, E.	Lear
	The Stone
	Saved
	The Woman
Bowen, J.	The Disorderly Women
Brecht, B.	Galileo
	The Resistible Rise of Arturo Ui
Brenton, H.	Christie in Love
	The Education of Skinny Spew
	Scott of the Antarctic
Buchner, G.	Woyzeck
	Danton's Death
Edgar, D.	Destiny
Euripides	Hyppolitus
Fugard, A.	Hello and Goodbye
	Siswe Bansi is Dead
	Statements After an Arrest under the Immorality Act
Genet, J.	The Balcony
Griffiths, T.	Comedians

246

PLAYS, BOOKS AND ARTICLES

Hare, D.	Teeth 'n' Smiles
Ibsen, H.	The Lady from the Sea
	John Gabriel Borkmann
	The Master Builder
Ionesco, E.	The Chairs
	The Lesson
Kaiser, G.	The Raft of the Medusa
Keeffe, B.	Gimme Shelter
Leonard, H.	Stephen D.
Nichols, P.	Forget Me Not Lane
Osborne, J.	Look Back in Anger
	Inadmissible Evidence
Orton, J.	Loot
Pinter, H.	The Birthday Party
	Silence
Pirandello, L.	Six Characters in Search of an Author
	Right You Are
Poliakoff, S.	City Sugar
Strindberg, A.	Miss Julie
	The Stronger

Some collections and series

Act One, ed. Self and Speakman (Hutchinson).
Act Two, ed. Self and Speakman (Hutchinson).
Act Three, ed. Self and Speakman (Hutchinson).
Conflicting Generations, ed. Marland (Longman).
Eight Plays, ed. Fellows (Cassell).
Four Greek Plays, ed. McLeish (Longman).
Harrap's Theatre Workshop, Adams and Leach (Harrap).
Hereford Plays (Heinemann).
Heritage of Literature Series (Longman).
Laughter and Fear, David Campton (Blackie).
Methuen Young Drama (Methuen).
Playbill One, Two and Three, ed. Durband (Hutchinson).
Second Playbill One, Two and Three, ed. Durband (Hutchinson).
Playspace (Methuen).
Play Ten, ed. Rook (Edward Arnold).
Prompt One, Two and Three, ed. Durband (Hutchinson).
Scene Scripts, ed. Marland (Longman).
Spotlight, ed. Marland (Blackie).
Steptoe and Son, ed. Marland (Longman).
Theatre Today, ed. Thomson (Longman).
Thieves and Angels, ed. Holbrook (Cambridge).
Two Ages of Man, ed. England (Oliver and Boyd).
Worth a Hearing, ed. Bradley (Blackie).
Z Cars Scripts, ed. Marland (Longman).

APPENDIX

Finally, a list of writings I hope will prove useful aids to thinking about the problems of teaching scripted drama in schools. Some describe procedures, some take a broader view of education, theatre or the arts.

Books

Adams, R. and Gould, G., *Into Shakespeare* (Ward Lock, 1977).

Adland, D., *The Group Approach to Shakespeare* (Volumes on *The Merchant of Venice, A Midsummer Night's Dream, Romeo and Juliet* and *Twelfth Night* — Longman, 1973).

Allen, John, *Drama in Schools* (Heinemann, 1979).

Argyle, M., *The Psychology of Interpersonal Behaviour* (Penguin, 1967).

Artaud, A., *Theatre and its Double* (Calder and Boyars, 1973).

Barker, C., *Theatre Games* (Eyre Methuen, 1977).

Bentley, E., *The Life of the Drama* (Methuen, 1965).

Berne, E., *Games People Play* (Penguin, 1964).

Berry, C., *Voice and the Actor* (Harrap, 1973).

Bolton, Gavin, *Towards a Theory of Drama in Education* (Longman, 1980).

Bowskill, D., *Drama and the Teacher* (Pitman, 1974).

Brook, P., *The Empty Space* (Penguin, 1972).

Brown, J. Russell, *Effective Theatre* (Heinemann, 1969).
  Free Shakespeare (Heinemann, 1974).
  Shakespeare's Plays in Performance (Penguin, 1968).
  Theatre Language (Allen Lane, The Penguin Press, 1972).

Chekhov, M., *To the Actor* (Harper and Row, 1953).

Collingwood, R.G., *The Principles of Art* (O.U.P., 1938).

Courtney, R., *Teaching Drama* (Cassell, 1965).
  The School Play (Cassell, 1966).

Fernald, J., *Sense of Direction* (Secker and Warburg, 1968).

Grotowski, J., *Towards a Poor Theatre* (Eyre Methuen, 1976).

Hayman, R., *How to Read a Play* (Methuen, 1977).
  Techniques of Acting (Methuen, 1969).

Hodgson, J., *The Uses of Drama* (Methuen, 1972).

Hodgson, J. and Richards, E., *Improvisation* (Methuen, 1966).

Holbrook, D., *Children's Games* (Gordon Fraser, 1957).

Hudson, A.K., *Shakespeare and the Classroom* (Heinemann, 1954).

Hunt, A., *Hopes for Great Happenings* (Eyre Methuen, 1976).

Hunt, H., *The Live Theatre* (Oxford, 1962).

Jones, R.M., *Fantasy and Feeling in Education* (Penguin, 1973).

Joseph, B., *Acting Shakespeare* (Routledge, 1960).

Laban, R., *The Mastery of Movement* (Macdonald and Evans, 1971).

Lowe, G.R., *The Growth of Personality* (Penguin, 1972).

MacGregor, Tate and Robinson, *Learning Through Drama* (Heinemann, 1977).

Male, D., *Approaches to Drama* (Unwin, 1973).

Marowitz, C., *The Act of Being* (Secker and Warburg, 1978).
  The Method as Means (Herbert Jenkins, 1961).
  A Macbeth (Calder and Boyars, 1971).

PLAYS, BOOKS AND ARTICLES

Moore, S., *An Actor's Training* (Gollancz, 1960).
O'Toole, J., *Theatre in Education* (Hodder and Stoughton, 1976).
Parry, C., *English Through Drama* (Cambridge, 1972).
Robinson, K. (ed.), *Exploring Theatre and Education* (Heinemann, 1980).
Saint-Denis, M., *Theatre: The Rediscovery of Style* (Theatre Art Books N.Y., 1960).
Seely, J., *In Context* (O.U.P., 1976).
Self, D., *Guidelines* (Mary Glasgow Publications).
Spolin, V., *Improvisation for the Theatre* (Pitman, 1973).
Stanislavsky, K., *An Actor Prepares* (Bles, 1937).
  Building a Character (Reinhardt, 1950).
Styan, J.L., *The Dramatic Experience* (Cambridge, 1965).
  Shakespeare's Stagecraft (Cambridge, 1967).
  Chekhov in Performance (Cambridge, 1971).
  The Elements of Drama (Cambridge, 1970).
Whitehead, F., *The Disappearing Dais* (Hart-Davis, 1966).
Willett, J., *Brecht on Theatre* (Eyre Methuen, 1978).
  The Theatre of Bertolt Brecht (Eyre Methuen, 1959).
Williams, R., *Drama from Ibsen to Brecht* (Pelican, 1973).
Witkin, R., *The Intelligence of Feeling* (Heinemann, 1974).

Articles

Bowskill, D., *Word-Play Word-Plays Word Play Word Splay* (*Young Drama*, 1973).
Durband, A., *Playing with Words: A Case for Short Scripted Plays* (*The Use of English*, Vol. 27, No. 3, Summer 1976).
England, A.W., *Maoris, Missionaries and Muskets* (*Drama in Education 3*, Pitman, 1975).
England, A.W., *Sheffield Crucible and "Gowky Arthur"* (*Theatre Quarterly*, Vol. 5, No. 17, 1975).
England, A.W., *Tape Recording and the End Product* (*The Use of English*, Vol. 21, No. 3, Spring 1970).
England, A.W., *Where Should We Go?* (*The Use of English*, Vol. 27, No. 3, Summer 1976).
Fay, H.C., *Performing Graeco-Roman Comedy in Schools* (*Didaskalos*, Vol. 2, No. 1, 1966, and Vol. 2, No. 2, 1967).
Hall, J., *'If You Like It' by Shakespeare and 4/2M: An Experiment in Drama* (*English in Education*, Vol. 1, No. 3, Autumn 1967).
Hall, P., *Directing Pinter* (*Theatre Quarterly*, Vol. 4, No. 16, Nov. 1974—Jan. 1975).
Kingsley, B., *Dramatic Poetry* (*The Use of English*, Vol. 30, No. 1, Autumn 1978).
Knights, L.C., *The Teaching of Shakespeare* (*The Use of English*, Vol. 19, No. 1, Autumn 1967).
Lewis, R., *An Approach to Hamlet with College Students* (*The Use of English*, Vol. 25, No. 1, Autumn 1973).

APPENDIX

Marland, M., *Plays for the Middle School* (*The Use of English*, Vol. 18, No. 2, Winter 1966).

Marland, M., *Z Cars and the Teacher* (*The Use of English*, Vol. 18, No. 3, Spring 1967).

Parry, C., *Taking Possession* (*English in Education*, Vol. 1, No. 3, Autumn 1967).

Payne, P., *Where We Are* (*The Use of English*, Vol. 27, No. 3, Summer 1976).

Pearce, J.J., *If You Can't Do Shakespeare Well* . . . (*English In Education*, Vol. 1, No. 3, Autumn 1967).

Povey, M., *Oh Godot* . . . (*The Use of English*, Vol. 27, No. 2, Spring 1976).

Raeburn, D., *Performing Greek Tragedy in School* (*Didaskalos*, Vol. 1, No. 1, 1963 and Vol. 1, No. 2, 1964).

Rostron, D., *Some Approaches to the Teaching of Shakespeare* (*The Use of English*, Vol. 26, No. 3, Spring 1975).

Self, D., *Who Is Afraid of Virginia Woolf?* (*The Use of English*, Vol. 23, No. 4, Summer 1972).

Stone, B., *Studying Drama* (Unit I of Course A307, Open University).

Vaughan, T., *Emotional Development* (*Observer Magazine*, 19 Nov. 1978).

Whittle, P., *King Lear in Dumb Show* (*The Use of English*, Vol. 27, No. 3, Summer 1976).

Index of names and titles

251

INDEX

INDEX

INDEX